JAVA™
by example

SECOND EDITION

THE SUNSOFT PRESS
JAVA SERIES

▼ **Core Java,** *Second Edition*
Gary Cornell & Cay S. Horstmann

▼ **Graphic Java**
David Geary & Alan L. McClellan

▼ **Instant Java,** *Second Edition*
John A. Pew

▼ **Java by Example,** *Second Edition*
Jerry R. Jackson & Alan L. McClellan

▼ **Just Java,** *Second Edition*
Peter van der Linden

JAVA™
by example

SECOND EDITION

JERRY R. JACKSON • ALAN L. MCCLELLAN

SunSoft Press
A Prentice Hall Title

The publisher offers discounts on this book when ordered in bulk quantities.
For more information, contact Corporate Sales Department, Prentice Hall PTR ,
One Lake Street, Upper Saddle River, NJ 07458. Phone: 800-382-3419; FAX: 201- 236-7141.
E-mail: corpsales@prenhall.com.

Editorial/production supervision: *Mary Sudul*
Cover design director: *Jerry Votta*
Cover designer: *Anthony Gemmellaro*
Cover illustration: *Karen Strelecki*
Manufacturing manager: *Alexis R. Heydt*
Marketing manager: *Stephen Solomon*
Acquisitions editor: *Gregory G. Doench*
SunSoft Press publisher: *Rachel Borden*

10 9 8 7 6 5 4 3 2 1

ISBN 0-13-272295-X

SunSoft Press
A Prentice Hall Title

To Kelly, who makes it all worthwhile.

Jerry

To Julie, my wife and best friend.

Alan

Contents

Part 1—Working With the Java Language

Part 2—Writing Java Applets

Chapter 14
Introduction to Applets, 227

Part 3—Appendixes

Appendix A
Object-Oriented Programming, 339

List of Tables

List of Examples

List of Figures

Preface

Why We Are Here

When we wrote the first edition of this book, we said that the hope of thousands of application developers and commercial software suppliers is to write and compile code once and run it on any number of target platforms, and that this would promote the use of Java as a general-purpose programming language. We're still firm believers that this is the case. While applets are still the sexy application of Java, there's clearly more and more interest in its general programming utility. In fact, this is evident from the focus of the new material in this edition—the Java Remote Method Invocation (RMI) mechanism and the Java Database Connectivity (JDBC). Java is an interpreted language powerful enough to use for sophisticated application development, yet simple in its design and implementation. Java is object oriented, encouraging the use of modular, maintainable code; it overcomes many of the deficiencies of other object-oriented languages, and it adds a robust set of features, including runtime extensibility, security, and simple multithreading.

Java is a great language that is only getting better, and it still has the world-wide web to promote its use and world-wide acceptance.

There are now hundreds of Java books available. However, few provide the same *focus* we do on the language and present it in practical terms showing nuances of writing elegant Java code. While we don't cover every Java class and method, we do take a pragmatic, illustrative approach to how programmers new to Java can learn the language.

Specifically, we have two basic goals. First, in Part 1 of the book, we aim to provide basics of the Java language, showing how to implement standard programming constructs such as reading and writing to a file, declaring arrays, allocating and initializing memory, using the Java RMI and JDBC, and so on. Second, in Part 2 of the book, we aim to provide basics of applet writing, specifically for programmers who are concentrating on programs that will run within a web browser. We include appendixes in Part 3 to cover the myriad of useful details that don't really fit with the focus of the first two parts.

Along the way, we hope to encourage good programming practices, using Java's object-oriented features to develop clean, maintainable, and readable code. And we try to do these things in practical terms, so that you can see and learn from examples of real programs.

Audience

This is not a book about authoring on the world-wide web, writing common-gateway interface (CGI) scripts, or maintaining web servers. This is a book for intermediate to experienced programmers interested in learning Java. Because of the sheer number of C and C++ programmers ready to make the transition to Java, we pay special attention to Java as it relates to C and C++.

For Windows 3.1 Programmers

As of the writing of the second edition of this book, the Java port to Windows 3.1 is in progress. In fact, an alpha version has just been made available. As this port matures and solidifies, we will test the programs in this book against that port of the JDK and make them available via the SunSoft Press web site:

```
http://www.sun.com/smi/ssoftpress/by_example
```

To check on the status of the JDK port to Windows 3.1, go to the following URL:

```
http://www.alphaWorks.ibm.com/
```

For Mac Programmers

There seems to be some confusion in the Macintosh community, from which we've had requests for Mac editions of *Java by Example*. This is actually counter to one of the great advantages of Java—it's platform independence. Granted, there are some restrictions on the Macintosh, namely, the 31 character file name limit imposed by MacOS. To address this issue, we've done two things:

- Provided modified files on the Mac partition of the CD that are within the 31 character boundary

- Provided the compiled programs in zip format for easy execution on the Mac

We hope these modifications ease use of this material by the Mac programming community.

For C Programmers

For C programmers who are coming to an object-oriented (OO) language for the first time, we provide an appendix that discusses the essential constructs used in object-oriented programming. Note, however, that this discussion is simply an introduction to OO as it relates to Java. There are several books and courses dedicated to OO programming, and novice OO programmers may want to consult some of these for more information.

Internet Sources of Information

There are several online sources of information on Java. You can find online guides and tutorials on Sun's home page:

```
http://java.sun.com/
```

There are active net newsgroups dedicated to Java:

```
comp.lang.java.misc
```

```
comp.lang.java.programmer
```

There is also a mailing list where Java aficionados exchange ideas, questions, and solutions. To subscribe, send mail to majordomo@xcf.berkeley.edu. The subject must be blank, and the body of email must be the following:

```
subscribe advanced-java
end
```

From these newsgroups, mail aliases, and web sites, you'll be able to locate countless other resources, tutorials, Frequently-Asked-Questions (FAQs), and online magazines dedicated to Java.

For updates about this book and information about other books in the SunSoft Press Java Series, look on the web at:

```
http://www.sun.com/smi/ssoftpress/catalog/java_series.html
```

Conventions Used in This Book

Table P-1 shows the coding conventions used in this book.

Table P-1 Coding Conventions

Convention	Example
Class names have initial capital letters.	`public class LineOfText`
Method names have initial lowercase and the rest of the words have an initial capital letter.	`public int getLength()`
Variable names have initial lowercase and the rest of the words have an initial capital letter.	`private int length` `private int bufferLength`
Public methods and variables are first in the file, because they represent the interface for the class.	N/A
Private methods and variables are last in the file, because users of the class do not need to see these.	N/A

Braces are used in every control structure, even when there is only one statement. This is not required by Java, but rather a personal preference.	`if (num < 5) {`
	`    count++;`
	`}`

Table P-2 shows the typographic conventions used in this book.

Table P-2 Typographic Conventions

Typeface or Symbol	Description
CD-Rom	Indicates that the accompanying code, command, or file is available on the CD that accompanies this book.
courier	Indicates a command, file name, class name, method, argument, Java keyword, HTML tag, file content, or code excerpt.
bold courier	Indicates a sample command-line entry.
italics	Indicates definitions, emphasis, a book title, or a variable that you should replace with a valid value.

Applets, Applications, and Programming Aids

The CD that accompanies this book includes several Java programs that you can use, modify, or simply study to help you learn the language. These programs include:

- Applets that show simple to complex use of the Java graphics library, multiple threads, and multimedia.

- Applications that show basic input/output, interfaces, memory use, and more.

- Programs such as a public class parser that you can use to extract information about Java classes or your program's classes. We provide these as simple aids you can use to better learn and understand the Java language.

Many of these programs are discussed throughout the book, but some are presented simply for you to examine, play with, or mimic. Feel free to borrow or adapt these for your own purposes.

Java by Example CD Contents

The CD accompanying this book includes a variety of Java programs and utilities. These include the applets and applications referred to within this book, as illustrated in Table P-3.

Table P-3 CD Contents

Directory	Contents
applets	This directory contains several sample applets, including the supporting audio and image files in .au and .gif format, respectively. This directory also includes sample HTML files that can be used to view the applets with the Java appletviewer.
applications	This directory contains several illustrative Java applications, some of which are described in the book, some of which are just provided for your use.

You do not have to copy the CD contents to run the applications and applets on it. To run the programs from the CD, set the CLASSPATH environment variable to point to the Java Development Kit on the CD.

Using the Java By Example CD-ROM

About the CD-ROM

Welcome to the Java By Example CD-ROM – a disc packed with all the Java tools and source code discussed in the book.

Since this CD-ROM has been designed for use by Windows 95, Windows NT, Macintosh and Unix users, you'll notice a directory for each of these operating systems.

NOTE: 1) Windows 95 and NT 4.0 files are located inside the "Windows" directory. The "Nt35" directory contains a version of the Road Map file described below that you should use if you are running Windows NT 3.5. 2) Because this is a cross-platform CD-ROM, Solaris users may encounter error messages when loading the CD indicating the presence of files that do not conform to the ISO-9660 specification. These error messages should be ignored. Follow the instructions below for touring the CD with your Web browser. 3) This CD was designed to work with a 100% compatible Windows 95/NT system. Some of the files use long file names, which is one of the features of Windows 95. If you are unable to see the long file names on the CD, then your system may not be 100% Windows 95/NT compatible. Windows 95/NT 4.0 users can check for compatibility by double-clicking on the "System" icon in the Control Panel and then clicking on the "Performance" tab. If the "Performance" section does not indicate that "Your system is configured for optimal performance" then you have some sort of system conflict which should be resolved. Consult Windows "Help" or contact Microsoft Technical Support for further assistance.

Road Map

In addition to the various operating systems directories, the top level of this CD-ROM also contains a file named RoadMap.html. RoadMap.html is actually a Web page designed to help make sense of the contents of this disc and is a convenient way to find and preview the Java code on the disc.

To begin your tour of the disc, open RoadMap.html with your Web browser. If you are running Windows NT 3.5, first open the "Nt35" folder and use the Road-map.html file in that directory.

You'll notice three distinct buttons: Examples, Tools and JDK. These buttons correspond to the main parts of this CD-ROM. Let's begin by taking a peek behind the first button on the RoadMap, "Examples."

Examples

Clicking on the "Examples" button on the RoadMap will open the various applications and applets discussed in the book. In this way, you can view the associated Java source code and all related files directly from the CD.

If you want to install the entire set of applets and applications and their associated Java source code files directly onto your own computer, open the "Code" subdirectory located inside the directory for your operating system.

Apple Macintosh users will find a file named "examples.sea" located in their "Code" directory. This file is a self-extracting archive, as indicated by the ".sea" extension. To begin the installation, drag this file to the desktop, double-click and choose the directory on your Macintosh where you want the source code to be installed.

Windows 95 and NT users will find a file named "examples.zip" located in their "Code" directory. This file is a ZIP archive, as indicated by the ".zip" extension. To open this archive, you must use a "ZIP" utility that understands how to deal with long file names. If you don't already have such a utility, first install the "WinZip" utility that is provided on this CD-ROM – see "Tools" below for details.

To begin the installation, simply open the "examples.zip" archive with the ZIP utility and specify the location on your Windows system where you want the applets and source code to be installed.

NOTE: Be sure to use a ZIP utility that understands long file names, since a number of files in this archive have long file names!

UNIX users will find a file named "examples.tar" located in their "Code" directory. This file is a tar archive. To open this archive, you must decompress and untar it using the *uncompress* and *tar* commands.

Tools

Clicking on the "Tools" button on the RoadMap page will load the page that describes the four utilities provided on the disc, and explains how to install them on your own computer. Let's take a look at each, beginning with the Java Workshop.

NOTE: The "Tools" provided on this disc are not available for Macintosh users. Java WorkShop is available only for Windows and Solaris 2.x.

Java Workshop

The Java WorkShop is an integrated Java development environment that helps you develop projects, manage those projects, and incorporate them into Web pages. A brief interactive tour is available as well as a 30-day trial version...

How do I install it?

See the instructions below for Windows and Solaris 2.x systems.

Windows NT & 95

1. Insert the Java By Example CD into your CD-ROM drive and change to the \windows\workshop directory.
2. Run the "Setupws.exe" installer — it will uncompress and copy all the necessary files to your hard drive (default directory is C:\Java-Workshop)
3. Follow the installation instructions, by clicking the appropriate buttons and entering the installation directory when, and if, needed.
4. After the installation is complete, double-click on the Java WorkShop icon to start the workshop (A program group containing all the icons will be created)
5. When Java WorkShop loads for the first time, you will be prompted to enter a serial number. Click on the "30-day trial" button and a serial number will be entered automatically.
6. To uninstall Java Workshop, double-click the uninstall icon in the Java WorkShop Program Group.

Solaris 2.x

1. Insert the Java By Example CD into your CD-ROM drive.
2. If Volume Manager is running on your machine, the CD-ROM is automatically mounted to the /cdrom/javabyexample directory. Skip to step 3.

    If the Volume Manager is NOT running on your machine, create a directory called /cdrom/javabyexample and mount the CD-ROM manually by becoming root and typing:

    ```
    # mkdir -p /cdrom/javabyexample
    # mount -rF hsfs /dev/dsk/c0t6d0s0
    /cdrom/javabyexample
    ```
3. Go to the directory where intend to install the Java WorkShop files:

    ```
    % cd /<destination_directory>
    ```

4. Extract the Java WorkShop files by typing:

    ```
    % tar -xvf
    /cdrom/javabyexample/unix/workshop/jw_<platform>.tar
    ```

    Where <platform> is either "sparc" or "intel" depending on whether you use a SPARC or Intel system.

5. If you mounted the CD-ROM manually, unmount the drive becoming root and typing:

    ```
    # cd /
    # umount /dev/dsk/c0t6d0s0
    ```

    Otherwise, go to Step 6.

6. Eject the CD by typing:

    ```
    % cd /
    % eject
    ```

    You can now use Java WorkShop.

7. Start Java WorkShop by typing:

    ```
    % /<destination_directory>/JWS/<platform>-S2/bin/jws &
    ```

Café Lite

Café Lite is a version of Symantec's integrated Java development environment for Windows 95 and Windows NT that allows you to edit, build, and execute Java programs from the Windows desktop.

How do I install it (Windows 95 & NT only)?

Locate the "Cafelite" installer inside the "Tools" folder in the Windows directory.

Double-click the Cafelite installer program. This will begin the installation process.

WinEdit

WinEdit is the Windows Editor that you can use to edit virtually any text file. It is specifically designed to be a programmer's editor and can execute compilers and check for error messages.

How do I install it?

This package contains all the pieces to install WinEdit for Windows NT and Windows 95

1. Locate the "WinEdit" installer inside the "Tools" folder in the Windows Directory.

2. Double-click the WinEdit installer program. This will begin the installation process.

The installation program adds the directory you specified for installing WinEdit to the PATH statement in your AUTOEXEC.BAT file.

WinZip

WinZip brings the convenience of Windows to the use of ZIP files. It features an intuitive point-and-click drag-and-drop interface for viewing, running, extracting, adding, deleting, and testing files in archives.

How do I install it?

1. Locate the "WinZip95" installer inside the "Tools" folder in the Windows Directory.
2. Double-click the WinZip95 installer program. This will begin the installation process.
3. The setup program will display a dialog box first prompting you to proceed with set up and then asking you where to install WinZip95.
4. Follow the on-screen installation instructions.

JDK

How do I install it?

To install the JDK, follow the instructions below for your particular operating system.

Windows NT & 95

1. Create a directory named "java" on the top level of your hard drive (usually the C drive). Copy the "Jdk_x86" ZIP archive file from the CD into the "java" directory you've just created. You can either drag and drop the file using your mouse, or issue the following command from the DOS prompt (where "d" is the drive containing the CD):

   ```
   copy d:\windows\Jdk\Jdk_x86.zip c:\java
   ```

   NOTE: The installation takes up about 5.5Mbytes. Be SURE to remove any previous version of the JDK that may already exist on your computer.

2. Open the "Jdk_x86" archive with a ZIP utility that supports long file names (such as WinZip, a popular ZIP program supplied on this CD-ROM) and unpack the files it contains into the "java" directory created in step 1.

   NOTE: This step will fill the "java" directory with the various files and subdirectories that make up the JDK. In the resulting "lab" directory you'll find a another ZIP archive named "classes.zip" — this archive should not be further unpacked, as the compiler needs to see it in this form. You can, however, unpack the "src.zip" archive to review the source for the runtime library. It's essential to use a ZIP utility that preserves long file names.

3. Once the JDK files have been unpacked onto your hard drive, you'll need to add (or modify) 2 variables in your autoexec.bat. To do this, open your autoexec.bat file with a text editor.

   First, add the "java\bin" directory to your path:

   ```
   SET PATH=c:\java\bin; (... the rest of your path follows...)
   ```

Next, set the CLASSPATH variable to point to the current directory and the Java runtime library (the classes.zip archive):

```
SET CLASSPATH=.;c:\java\lib\classes.zip
```

4. Save these changes to your autoexec.bat, and restart your computer so the new variables take effect.

NOTE: Once installed, you can delete the installer archive (JDK_x86.zip) from your hard drive.

Macintosh

Macintosh System Requirements: A Macintosh with at least a 68030/25MHz or better CPU or a Power Mac. System 7.5.3. revision 2 is recommended. Approximately 7MB of free disk space is also required.

1. Copy the "JDK-1_0_2-MacOS.sea" installer file found in the JDK folder onto your hard disk.

2. Double-click on the "JDK-1_0_2-MacOS.sea" installer icon, and follow the instructions that appear.

NOTE: Quicktime 2.0 or later is needed for the installation to work properly. Some people have reported problems due to old Mac software installing a down-rev version of the Quicktime extension. If you run into a problem, reinstall Quicktime 2.x and try again.

Solaris 2.x

Installation instructions are the same for Solaris 2.x for SPARC and Solaris 2.x for x86. On Intel systems, use "x86" instead of "sparc" in the filenames below. Make sure you are running an up-to-date version of Solaris 2.x, preferably Solaris 2.5.1.

1. Change directory to the location where you want to install the JDK. Let's assume you're installing it in /home/jones:

```
cd /home/jones
```

2. Untar the file:

```
tar -xvf /cdrom/javabyexample/unix/jdk/sparc.tar
```

This is a 4.7Mbyte file, so it will take a few seconds to pull off the CD.

You should see dozens of lines indicating the files being untar'd.

3. Add the JAVA_HOME environment variable to your .cshrc (or whatever initialization for the shell you use). For the cshell, add the following line:

```
setenv JAVA_HOME /home/jones/java
```

Also add $JAVA_HOME/bin to your existing search path:

```
set path=($JAVA_HOME/bin ... rest of path ...)
```

4. Logout and login again so the new variables take effect.

NOTE: If you experience any problems with the Java By Example CD, check the SunSoft Press Java Series Web page for updates:

http://www.prenhall.com/~java_sun

Acknowledgments

With the second edition of this book, we'd like to extend our appreciation to the people who have been using our book and have pointed out areas where we could improve our coverage or avoid confusion. We're most appreciative of the help given by Spencer Roberts, Software Consultant for MCI, Inc. Spencer provided excellent inputs on all the new material. We'd also like to thank Shawn Wass, Rod King, and Dale Passmore who, through their use of the book, have pointed out several routine problems we missed in the first edition.

We still owe so much to all the people who originally helped on the first edition. That list of people includes Vasanthan S. Dasan, Paul Kasper, Rob Gordon, Brian Smithey, Craig A. Lindley, David Geary, Margaret McCormack, Andrea Mankoski, Mike Jessie (third base coach), Jerry Jelinek, Steve Senator, Bob Hendrich, Bill Birnbaum, Don Allen, Ph.D., and Lou Ordorica.

Our book is still on the shelves in part to the thorough reviews we received from professionals in the industry. For those reviews, we extend our thanks to Michael K. Mahoney, Ph.D., of California State University, Long Beach, Claude W. Anderson, III, of Rose-Hulman Institute of Technology, Len Dorfman, Ph.D., of Hofstra University, Clovis Tondo, Ph.D., President of T&T TechWorks, Doug Langston, Programmer/Analyst, Andrew Nathanson, and Tim Davis, System Design Engineer for Hewlett Packard.

We've continued to enjoy the support of our management at SunSoft's Rocky Mountain Technology Center (RMTC). That support has come from Eric H. Corwin, the Director of SunSoft's RMTC, Randy Kalmeta, Dale E. Ferrario, Chris Silveri, and Dave Sample, Software Engineering Managers, Lynn Rohrer and Diane Plampin, Publications Managers, and Beth Papiano, Human Resources Director.

As always, the people at Prentice Hall and SunSoft Press have been extremely helpful. We owe much to Greg Doench, Mary Sudul, Jim Markham, Leabe Berman, Lisa Iarkowski, and Camille Trentacoste of Prentice Hall. Rachel Borden and John Bortner of SunSoft Press continue to provide all the support we could ask for.

We're also grateful for the work of our editor, Lunaea Hougland and our indexer, Mary Lou Nohr.

Lastly, we'd like to thank our wives and families. Just when they thought they might have us back, we began working on this second edition. Once again, they've helped make this edition possible by giving us the time to write this book. Also, Julie is a great proofreader.

Oh, the Celebese Kalossi from BB Bean coffee roasters in Colorado Springs is still inspiring.

PART ONE

Working With the Java Language

CHAPTER
1

- Java Overview

- Using the Java Compiler and Interpreter

- Using the appletviewer

- The Difference Between Java Applications and Applets

- Applets and Web Pages

About Java

What Is Java?

Java is a general purpose object-oriented programming language. It provides a number of extensions that support development of GUI applications, as well as development of client/server applications over local and wide area networks. Given all the attention and interest in the Java programming language, it's somewhat surprising that there is very little new in it. However, that may account for its sudden popularity. It is mostly a collection of familiar constructs and features from programming languages such as C, C++, Objective-C, SmallTalk, and Common Lisp. From C and C++, Java borrows its syntax and its variable scoping model. From Objective-C, Java uses the concept of interfaces. From SmallTalk, Java borrows its model of runtime extensibility, dynamic memory management, and multiple threads of execution (multithreading). To these, Java adds security, a simple programming paradigm, and more.

Another reason for Java's popularity among programmers is that it is architecturally neutral. It is an interpreted language, and you can run Java programs on any platform that has the Java interpreter and runtime environment. This enables programmers to write code (and write it once) that can execute on a variety of hardware platforms and operating systems, as illustrated in Table 1-1.

Table 1-1 Platforms/Operating Systems Supporting Java

Hardware Platform	Operating System
SPARC	Solaris
Intel	WindowsNT, Windows95
Macintosh	MacOS 7.5

It is likely that several other platforms and operating systems will soon have their own ports of Java. These include Windows 3.1, OS/2, OSF/1, HP-UX, Linux, NEXTSTEP, Solaris for Intel, and SunOS 4.x.

Java and the World-Wide Web

It's safe to say that the merits of the Java programming language have been highlighted by its suitability for use on the world-wide web. It is, in fact, the programming language of the web. Its popularity has grown with the web's growth and with the advent of web browsers (such as Netscape Navigator, Internet Explorer, and HotJava) that are capable of running Java programs to incorporate audio, video, and animation directly into a web page. The Java programming language gives commercial, educational, and recreational programmers a language they can use to change web pages that are static and flat into web pages that are dynamic, lively, and rich.

The Java Compiler and the Java Interpreter

Even though Java is an interpreted language, Java programs must be compiled first. The Java compiler (`javac`) converts the program source code into bytecodes that can be executed in the Java runtime environment. The Java interpreter (`java`) executes the compiled bytecode on the local system. The `javac` and `java` programs reside in the `bin` directory of the Java Development Kit (JDK). For example, if the JDK were installed in a directory named `/local/jdk`, you'd find the `javac` compiler and `java` interpreter in the `/local/jdk/bin` directory.

The Appletviewer Program

An *applet* is simply a Java program that executes in the context of a web browser capable of executing that program. The JDK also includes an `appletviewer` program to enable you to view applets without having to start a web browser. Like the `javac` compiler and the `java` interpreter, the `appletviewer` program resides in the `bin` directory of the JDK. (*Writing, Compiling, and Viewing an Applet* on page 6 shows how to invoke the `appletviewer` program.)

Applications and Applets

Java programs come in two flavors: standalone applications and web browser applets. Java applications and applets differ slightly in their structure. C programmers can find an equivalent to main() in a Java application, but it is missing altogether in applet code.

Writing, Compiling, and Running an Application

Example 1-1 shows a simple hello world application in Java.

Example 1-1 Hello World Application

```
public class HelloWorld {
  public static void main(String[] args) {
    System.out.println("Hello Brave New World!");
  }
}
```

Just as in a C or C++ program, main() is the first piece of code that is executed in a Java application.

To produce an executable program, you have to first compile the hello world program into bytecodes. Assume for the moment that the source file is named HelloWorld.java. (By convention, Java source files must be named *filename*.java.) Example 1-2 shows the command line to compile the program.

Example 1-2 Compiling Hello World

```
javac HelloWorld.java
```

The javac compiler produces a compiled bytecode file named *filename*.class. For instance, compiling the HelloWorld.java file produces a file named HelloWorld.class. To execute the program, you invoke the java interpreter, as in Example 1-3.

Example 1-3 Invoking the Java Interpreter

```
java HelloWorld
```

The compiled program is stored in a file named HelloWorld.class,. The java interpreter requires class name (in this case, HelloWorld) as an argument.

Running the `java` interpreter on the `HelloWorld` program would produce the following output:

```
Hello Brave New World!
```

Writing, Compiling, and Viewing an Applet

A Java applet looks quite a bit different from a Java application. Example 1-4 shows a hello world applet.

Example 1-4 Hello World Applet

```
import java.applet.Applet;
import java.awt.Graphics;

public class HelloWorldApplet extends Applet {
  public void paint(Graphics g) {
     g.drawString("Hello Brave New World!", 50, 25);
  }
}
```

You'll notice that there's no `main()` statement. It is not required for applets. (An applet can also have a `main()` and execute as a standalone application. However, this means you have to manually add some support that is normally handled by the browser.) Java applets are invoked differently than Java applications. We'll get into the nitty-gritty of these differences later. For now, understand that applets use a special set of browser and graphics support, while applications are similar to conventional programs written in an object-oriented language.

You use the `javac` compiler to compile all Java programs in the same way (see Example 1-2), whether they are applications or applets. However, an applet is normally going to execute within a web browser. Instead of invoking the `java` interpreter from the command line to execute an applet, you embed HTML tags that reference the applet within a web page. For developing rapid applet prototypes, it's helpful to use the `appletviewer`. To do so, create a minimal HTML file, as in Example 1-5 and include the name of the compiled applet (in this case, `HelloWorldApplet.class`).

Example 1-5 Minimal HTML File With an Applet Reference

```
<title>Hello World Applet</title>
<hr>
<applet code="HelloWorldApplet.class" width=250 height=80>
</applet>
<hr>
```

After you've created a minimal HTML file, you can use the `appletviewer` to view the applet. Simply run `appletviewer` from the command line and specify the HTML file as an argument. For instance, assuming an HTML file named `HelloWorldApplet.html`, you could use the command in Example 1-6 to view the applet with the `appletviewer`.

Example 1-6 Invoking the `appletviewer` Program

```
appletviewer HelloWorldApplet.html
```

Figure 1-1 shows sample output from this command.

Figure 1-1 Displaying an Applet in the `appletviewer`

Of course, you can also include the HTML code in a web page and view the applet in a Java-enabled web browser. Then, when activated from the web page, the applet executes.

Incorporating Applets Into a Web Page

As previously mentioned, a Java program that runs within a web page is called an applet. However, not all web browsers are capable of executing Java applets. Netscape Navigator, Internet Explorer, and HotJava are the most prominent of the browsers currently capable of executing Java applets.

Although Java is a programming language, you don't have to be a programmer to incorporate a Java applet into your home page. A Java applet can be integrated easily into the HTML code that defines a web page. You just need to use the HTML `applet` tag, as in Example 1-7.

Example 1-7 The Basic HTML `applet` Tag Syntax

```
<applet code="applet_name.class" width=width height=height> </applet>
```

In this example, *applet_name* is name of the applet, including the `.class` extension of a compiled Java program. The *width* and *height* are numbers representing the width and height of the applet in pixels.

You can also include a set of parameters to specify exactly how you want the applet displayed. However, this only makes sense in the context of an applet with parameters, which we describe in *The HTML applet and param Tags* on page 380.

Summary

Java is a general purpose object-oriented programming language based on several already popular and familiar languages. Java programs can be written to be executed from a command line or from within a web browser. The former programs are Java applications, and the latter are referred to as Java applets. Applets can only execute in browsers that support Java. Those include Netscape Navigator, and Microsoft Internet Explorer 3.0. The HTML `applet` tag is used to specify an applet within a web page.

Although Java is an interpreted language, Java programs must be compiled using the Java compiler (`javac`). The compiler converts the program source code into bytecodes that can be executed in the Java runtime environment. The Java interpreter (`java`) executes the compiled bytecode on the local system.

CHAPTER
2

Beginning With a Program

A Line Counter Program

To begin our discussion of Java, let's look at a simple program that counts the number of lines in a file. The program is used in the following way:

```
java CountLines file1  [file2 ... fileN]
```

The program will output the sum of lines in the files listed as arguments on the command line.

Much of the program will probably look familiar. You'll notice that Java looks a lot like C or C++. Java syntax was designed to be consistent with C usage where possible. First, we'll show the entire program in Example 2-1. Then, we'll take you through it, highlighting some key features.

Example 2-1 A Line Counter Program

```java
import java.io.*;

// The CountLines class will count and sum up the number of
// lines in the text files passed as arguments on the command line.

public class CountLines {

  public static void main(String[] args) {
    // Check usage. CountLines expects at least one file to count.

    if (args.length < 1) {
      System.err.println(
         "Usage: java CountLines <file1>...<fileN>");
       return;
    }

    // Initialize the line count.

    int lineCount = 0;

    // Loop through the file arguments and count the lines in each
    // file.

    for (int i = 0; i < args.length; i++) {

      // Wrap the processing of each file in a try/catch block in
      // case a read error occurs or the file can't be opened.
      // Save the current line count and revert to it if there
      // is an error processing the current file.

      int       savedLineCount = lineCount;
      InputStream in           = null;

      try {

        // Create a buffered stream connected to the current
        // file.

        in = new BufferedInputStream(
           new FileInputStream(args[i]));

        // The wasNewline flag is used to make sure we count a
        // final line that is terminated with EOF and has no
        // newline.
```

CD-Rom

```java
        boolean wasNewline = true;
        int    ch;

        // Loop through the characters and increment the
        // linecount when a newline is seen. The stream is
        // buffered so reading a character at a time is
        // efficient.

        while ((ch = in.read()) != EOF) {
            if (ch == '\n') {
                lineCount++;
                wasNewline = true;
            } else {
                wasNewline = false;
            }
        }

        // If we reached EOF and the previous character was not
        // a newline, increment the linecount.

        if (wasNewline == false) {
            lineCount++;
        }

    } catch (IOException e) {

        // If an exception occurred during the processing of
        // the current file, print a message and reset the
        // linecount.

        System.err.println(
            "Error while processing \"" + args[i] +
            "\": not counted.");
        lineCount = savedLineCount;
    }

    // Close the stream for this file. The in variable might be
    // null if an exception occurred during stream creation

    if (in != null) {
        try {
            in.close();
        } catch (IOException e) {
        }

        in = null;
    }
}
```

```
   // Display the final count.

   System.out.println(lineCount);
  }
  // A constant representing end of file.

  private static final int EOF = -1;
}
```

A Closer Look at the Line Counter

Now that you've had a chance to see a simple Java program, let's take a closer look at it. (Rather than define all the new terms and features right here, we'll point you to sections of this book where various topics are covered in more detail.)

Let's go through the program a piece at a time:

```
import java.io.*;
```

The first line is similar to an `include` statement in C or C++, except that an `import` doesn't actually insert anything into the current file. It just tells the compiler that the program will reference definitions in the named package. (Packages are described in more detail in *Packages and the import Statement* on page 44.) In this case, this class will reference definitions in the `java.io` package. The asterisk (*) is a wildcard character indicating that this class will have access to any class in the `java.io` package.

```
   // The CountLines class will count and sum up the number of
   // lines in the text files passed as arguments on the command line.
```

A series of comments follows the `import` statement. Java supports both C style (`/* */`) and C++ style (`//`) comments.

```
   public class CountLines {
```

A Java program consists of a set of class definitions. The first class defined in this program is called `CountLines`. The `public` keyword means that any other class may use this class. (Classes are discussed in *The Java Language Structure* on page 21, and scope modifiers such as `public` are discussed in *Method Modifiers and Their Scope* on page 32.) This is a standard opening statement for a class definition.

```
   public static void main(String[] args) {
```

A Java class that is used as the top level of an application must provide a `main()` method just as a C or C++ program provides a `main()` function. In Java, a `main()` method takes an array of `String` objects as its arguments and has no return value. (The `static` modifier is described in *Method Modifiers and Their Scope* on page 32.)

Unlike C or C++, the argument array for a `main()` method in Java does not contain the name of the program. The first element in the array is the first argument.

```
// Check usage. CountLines expects at least one file to
// count.

if (args.length < 1) {
    System.err.println(
        "Usage: java CountLines <file1>...<fileN>");
    return;
}

// Initialize the line count.
```

`System.err` is the standard error stream for a Java program. Java has predefined standard input, output, and error streams just like C and C++.

```
int lineCount = 0;

// Loop through the file arguments and count the lines in
// each file.
```

Variables may be declared anywhere in Java and not just at the top of a block as in C.

```
for (int i = 0; i < args.length; i++) {

    // Wrap the processing of each file in a try/catch block
    // in case a read error occurs or the file can't be
    // opened.
    // Save the current line count and revert to it if
    // there in an error processing the current file.

    int         savedLineCount = lineCount;
    InputStream in             = null;
```

Arrays in Java have lengths associated with them. `args.length` returns the size of the argument array. Also note that the `in` variable is assigned `null`. This is an explicit `null` value that is distinct from all objects.

```
try {
```

This line is the start of the `try` block, used for *exception handling*. (Exceptions are described in detail *Exception Handling* on page 99.) Java deals with errors through an exception handling model. The Java exception handling model is almost identical to the one used in C++, but Java relies much more heavily on exceptions than does C++. Any error condition that arises within this `try` block will cause control to transfer to the `catch` block.

```
// Create a buffered stream connected to the current
// file.

in = new BufferedInputStream(

         new FileInputStream(args[i]));
```

Java provides a building block approach to I/O. (See *Input/Output* on page 111 for details about the Java I/O.) This section of the `CountLines` program creates a `FileInputStream` to read from a file and obtains buffering by wrapping a `BufferedInputStream` around it.

```
// The wasNewline flag is used to make sure we count a
// final line that is terminated with EOF and has no
// newline.

boolean wasNewline = true;
int     ch;
```

Java has a primitive `boolean` type that is unrelated to the integer type. The `boolean` values are `true` and `false`.

```
// Loop through the characters and increment the
// linecount when a newline is seen. The stream is
// buffered so reading a character at a time is
// efficient.

while ((ch = in.read()) != EOF) {
   if (ch == '\n') {
       lineCount++;
       wasNewline = true;

   } else {
       wasNewline = false;
   }
}

// If we reached EOF and the previous character was
// not a newline, increment the linecount.
```

```
    if (wasNewline == false) {
        lineCount++;
    }
```

The previous block of code looks almost exactly like C.

```
catch (IOException e) {

    // If an exception occurred during the processing of
    // the current file, print a message and reset the
    // linecount.

    System.err.println(
    "Error while processing \"" + args[i] +
        "\": not counted.");
    lineCount = savedLineCount;
}
```

This is the catch block that goes with the previous try block. If an error occurs in the try block, control will transfer to this catch block. In this case the errors are file I/O errors so we print a message and go on to the next file. Note that strings in Java may be concatenated using + .

```
    // Close the stream for this file. The in variable might
    // be null if an exception occurred during stream
    // creation.

    if (in != null) {
        try {
            in.close();
        } catch (IOException e) {
        }

        in = null;
    }
}
```

In the previous block, the program closes each file before going to the next one. If an error occurs when closing the file, the catch block will trap the error.

```
    // Display the final count.

    System.out.println(lineCount);
}
```

This is the end of the main() method. The System.out.println() method will display the sum of lines in all files listed as arguments to the program.

```
// A constant representing end of file.
private static final int EOF = -1;
}
```

This variable declaration defines the `EOF` constant used earlier in the program. The `InputStream read()` method returns `-1` on the end of file. The `final` modifier means the value of the variable will not change; it is treated as a constant.

Output From the Line Counter

The `CountLines` program outputs the number of lines in all files specified on the command line. For example, assuming a single file with 227 lines, the command line and output would look like this:

java CountLines file
227

Summary

This example shows that Java is closely related to C and C++. A programmer familiar with these languages can read simple Java programs fairly easily right away. Throughout the rest of this book, we will discuss the unique features of Java and the differences between it and the C family of languages.

In the next chapter, we'll delve into some necessary details about the Java language structure.

CHAPTER
3

- All About Classes and Methods
- Method Modifiers and Their Scope
- Variables, Methods, and Superclasses
- Packages and the import Statement

The Java Language Structure

Introduction

When working with a new programming language, there are basic language constructs and features that influence the way you develop your programs. We'll spend some time in the next few chapters describing these. We'll begin in this chapter by giving an overview of the basic structure of the Java language.

Classes and Methods

As we alluded to in the previous chapter, the fundamental structure in Java is a class. A class definition in Java corresponds to the definition of a structured type in C, and an *instance* of a class corresponds to a C structure. The fields or members of a structure in C also have an equivalent in Java. They are the *instance variables* of an instance of a Java class. For example, consider the following C structure:

```
struct point {
   int x;      /* a field/member */
   int y;
};
```

Now, here's a corresponding Java class definition:

```
class Point {
   int x;      // an instance variable
   int y;
}
```

An instance of a Java class can also have functions associated with it. These functions are called *methods*, and they act on the instance variables of the class, as illustrated in the following:

```
class Point {
   int x;
   int y;

   // A method that returns how far this Point is from (0,0).

   double distanceFromOrigin() {
     return Math.sqrt(x * x + y * y);
   }
}
```

Java has nothing that corresponds to C's global, free-standing functions (such as `printf`, `strcmp`, etc.). Each method is associated with a particular class and is referred to as a method of that class. Example 3-1 shows a sample class definition and the methods of that class. We'll present several new terms in this example and then explain them throughout the rest of this chapter

Example 3-1 Anatomy of a Class Definition

CD-Rom

```
public class Card {

   // INSTANCE METHODS

   // Methods that return the suit and rank of a
   // particular card as Strings.

❶ public String getRank() {
     return ranks[rank];
   }

❷ public String getSuit() {
```

```
    return suits[suit];
  }

  // A method that returns whether the current card
  // is of higher rank than the argument card.

❸ public boolean higherRank(Card otherCard) {
    return rank > otherCard.rank;
  }

  // CLASS METHODS

  // Shuffle the deck.

❹ public static void shuffle() {
    for (int card = 0; card < cards.length; card++) {
      int otherCard     =
          (int)(Math.random() * 100) % DECKSIZE;
      Card temp          = cards[otherCard];
      cards[otherCard] = cards[card];
      cards[card]       = temp;
    }

    nextCard = 0;
  }

  // Deal a card.

❺ public static Card deal() {
    if (nextCard == DECKSIZE) {
      return null;
    } else {
      return cards[nextCard++];
    }
  }

  // INSTANCE VARIABLES

  // Variables representing the rank and suit of a particular
  // card.

❻ private int rank;
❼ private int suit;
```

```
// CONSTRUCTORS

// Construct a new card. Since there is a fixed set of 52 cards,
// don't let anyone else call this.
```

❽
```
private Card(int newSuit, int newRank) {
  suit = newSuit;
  rank = newRank;
}

// CLASS VARIABLES

// The deck.

private static final int    DECKSIZE = 52;
private static final Card[] cards    = new Card[DECKSIZE];

// Class variables representing different card suits and ranks.
```

❾
```
private static final int    NUMRANKS = 13;
private static final int    NUMSUITS = 4;
private static final String[] suits = {"C", "D", "H", "S"};
private static final String[] ranks =
  {"A",  "2", "3", "4", "5", "6", "7", "8", "9",
   "10", "J", "Q", "K"};

// Class variable holding the index of the next card to deal.

private static int nextCard;

// STATIC INITIALIZER

// A static initializer that initializes the deck of cards.
```

❿
```
static {
  int cardNumber = 0;

  for (int cardSuit = 0; cardSuit < NUMSUITS; cardSuit++) {
    for (int cardRank = 0; cardRank < NUMRANKS; cardRank++) {
      cards[cardNumber++] = new Card(cardSuit, cardRank);
    }
  }
  shuffle();
}
}
```

In Example 3-1:

❶, ❷, and ❸ on page 22 are instance methods of the Card class. Instance methods are associated with a particular instance of a class.

❹ and ❺ on page 23 are class methods of the Card class. Class methods deal with the class as a whole rather than with individual instances of the class.

❻ and ❼ on page 23 are instance variables for the Card class. Each card has its own copies of rank and suit just as a C structure would.

❽ on page 24 is the *constructor* for the Card class. A call to it creates a new instance of Card. (The next chapter, *Memory and Constructors*, describes constructors in more detail.)

❾ on page 24 begins a set of class variable definitions for the Card class. There is only one copy of each of these variables for the whole class.

❿ on page 24 is a *static initializer* for the Card class. It is used to initialize class data when a class is first created.

Now, having dissected the Card class, let's look at each feature in more detail.

Instance Methods

In Java, an *instance method* is a method associated with a particular instance of a class. When an instance method is called, it has access to the data contained in the instance it's associated with.

In the Card class example, the getSuit() method will return a String representing the suit of a particular card. Assume, for example, two cards—card1 and card2:

```
❶ card1.getSuit();
❷ card2.getSuit();
```

These are calls to instance methods. The call in line ❶ would return either C, D, H, or S, depending on the suit of card1. Likewise, the call in line ❷ would return either C, D, H, or S, depending on the suit of card2.

The Java syntax for invoking a method is:

<object> . *<method_name>* (*arg1*, *arg2*, ... *argN*)

In the case of an instance method, *<object>* must refer to an instance of a class that defines *<method_name>*.

Class Methods

Class methods are associated with a class as a whole, not with a particular instance. They are declared `static` in the class definition, in a manner similar to C++. The `shuffle()` and `deal()` methods in the `Card` class are class methods. They could be used as follows:

```
Card.shuffle();
Card nextCard = Card.deal();
```

Instead of calling the method on a particular instance of the `Card` class, you would call the method using the name of the class itself. The Java syntax for calling a class method is:

<class_name> . *<method_name>* (*arg1*, *arg2*, ... *argN*)

Class methods have a broader focus than instance methods. They can deal with information that is meaningful for the entire class. For instance, in the `Card` class example, the `shuffle()` and `deal()` methods manipulate an entire deck of cards, not just a single individual card.

Java allows class methods to be called in the same way as instance methods, but when this is done, the actual instance it is called on is irrelevant. For example:

```
❶ Card card1 = Card.deal();
❷ Card card2 = card1.deal();
```

In this example, line ❶ is a normal call to a class method. Line ❷ is a call to a class method, but using an instance-style reference to that method. Using `card1.deal()` is equivalent to finding the `deal()` method in `card1`'s class. This call is valid, but `card1` is only used to determine its class so the proper method can be called.

All class methods are implicitly *final* methods. As such, they cannot be overridden. (See *Final Methods* on page 32 for information.)

The main() Method

All Java applications include the equivalent of `main()`. It is a method declared in the top-level class in the program. (By top-level class here, we mean the class that is used as an argument to the `java` interpreter. The `main()` method in that top-level class controls the program's execution.)

You always define the `main()` method as in Example 3-2.

Example 3-2 The Java `main()` Method Declaration

```
   public class RunCalculator {
❶     public static void main (String[] args) {
          .
          .
          .
      }
   }
```

There are several things worth pointing out about the `main()` declaration. Note in line ❶ that the `main()` statement returns a `void`. Whereas in C and C++, `main()` returns a value (a status code), there is no return value associated with `main()` in Java. That is because `main()` status is handled by means of the Java exception handling model. (See *Exception Handling* on page 99 for details.)

You can actually have multiple `main()` methods within the classes used by a Java program. However, the only one that is recognized is the one in the class used as an argument to the `java` interpreter. For example, if the top-level `main()` method is in a class named `RunCalculator`, that `main()` method is executed by virtue of the command:

```
java RunCalculator
```

Overriding Methods

Java allows one class to be a subclass of another class. (See *Inheritance* on page 347 for more details about how this works.) All the attributes and methods of one class are applicable to the subclass as well. (This is not *strictly* true in Java, as we will see later in the discussion of method scope, but the reasons for its inaccuracy aren't relevant at the moment.) These attributes and methods are said to be *inherited* from the parent class, which is referred to as the *superclass*. If the new class you're defining behaves exactly like its superclass, except in areas that aren't defined for the superclass, then just inheriting everything from the superclass works fine. For instance, a RedWagon class is just like a Wagon class except in the area of color, which isn't defined for Wagon.

Consider, however, a class Window that represents windows on a computer screen. Let's say it has an instance method called draw() that displays windows on the screen. Now we want to create a window with a border. We could say that the WindowWithBorder class behaves just like Window, but we want to add a new drawBorder() method that covers the border area that isn't defined for Window. This approach seems reasonable, but what if we have a program that iterates through a list of windows and redraws them? Does it have to check each Window to see if it's a WindowWithBorder and, if so, call drawBorder() on it? What if there is also a WindowWithTitle?

To avoid building extensive knowledge about the structure of the Window class hierarchy into every program that wants to draw a Window, we need to take a different approach. We can say that drawing a WindowWithBorder means something different than just drawing a Window. We'd like draw() to do the normal Window drawing *and* draw the border for a WindowWithBorder. Java provides support for this approach by allowing you to override methods. You can create a WindowWithBorder class that inherits all the attributes and methods of the Window class, but you can redefine the draw() method. For instance, consider the code in Example 3-3.

Example 3-3 Overriding Methods

```
❶ public class WindowWithBorder extends Window {
     .
     .
     .
❷    public void draw() {
❸      super.draw();
❹      drawBorder();
     }

     private void drawBorder() {
       .
       .
       .
     }
   }
```

In line ❶ the use of the extends keyword guarantees that the WindowWithBorder class will inherit everything in the Window class.

Now, when the program iterates through a list of windows and calls the draw() method in line ❷ on a WindowWithBorder, it will draw the Window part and then draw the border. The program can now just call draw() on any type of Window and the right thing will happen.

To override a method, the new method (WindowWithBorder.draw() in our example) must have the same name, argument types, and return type as the corresponding method in its superclass. (The method name, argument types, and return type are referred to as the *signature* of the method.) If you just want to override the method in the superclass, that's all there is to it. If you want to extend the method, as in Example 3-3, Java provides the super reserved word (as in line ❸) to invoke the superclass method from within the new method. A method defined in the superclass may be invoked as follows:

```
super.<method_name>(arg1, arg2, ... argN)
```

In our example, we call super.draw() to draw the normal Window features (that is, we call the draw() method of the superclass). Then we call drawBorder() in line ❹ to complete the task.

Abstract Methods

Java provides the ability to specify the interface of a method without defining that method. Doing this can be very useful when you know that classes in your program will have to provide a particular operation, but the specifics of that operation may vary from subclass to subclass. For instance, in Example 3-4 we're writing a set of classes to support bank accounts.

Example 3-4 Abstract Methods

```
❶ public abstract class BankAccount {
     // Create a new BankAccount.
     public BankAccount(double balance, double interestRate) {
       accountBalance      = balance;
       accountInterestRate = interestRate;
       accountNumber       = nextAccountNumber++;
     }
     public double getbalance() {
       return accountBalance;
     }

     public double getInterestRate() {
       return accountInterestRate;
     }

     public int getAccountNumber() {
       return accountNumber;
     }

     // Compute interest. The method varies depending on the type of
     // account, so we declare it to be abstract.
❷    public abstract computeInterest();

     // The next account number is incremented each time an account
     // is created.
     private static int nextAccountNumber = 1;

     private double accountBalance;
     private double accountInterestRate;
     private int    accountNumber;
   }
```

We must declare BankAccount to be an abstract class as in line ❶ because it contains the abstract method, computeInterest(), which is not fully specified.

In line ❷, we declare computeInterest() to be an abstract method because there isn't any general body of code we could give it. However, we know that it needs to be defined in the subclasses of the BankAccount class. If we were to leave computeInterest() out of the BankAccount class definition and define it only in subclasses of BankAccount, we couldn't deal with BankAccount objects in a generic way. For example, if we wanted to write a method to calculate interest for all the BankAccount objects and print the results, we wouldn't be able to write the following loop because computeInterest() would not be defined for the BankAccount class:

```
for (int i = 0; i < numBankAccounts; i++) {
   BankAccount account = bankAccounts[i];
   System.out.println(account.getAccountNumber() + ": "
                  + account.computeInterest());
}
```

By making computeInterest() an abstract method, we can specify that it's part of the BankAccount abstraction without being forced to put in some kind of dummy definition.

Native Methods

Not all code can be written in Java. Java is platform-independent, and it is sometimes necessary to write platform-specific code. Java programmers may also need to reuse code they've already written in other languages.

Java provides the capability to do this with a facility called *native methods*. Example 3-5 shows how to declare a native method in Java.

Example 3-5 Declaring a Native Method

```
// blink the dashboard lights
native void blinkLights(int numtimes);
```

Note that there is only a declaration; no method body is included.

The Java developers picked C as the default native method language, and they provided support for hooking C code into the Java interpreter. We'll describe the support for creating native methods in our section on *Linking With C Code* on page 133.

Final Methods

Final methods are methods that cannot be overridden by methods in subclasses. (Recall that class methods are `final` methods.) When you declare a method `final`, you are saying that the implementation provided will never change. This allows the Java compiler to optimize by inlining final methods. (*Inlining* refers to replacing a call to a method with the body of the method after substituting for arguments—similar to macroexpansion.) This means that in many cases, the compiler can avoid looking up a method, which can lead to large speedups if the method-calling overhead is a significant part of the time required to execute the method.

Method Modifiers and Their Scope

Method modifiers in Java can be divided into two groups, based on whether or not they affect the scope of a method. *Scope* in a programming language refers to the region of a program in which a particular item such as a class, method, or variable may be accessed.

First, let's look at those modifiers that do not affect the scope of a method. Table 3-1 describes these modifiers.

Table 3-1 Method Modifiers That Do Not Affect Scope

Method Modifier Is...	Then...	Use for...
`final`	The method cannot be overridden by a method in a subclass.	Methods you do not want to change or methods you want the `javac` compiler to inline for performance reasons. (The `javac` compiler attempts to inline small `final` methods.)
`static`	The method is a class method.	Methods that do not rely on data internal to a particular instance of the class.

Table 3-1 Method Modifiers That Do Not Affect Scope (Continued)

Method Modifier Is...	Then...	Use for...
native	The method body will be written in C and linked into the interpreter.	Methods you want to be platform specific or methods you want to use to link in pre-existing code.
abstract	The method is not defined in the class. It must be defined in a subclass.	General-purpose methods that have no meaningful default operations. These methods are fully defined in subclasses.
synchronized	The method will acquire a lock on the instance (or on the class, if it is a class method) before running and will relinquish the lock when it completes. We describe synchronized methods in detail in *Multiple Threads of Execution* on page 147.	Methods that might interfere with each other in a threaded application.

Now let's look at those method modifiers that do affect a method's scope.

Methods in Java can have one of three primary scopes assigned to them: public, private, and *friendly*. Additionally, the protected modifier can be used to further define a method's scope. Table 3-2 summarizes how these modifiers affect the scope of a method.

Table 3-2 Method Modifiers That Affect Scope

Method Modifier Is...	Then...	Use to Define...
public	The method can be accessed by any class.	The external interfaces of your classes.
private	The method can be accessed only by methods within the same class.	Methods that are internal and only relevant to a particular class (and irrelevant to users of the class).
Not Explicitly Specified (a *friendly* Modifier)	The method can be accessed by methods in the class or methods in other classes in the same package as the class.	Methods you want other related classes to be able to access.
protected	The method can be accessed by methods in subclasses of the class.	Friendly methods that you want subclasses to also be able to access.

Method scope is important because the more narrowly the scope is defined on a part of a program, the simpler and more straightforward the program can be. This is evident by contrast. For example, in a traditional Basic program, there is only one scope. Everything in the program is accessible from everywhere. Unfortunately, this means that any part of the program might be dependent on any other part. Limiting the scope of each part of a program to the minimum necessary is one of the best ways of reducing program complexity, and the scope method modifiers in Java make this possible. With that in mind, let's look at these modifiers in a little more detail.

Scope of a public Method

A method defined to be `public` can be called by any part of the program. This is just like the Basic programming model. You would use the `public` modifier for the methods that define the external interfaces of your classes. The collection of publicly scoped methods defines the class as seen by users of the class.

Scope of a private Method

A method defined to be `private` can be called only by other methods in the same class. You would use the `private` modifier for methods that make up the implementation of the class. Users of the class have no reason to call these methods. For example, if you were writing a class that parsed input lines, you might have a `private` method named `getCharacter()` that extracted the next character from an internal buffer. This would be a useful abstraction in implementing a parsing class, but users of the class clearly have no reason to even know of its existence.

Scope of a friendly Method

By default, Java methods are *friendly*. A method that does not have an explicit scope modifier can be called by other methods in the class or by methods in any class in the same package.

Friendly method behavior in Java is similar to the `friend` access concept in C++. It is often the case when designing an object library that the abstraction presented to the users of the library consists of several interconnected classes. These interconnected classes commonly need access to parts of each other that aren't intended to be included in the external interfaces of the classes. In C++, a class can be made a friend of another class, giving it access to all the internals of the other class. In Java, friendship is supported by making the friendly classes part of the same package.

C++ programmers may be puzzled by the absence of the `friend` access concept in Java. However, C++ originally had no package concept. Without packages (or something like them) to provide *implicitly* friendly relationships between methods, the C++ developers implemented the `friend` method modifier, which provides *explicitly* friendly relationships between methods.

One significant difference between C++ friendship and Java friendly behavior is that friends in C++ actually have access to `private` members of their friends. In some cases, this gives friends greater access to class internals than the subclasses of the class enjoy.

Scope of a protected Method

A `protected` method is like a friendly method except that it can also be accessed by the subclasses of the class in which the method is defined.

Allowing subclasses access to a method that cannot be accessed by users of the class is often useful for extending a class. Allowing subclass access to class *data* is much less useful and is generally not recommended. (See Bjarne Stroustrup's *The Design and Evolution of C++*, page 301, for a discussion of the dangers of protected data.)

One additional constraint is placed on `protected` access. A method declared `protected` may only be accessed through a reference to the class attempting access or through one of its subclasses. For instance, consider the next example:

```
class A {
  protected void aMethod() {
  }
  protected void aFriendlyMethod() {
  }
}
class B extends A {
  void anotherMethod() {
    aMethod();                // Correct. B is a subclass of A and
                              // the method is being called through
                              // a reference to B or one of its
                              // subclasses. (Through the "this"
                              // reference).
  }
  void aFourthMethod(A anA) {
    anA.aMethod();            // WRONG! The method is not being
                              // called through a reference to B or
                              // one of its subclasses. It's being
                              // called through a reference to A
                              // since anA is declared as being of
                              // type A.
  }
  void aFifthMethod(B aB) {
    aB.aMethod();             // Correct. The method is again being
                              // called through a reference to B or
                              // one of its subclasses.
  }
}
class C {
  void oneMoreMethod(A anA) {
```

```
anA.aFriendlyMethod(); // Correct. aFriendlyMethod() is
                       // declared as "friendly" protected
                       // so other classes in the same
                       // package can access it.
    }
}
```

Variables

There are three kinds of variables in Java:

- Instance variables — Variables that hold data for an instance of a class

- Class variables — Variables that hold data that will be shared among all instances of a class

- Local variables — Variables that pertain only to a block of code

We introduce these here because they are important to understanding variables in Java. However, before examining instance, class, and local variables in more detail, we first need to describe some basic features of all Java variables: supported types, modifiers, scopes and extents, and initial values.

Variable Type

A variable's type refers to the kinds of values that may be stored in it. Java variables can hold any of the Java primitive types—`boolean`, `char`, `int`, `float`, `double`—or an instance of a particular class. A variable of type `Object` can hold an instance of any class, since all classes are subclasses of `Object`.[1] Example 3-6 shows some sample variable type declarations.

Example 3-6 Sample Variable Type Declarations

```
   int a = 1;
   boolean flag = true;
❶ String s = "a string";
❷ Object o = s;
❸ s = o;                 // s = o Generates an error.
```

Note that in this example:

❶ Assigns an instance of the class `String` to `s`.

---

1. Unlike C++, but similar to Objective-C and SmallTalk, Java includes an `Object` class, which is the root of all other classes.

❷ Assigns s, a `String`, to o, an `Object`. This is okay, because the `String` class is a subclass of `Object`.

❸ Generates an error. Assigning the value of o to s fails because `Object` is not a subclass of `String`. (Not all objects are strings). In this case, of course, we know that o is a `String`. We'll see how to make this assignment work later in our discussion of casting in *Runtime Typing, Class Loading, and Native Methods* on page 127.

Variable Modifiers

You can use some of the same modifiers on variables that you can use on methods: `public`, `private`, `protected`, `final`, and `static`. Table 3-3 shows variable modifiers and describes their meaning.

Table 3-3 Variable Modifiers

Variable Modifier Is...	Then...
public	The variable can be accessed by any class.
private	The variable can be accessed only by methods within the same class.
protected	The variable can be accessed by subclasses of this class and classes in the same package.
static	The variable is a class variable.
final	The variable's value cannot be changed.
transient	The variable is not part of the persistent state of an object. (This is intended for future use.)
volatile	The variable can be changed asynchronously. The compiler will keep it in memory.

Variable Scope and Extent

Variables in a programming language are typically described in terms of two concepts: extent and scope. In Java, the scope of a variable is the same thing as the scope of a method. It is the region of the program from which the variable can be accessed.

Instance variables and class variables have the same scope modifiers as methods: they can be:

- public
- private
- friendly
- protected

(Local variables are completely different, so we'll talk about the scope of local variables separately.)

The *extent* of a variable refers to the duration for which the variable has meaning within the program. For example, the extent of an argument to a function is from the invocation of that function until it exits.

Table 3-4 summarizes variable scope and extent in Java.

Table 3-4 Variable Scope and Extent in Java

Variable Type	Scope Is...	Extent Is...
Instance Variable	Subject to these conditions: 1. `private` – only methods in this class can access the variable. 2. `public` – any class can access the variable. 3. *friendly* – this class or any class within the package can access the variable. 4. `protected` – any subclasses of this class or any class within the package can access the variable.	The time the instance is created until there are no more references to that instance.
Class Variables	Subject to the same scope as instance variables.	The time the class is loaded until there are no more references to that class.
Local Variables	Within the current block of code.	The time that the code block is active.

Instance Variables

Instance variables hold the data for an instance of a class. For example, recall the Card class:

Example 3-7 Sample Instance Variables

```
public class Card {
    .
    .
    .
    // INSTANCE VARIABLES

    // Variables representing the rank and suit of a particular
    // card.
❶   private int rank;
❷   private int suit;
```

In Example 3-7, rank and suit in lines ❶ and ❷ are instance variables. The extent of an instance variable is from the time the instance is created until all references to the instance are gone, at which point the instance may be *garbage collected*. (Java uses a garbage collection memory management model, which we'll describe in *Memory and Constructors* on page 49.)

You can explicitly specify the initial value of an instance variable, for example:

```
int a = 1;
```

However, if you do not specify the initial value of an instance variable, Java assigns a default value. Table 3-5 shows the default values assigned for each type of variable.

Table 3-5 Initialized Values of Primitive Types

If the Variable Is of Type...	Then the Java Compiler Initializes It to...
float	0.0f
double	0.0d
int	0
byte	0
short	0
char	'\u0000'

Table 3-5 Initialized Values of Primitive Types (Continued)

If the Variable Is of Type...	Then the Java Compiler Initializes It to...
`long`	`0L`
`boolean`	`false`
all others	`null`

Note that `null` is a special value that can be assigned to any variable that holds an object. It is guaranteed to be distinct from any instance.

Class Variables

Class variables hold data that is shared among all the instances of a class. Conceptually, instead of there being a separate variable for each instance, there is just one variable for the whole class. If, for example, we wanted to keep a list of all the instances of a class, we could use a class variable like the one in Example 3-8.

Example 3-8 Class Variables

```java
import java.util.Vector;

public class ClassWithMemberList {

  // Construct a new member of the class and add it to the list.

  public ClassWithMemberList() {
    memberList.addElement(this);
  }

  // Return the list of members for this class.

  public static Vector getMembers() {
    return memberList;
  }

  // List of members of this class. It's static (and thereby, a
  // class variable) so that it is shared among all the members.

  private static Vector memberList = new Vector();
```

❶

The `memberList` variable in line ❶ is a class variable. All instances of `ClassWithMemberList` will share a `memberList`.

The extent of a class variable is from the time a class is loaded until the last reference to the class is lost. (Class loading is discussed in *Class Loading at Runtime* on page 131.) Class variables are initialized in exactly the same way as instance variables.

Local Variables

Java has local variables that are much like local variables in other languages. A local variable's scope is from its declaration until the end of the enclosing block. You may have already noticed in our examples that Java is like C++ in that you can declare local variables anywhere a statement is valid. This is useful because it allows a programmer to limit the scope of a variable to the smallest possible region of a program. The extent of a local variable is from the time it is initialized until its block is exited. Java requires that you initialize local variables before they are used. There are no default initial values for local variables.

Java also has a special declaration model for the variables in `for` loops. For example, look at this `for` loop:

```
for (int i=0; i<100; i++);
```

You can declare and assign the variable a value at the head of the `for` loop. This is similar to C++, which allows a declaration in the head of the loop. However, in C++, the variable is accessible until the end of the block that contains the loop. In Java, it is only valid until the loop ends.

Constants

Java does not really have constants as you may be accustomed to in other languages. To provide similar capability, Java includes the variable modifier `final`. When applied to a variable, `final` indicates that the value of the variable will not change. (Note that Java does not allow a local variable to be declared `final`.)

It is fairly common to use `switch` statements with `case` values that are constants. In Java, you can accomplish this by declaring variables to be `final static`, as in Example 3-9.

Example 3-9 Using `final static` to Create a Constant

```
class Reader {

    private final static char SPACE   = ' ';
    private final static char TAB     = '\t';
    private final static char NEWLINE = '\n';
    private final static char DOT     = '.';
    private final static char MINUS   = '-';
        .
        .
        .
}
```

The variables TAB, NEWLINE, DOT, and MINUS can then be used as you would constants, since the `final` declaration means the variable's value cannot be changed.

Variables, Methods, and Superclasses

When you have variables and methods defined in the superclass of a class, you can access them by using the name of the superclass. For example, the following Foo class extends the Bar class, so you can directly access the variable x in the superclass.

```
public class Foo extends Bar {
    .
    .
    .
    public void setBar(int val) {
        Bar.x = val;
    }
}
```

Static Initializers

A static initializer is a block of code that is executed when the class containing it is loaded. Static initializers and variable initializers are executed in the order that they appear. For instance, consider the program in Example 3-10.

Example 3-10 Static Initializers

```java
public class StaticInitExample {
   static string str  = "yes";
   static boolean flag;

   static {
     System.out.println(str);
     flag = true;
   }

   static boolean anotherFlag = flag;

   static {
     System.out.println(anotherFlag);
   }

   public static void main(String[] args) {
   }
}
```

This program would print the following output:

```
yes
true
```

A common use of static initializers is the loading of native libraries, as described in *Runtime Typing, Class Loading, and Native Methods* on page 127.

Packages and the import Statement

Java allows related classes to be grouped together into a *package*. From within a package, all classes can access each other's friendly members. From outside a package, only `public` and `protected` classes, methods, and variables may be accessed.

To specify the package in which to place the classes in a file, you use the `package` statement. It is the first statement in a file. For example, the calculator program described in *Putting the Pieces Together* on page 155, begins with the following `package` statement:

```
package calc;
```

This line says that this class will be in the `calc` package and that this class will have access to all the classes in the `calc` package.

If there is no explicit package statement in a source file, the Java runtime system assigns the source file a default package with no name.

You can only use one package per Java source file, so if you want to access classes from other packages, you have to use the `import` statement. Table 3-6 shows acceptable syntax for an `import` statement.

Table 3-6 Forms of an `import` Statement

This `import` Syntax in a Source File...	Specifies...
`import <package_name>.<class_name>;`	The source file can access a single class in the package named *package_name*. For example, the following `import` statement enables the source file to access the `Stack` class in the `java.util` package: `import java.util.Stack;` Using this `import` syntax, you can then access the `Stack` class either as `java.util.Stack` or simply as `Stack`.
`import <package_name>.*;`	The source file can access any class in the package named *package_name*. The wildcard (`*`) in the `import` statement matches all the `public` classes in the package. This `import` syntax is referred to as import-on-demand. For example, the following `import` statement enables the source file to import-on-demand all the classes in the `java.io` package: `import java.io.*;`

An explicit single class `import` statement (as described in the first row of Table 3-6) or a local definition is intended to override a type name obtained through an import-on-demand statement. However, in Java 1.0, the compiler will signal an error if a conflict occurs.

Java assumes that the directory structure of your program files matches the package structure of your program. There is a CLASSPATH environment variable you can set so that the Java runtime system knows where to find the classes in your program. The top-level directory containing the class definitions for Java is implicitly in your CLASSPATH. Say the top-level Java directory was named `classes`. Then the `java.util` package would be in the directory `util` under the directory `java` under the directory `classes`. Figure 3-1 shows this directory structure.

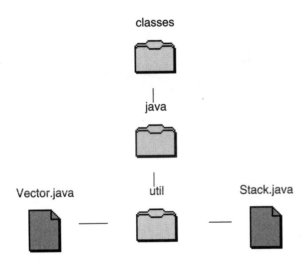

Figure 3-1 Sample Package Hierarchy

Summary

In this chapter, we've covered a lot of basic material about the Java language. Remember that classes and methods are the fundamental building blocks of Java programs. Classes can *inherit* characteristics of other classes, and classes can access other, supporting classes by importing packages. Also, keep in mind the Java method and variable modifiers, which provide support for structuring applications and limiting access to the internal parts of a class.

CHAPTER
4

- Dynamic Memory Allocation and Garbage Collection

- Using Constructors and Creating Instances

- The Default Constructor

- Cleaning Up Resources (Finalization)

- Creating Linked Lists in Java

Memory and Constructors

Dynamic Allocation and Garbage Collection

Java implements a simple memory management scheme. You dynamically allocate memory within your program. Java frees it when that memory is no longer referenced.

Programming languages often implement a memory management scheme that optimizes for performance—at the expense of all other factors. Java, on the other hand, optimizes for reliability. Java programmers never explicitly free memory. It is always *garbage collected*, meaning that Java frees that memory and reuses it when there are no longer any references to it.

The current Java implementation is not guaranteed to garbage collect all unused memory. It uses a conservative garbage collector. Conservative garbage collectors are often used to add garbage collection to languages such as C and C++ [1], in which it is impossible to be sure if an address actually points to useful memory or not. The collectors are called conservative because in these cases, they will not collect memory that looks as if it might be in use.

---

1. For an overview of different garbage collection strategies, see Paul Wilson's paper, "Uniprocessor Garbage Collection Techniques," in the Proceedings of the International Workshop on Memory Management, St. Malo, France, September 1992. This has been published as Springer-Verlag Lecture Notes in Computer Science, no. 637.

The emphasis on reliability is at least one contributing factor in Java being garbage collected. Explicit memory deallocation is unsafe. If two parts of a program hold references to a piece of memory, and one of them frees it, the other part may perform an operation on corrupted data. Java keeps track of memory in use, and when that memory is no longer referenced within a program, Java automatically frees that memory (it *collects* the *garbage*) and reuses that memory.

Two sets of data types are available in Java, and allocating memory is handled differently for each. One set of data types is the Java primitive types—`char`, `int`, `boolean`, `float`, `byte`, `short`, `long`, `double`. These are allocated directly on the stack or in an instance. All other data types are subclasses of `Object`, and you must dynamically allocate them in your program.

Unlike C and C++, Java does not support global or stack allocation of structures and arrays. For example, Java does not have an equivalent to the C statement:

```
struct complex cnum;
```

In C, this might allocate space for a `complex` number on the stack. In Java, if you require a local structure, you need to dynamically allocate it—that is, you need to do something analogous to the C statement:

```
struct complex *cnum = malloc(sizeof(struct complex));
```

This line says to allocate space for a pointer to a `complex` number on the stack, and then allocate memory dynamically and place its address in cnum. To accomplish the same thing in Java, you would use the following declaration:

```
Complex cnum = new Complex();
```

The new Operator and Constructors

There are two components involved in allocating and initializing memory in Java: 1) the new operator and 2) a special method in each class called a *constructor*. Here is how they work. You use the new operator to create a new instance of a class. When the Java runtime system encounters a statement with the new operator in it, the runtime system allocates memory for that instance. Then the constructor [2] is called to initialize the newly allocated memory. For instance, in *Putting the Pieces*

Together on page 155, we show a calculator written in Java. Example 4-1 shows use of the `new` operator to create an instance of a `Calculator` class from that program.

Example 4-1 Creating an Instance With the `new` **Operator**

```
Calculator calc = new Calculator(System.in, System.out);
```

In Example 4-1, the `new` operator first *allocates* memory for an instance of the `Calculator` class. Then, the constructor for the `Calculator` class is called to *initialize* that memory. Example 4-2 shows a `Calculator` class constructor.

2. Note that most object-oriented languages that support dynamic memory allocation provide something similar to a Java constructor.

Java by Example

Example 4-2 Initializing Memory With a Constructor

```
public class Calculator {

❶ public Calculator(InputStream in, OutputStream out) {

    DataInputStream dataIn;
    PrintStream     printOut;

❷   if (!(in instanceof DataInputStream)) {
       dataIn = new DataInputStream(in);
    } else {
       dataIn = (DataInputStream)in;
    }

    if (!(out instanceof PrintStream)) {
       printOut = new PrintStream(out);
    } else {
       printOut = (PrintStream)out;
    }

❸   reader= new Reader(dataIn); // Object that handles input.
    stack = new CalcStack();    // Operand stack.
    output= printOut;           // Output stream
  }
  .
  .
  .

}
```

In Example 4-2:

❶ Is the constructor declaration. The constructor *must* have the same name as the class and no return type.

❷ This is our first use of the `instanceof` operator, which performs type comparisons. Although not directly relevant to constructors, we mention it here for completeness.

❸ Is a series of items to be initialized when there is a new instance of the `Calculator` class. Specifically, after a new instance of the `Calculator` class is created (and memory is allocated for it), the `Calculator` constructor will create a reader instance to handle all input and an operand stack instance for the calculator. (Note that `reader`, `stack`, and `output` are all `private` `instance` variables of the `Calculator` class.)

Using Multiple Constructors Within a Class

Although it's not illustrated in the previous example, you can include multiple constructors within a class. Doing so is useful if there is a common default initialization for a class. For example, if defining a complex number class, we might want a constructor that initializes the real and imaginary parts to 0.0 and another constructor that lets the user specify the initial values, as in Example 4-3.

Example 4-3 Using Multiple Constructors

```
public class Complex {
   public Complex() {
     realValue       = 0.0;
     imaginaryValue = 0.0;
   }

   public Complex(double real, double imaginary) {
     realValue       = real;
     imaginaryValue = imaginary;
   }
   .
   .
   .
   private double realValue;
   private double imaginaryValue;
}
```

In a program, we could use these constructors like this:

```
❶ Complex cnum1 = new Complex();
❷ Complex cnum2 = new Complex(0.0 1.0);
```

In this example, line ❶ allocates memory for a new instance of the `Complex` class and initializes that memory with a real value of 0.0 and an imaginary value of 0.0. Line ❷ allocates memory for a new instance of the `Complex` class and initializes that memory with programmer-defined values (0.0 and 1.0) for the real and imaginary parts.

The Default Constructor

If for some reason a class doesn't have a constructor defined in it, Java defines a default constructor. The default constructor does not have any arguments. What it does is call the constructor (with no arguments) for the immediate superclass. Once a class has at least one constructor, the default constructor is ignored.

It's important to note that instance variables in a new instance are initialized to the default values for their types (or to explicit initial values) before a constructor is called. If default initial values are all you require, an explicit constructor is not strictly necessary.

Using super and this in Constructors

There are two reserved words that have special meaning in constructors: super and this. You can use super to explicitly call a constructor from the superclass of the current class, and you can use this to call a constructor already defined within the same class. For instance, Example 4-4 shows use of super to call the constructor of the superclass.

Example 4-4 Using super to Call the Superclass Constructor

```
class A {
  A(int x) {
    aValue = x;
  }

  int aValue;
}

class B extends A {
  B() {
❶    super(0);
  }
}
```

In this example, super(0) in line ❶ calls A(0).

Without the call to `super()`, class B would fail to compile, since by default the first thing done in a constructor is to call the superclass constructor with no arguments, and class A has no constructor without arguments. (Note that since class A has a constructor defined, the default constructor is no longer available.) The empty constructor:

```
B() {}
```

is equivalent to:

```
B() {
    super();
}
```

You can use `this` to call other constructors in the same class. Example 4-5 shows how our previous complex number example could have been written using `this`.

Example 4-5 Using `this` to Call a Constructor in the Same Class

```
   public class Complex {
     public Complex() {
❶      this(0.0, 0.0);
     }

❷    public Complex(double real, double imaginary) {
       realValue       = real;
       imaginaryValue = imaginary;
     }
       .
       .
       .
   }
```

In this example, `this(0.0, 0.0)` in line ❶ calls `Complex(double, double)`, which is defined in line ❷.

The constructor to call is determined by matching the number and types of arguments. It is useful to use `this` when one constructor does a lot of setup work that all of the constructors need. This helps reduce redundant code.

When using `super` or `this` to call a constructor, you must make the call the first statement of the constructor.

Finalization

If an object has resources other than memory associated with it, such as open files or sockets, and the last reference to it is lost, Java provides a way for the programmer to release the resources. This is called *finalization*. In each class, you can define a method called `finalize()` with no arguments. Immediately before the object is garbage collected, the Java runtime system will call the `finalize()` method to clean up any outstanding resources. (The `finalize()` method is similar to a C++ destructor.) When defining a `finalize()` method, it is recommended that you *always* call `super.finalize()`.

A Sample Program Showing Linked Lists in Java

The following example demonstrates the use of linked lists in Java. It is a program for multiplying very long integers together. Each integer is represented as a linked list of digits. This example is particularly important for programmers wondering about the lack of *pointers* in Java. As the example will show, Java makes it very easy to build linked structures. In fact, each object reference in Java is actually a pointer, but its use is much more constrained than in C. The only operation defined on a Java pointer is to fetch a field from the object it points to.

The program is used in the following way:

```
java LongMult long_number1 long_number2 ... long_numberN
```

This long multiplication program uses the standard long multiplication algorithm taught in school. Multiply one number by each digit of the other and add the intermediate results. The addition of results uses the standard long addition algorithm. The program is optimized for clarity rather than speed; the only optimization applied is to always multiply the longer number by each digit of the shorter one to reduce the number of temporary results.

Figure 4-1 shows the simple structure of the long multiplier program, which consists of four classes. Table 4-1 shows a little more detail about the structure and function of these classes.

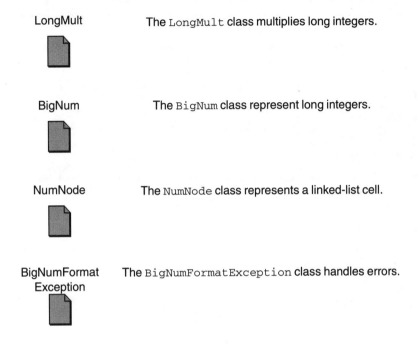

LongMult   The `LongMult` class multiplies long integers.

BigNum   The `BigNum` class represent long integers.

NumNode   The `NumNode` class represents a linked-list cell.

BigNumFormat Exception   The `BigNumFormatException` class handles errors.

Figure 4-1 Long Multiplier Class Structure
All the classes are defined in one source file, `LongMult.java`.

Table 4-1 Long Multiplier Program Class Summary

`LongMult` **Class**	
Package	`null`
Imports	`java.io.*` `java.util.Vector`
Subclass of	`Object`
Description	The `LongMult` class takes a list of long integers on the command line, multiples them together, and prints the result. This is the only `public` class in this program.

`Bignum` **Class**	
Package	`null`
Imports	None

Table 4-1 Long Multiplier Program Class Summary (Continued)

Subclass of	Object
Description	The Bignum class represents a long integer. It stores the digits of the integer in a linked list and provides add() and mul() methods.

NumNode **Class**	
Package	null
Imports	None
Subclass of	Object
Description	The NumNode class represents a single linked-list cell. It contains a numeric value and a reference to the next node in the list.

BigNumFormatException **Class**	
Package	null
Imports	None
Subclass of	Object
Description	The BigNumFormatException class represents all errors that occur during the construction of a Bignum object.

We will discuss each of these classes separately, but on the CD accompanying this book, all the classes are defined in one source file, LongMult.java. Now let's look at the long multiplier program in closer detail.

The LongMult Class and the main() Method

The LongMult class multiplies an arbitrary number of large integers (Bignum objects) together. The digits of a Bignum are stored in a linked list, and the multiplication is done using the standard long multiplication algorithm taught in school:

```java
import java.io.*;
import java.util.Vector;

public class LongMult {
  public static void main(String[] args) {

    // Check usage. Any number of Bignum arguments may be
    // specified.

    if (args.length < 1) {
      System.err.println(
          "Usage: java LongMult <num1> ... <numN>");
      return;
    }

    try {

      // Initialize the total with the first argument translated
      // into a Bignum.

      Bignum total = new Bignum(args[0]);

      // Call Bignum.mul on the total and each new argument.

      for (int i = 1; i < args.length; i++) {
        total = total.mul(new Bignum(args[i]));
      }

      // Display the result.

      System.out.println(total);

    } catch (Exception e) {
      e.printStackTrace();
      return;
    }
  }
}
```

The BigNum Class

The `Bignum` class represents large integers. Each digit is stored independently in a linked list node. The number of digits is stored separately so that the smaller of two `Bignum` objects can be easily determined:

```java
class Bignum {

   // Create a new Bignum from a String of digits. If any of the
   // characters in the String are not digit characters, a
   // BignumFormatException is thrown.

   Bignum(String stringNum) throws BignumFormatException {

     // Store the number of digits.

     digits = stringNum.length();

     if (digits == 0) {
        System.err.println("Bignum has no value.");
        throw new BignumFormatException();
     }
```

Here, we add each digit to the linked list of nodes for the `Bignum`. The digits are stored in reverse order so we can process them later from right to left:

```java
     for (int index = 0; index < digits; index++) {
```

The `Character.digit()` method is used to get the numeric value of a digit character. It returns -1 if the character does not represent a digit in the specified base:

```java
        int digitVal = Character.digit(stringNum.charAt(index),
           10);

        if (digitVal == -1) {
           System.err.println(
              stringNum.charAt(index) + " is not a digit.");
           throw new BignumFormatException();
        }

        nodes = new NumNode(digitVal, nodes);
     }
   }

   // Create a Bignum from a list of nodes. This is used to create
   // intermediate results for multiplication.

   Bignum(NumNode nodeList) {
     nodes  = nodeList;
```

```
   digits = 0;

   for (NumNode node = nodes; node != null; node = node.next) {
      digits++;
   }
}
```

In this code, we multiply two `Bignum` objects. The longer `Bignum` is multiplied by each digit of the shorter `Bignum`, and then the intermediate results are added:

```
Bignum mul(Bignum other) {
  Bignum arg1;
  Bignum arg2;

  // Put the shorter number at the bottom of the long
  // multiplication to reduce the number of intermediate
  // results.

  if (digits > other.digits) {
     arg1 = other;
     arg2 = this;
  } else {
     arg1 = this;
     arg2 = other;
  }

  // Create the first intermediate result.

  Bignum total = arg2.mul(arg1.nodes.val);

  // Initialize the zeros counter. This is the number of zeros
  // to tack on at the right of an intermediate result. Each
  // intermediate result will be shifted left by one more
  // position.

  int    numZeros = 1;

  // For each successive digit of the shorter number, multiply
  // it by the longer number, scale the result by the
  // appropriate power of ten and add it to the running total.

  for (NumNode current = arg1.nodes.next; current != null;
     current = current.next) {

     // Multiply the longer Bignum by a digit of the shorter.

     Bignum partial = arg2.mul(current.val);
```

```
    // Scale the result to the correct tens position.

    partial.shift(numZeros);

    // Add the result to the running total.

    total = total.add(partial);

    // Add another zero.

    numZeros++;
  }

  return total;
}
```

The add() method adds two Bignum objects together. This method is used to add up intermediate results of a multiplication. Each corresponding digit of the two numbers is added with a carry. When the digits of one number run out, zeros are added until the other runs out:

```
Bignum add(Bignum other) {

  // The list of nodes that will make up the resulting Bignum.

  NumNode total = null;

  // The current carry. Always 1 or 0.

  int     carry = 0;

  // The current nodes from each Bignum. We traverse them right
  // to left using the standard long addition algorithm.

  NumNode current;
  NumNode current2;
  // Step through the nodes of each Bignum. The next() method
  // keeps returning null once null is reached so we can
  // keep stepping through whichever number is longer.

  for (current = nodes, current2 = other.nodes;
     current != null || current2 != null || carry != 0;
     current = next(current), current2 = next(current2)) {

    // valof() returns the digit stored in a node or 0
    // if the node is null.

    int tempVal = valof(current) + valof(current2) + carry;
```

```
    // If the temporary result is greater than ten, carry
    // one.

    if (tempVal >= 10) {
        carry   = 1;
        tempVal = tempVal % 10;

    } else {
        carry = 0;
    }

    // Add the current result digit to the result list of
    // digits.

    total = new NumNode(tempVal, total);
}

// Reverse the order of the digits to the normal Bignum
// right to left order.

return new Bignum(reverse(total));
}

// Return a String representation of the Bignum.

public String toString() {
    StringBuffer buf = new StringBuffer();

    fillBuffer(buf, nodes);

    return buf.toString();
}

// Multiply a Bignum by a single decimal digit. This method is
// used by the general Bignum * Bignum multiplication method.

    private Bignum mul(int other) {
```

The total variable holds the list of digits resulting from multiplying the current Bignum by a single digit. Each digit of the Bignum is multiplied by the argument digit, and then the carry is added:

```
NumNode total    = null;
int      carry   = 0;
```

```
// For each digit in the Bignum, multiply it by the argument
// digit leaving the ones place in the current node and
// passing the tens place on as the carry.

for (NumNode current = nodes; current != null;
  current = current.next) {

  // Calculate the result for the current digit. Multiply
  // the current digit by the argument and add the carry.

  int tempVal = other * current.val + carry;

  // If the current result is greater than ten, leave the
  // ones place and pass the tens place on as a carry.

  if (tempVal >= 10) {
     carry   = tempVal / 10;
     tempVal = tempVal % 10;

  } else {
     carry = 0;
  }

  // Add the current result digit to the list of nodes.

  total = new NumNode(tempVal, total);
}

// If there is a carry left over after all the digits have
// been multiplied, it becomes the leftmost digit.

if (carry != 0) {
  total = new NumNode(carry, total);
}
// Reverse the order of the digits to the normal Bignum
// right to left order.

return new Bignum(reverse(total));
}

// The reverse() method destructively reverses the order of the
// nodes in a list.

private NumNode reverse(NumNode nodes) {

  // Save the next node before setting the next field of the
  // first node to null.
```

```
NumNode after    = nodes.next;
nodes.next       = null;

// For each node in the list, save the value in its next
// field, change the next field to point to the previous node
// and continue with the saved value.

while (after != null) {
    NumNode temp = after.next;
    after.next = nodes;
    nodes = after;
    after = temp;
}

  return nodes;
}

// Add n zeros to the right end of a Bignum thus multiplying it
// by 10^n.

private void shift(int n) {
  while (n-- > 0) {
    nodes = new NumNode(0, nodes);
  }
}
```

Here, we fill a `StringBuffer` with the nodes of a `Bignum`. Since the nodes are in reverse order, we call `fillBuffer()` recursively to generate the later nodes, and then add the current node:

```
private void fillBuffer(StringBuffer buf, NumNode nodes) {
  if (nodes == null) {
    return;
  }
  // Add all the nodes after the current node first to
  // reverse the node order.

  fillBuffer(buf, nodes.next);

  // Now add the current node.

  buf.append(nodes.val);

}

// Return the digit value of a node. If the node is null, return
// 0. This is used by add() to return a value when the nodes of one
// Bignum have run out.
```

```
    private int valof(NumNode node) {
      if (node == null) {
        return 0;
      } else {
        return node.val;
      }
    }


    // Return the node after the current node. If the current node is
    // null, return null. This is used by add() to continue stepping
    // through the digits of one Bignum when the other has run out.

    private NumNode next(NumNode node) {
      if (node == null) {
        return null;
      } else {
        return node.next;
      }
    }


    // A Bignum consists of a list of digits and its length.

    private NumNode nodes = null;
    private int     digits;
}
```

The NumNode Class

The NumNode class holds a single digit of a `Bignum` and contains a reference to
the next NumNode in a list.

```
class NumNode {
  NumNode(int intVal, NumNode nextNode) {
    val  = intVal;
    next = nextNode;
  }

  int     val;
  NumNode next;
}
```

The BigNumFormatException Class

Instances of the `BignumFormatException` class are returned whenever any
error occurs trying to construct a `Bignum` object.

```
class BignumFormatException extends Exception {}
```

Output From the Long Multiplier Program

After all the classes in the program have been compiled, you can call the `java`
interpreter from the command line and multiply several long numbers:

java LongMult 594930002929 4332499002934 4545421112 123900922
145162020927879257333688982538426261232 3104

Summary

Java is a garbage-collected language. You never have to explicitly free memory,
because the Java runtime system frees memory when there are no longer any
references to it. To allocate memory in Java, you use the new operator to create a
new instance of an object. The Java runtime system then creates a new object and
allocates memory for it. To initialize that memory, the Java runtime system calls a
special method, called a constructor, defined in the new object's class. The
constructor defines how to initialize memory for the new object.

Also, the long multiplier example shows how to build linked structures in Java.
For programmers accustomed to using C-style pointers, this example illustrates
how to accomplish the same result in Java.

CHAPTER
5

- Using Interfaces as Types
- Extending Interfaces
- A Tree Sort Program

Interfaces as Types

What Is an Interface?

Besides creating classes in your Java programs, you can also create special structures called *interfaces*. A Java interface is similar to a class, except there is no data associated with the interface. (We'll elaborate on that shortly.)

As we've seen, a class definition looks something like this:

```
public class MyClass {
    <class constructor, methods, and variables>
}
```

Similarly, you can define an interface:

```
public interface MyInterface {
    <methods—with no implementation details>
    <final variables>
}
```

The primary difference between a class and an interface is that the variables in an interface must be `final`, and the methods in the interface are only declarations. The way the method works is specified in any class that `implements` the interface. We'll show you exactly what this means in *Using Interfaces* on page 72, but first, let's consider the reason for interfaces.

Why Use an Interface?

We said earlier that the `public` methods of a class make up its external interface. In many ways, the external interface of a class is like a contract with users of the class. It defines the operations in the class that its instances can be counted on to perform. To draw a comparison to everyday life, we could say that people also enter into contracts that define the actions that are expected of them. It's not uncommon, however, for people to enter into multiple contracts with distinct sets of requirements: for example, a person might primarily be a family member, but also have responsibilities to the community, the church, the employer, and so on. In Java, a class may enter into multiple contracts by specifying multiple *interfaces* that it supports.

A class that *extends* another class is guaranteed to support the contracts entered into by its superclass. In Java, however, the extension mechanism alone does not provide the ability to enter into multiple contracts. (Java is a *single inheritance* language, and for C++ programmers, interfaces are used to approximate *multiple inheritance*.) Let's look at an example to illustrate this point:

```
❶ public class ColoredObject {
     public Color getColor() {
       return color;
     }

     public void setColor(Color newColor) {
       color = newColor;
     }

     private Color color = Color.white;
   }
❷ public class NamedObject {
     public String getName() {
       return name;
     }

     public void setName(String newName) {
       name = newName;
     }

     private String name = "";
   }
```

In this example, line ❶ is a class definition for ColoredObject, which includes methods for getting and setting color values. Line ❷ is a class definition for NamedObject, which includes methods for getting and setting name values.

Now assume we wanted to define a new class that extended both NamedObject and ColoredObject, as in the following:

```
   // The following is WRONG, because we can only extend one class.
❸ class NamedAndColoredObject extends NamedObject, ColoredObject {
   }
```

Line ❸ is an *invalid* class definition for NamedAndColoredObject because it extends both NamedObject and ColoredObject, which is illegal. We can't achieve what we want with NamedAndColoredObject because we can't extend more than one superclass. However, by using interfaces, we can achieve what we're trying to accomplish with NamedAndColoredObject.

Using Interfaces

Suppose we had an application that needed to determine if certain objects it manipulated were blue. We wouldn't expect each object to have a flag indicating whether or not it was blue, but we might want to fetch the object's color and compare it to blue. We know we can perform `getColor()` on instances of the `ColoredObject` class, and it seems right to have our `isBlue()` method operate on a `ColoredObject`. However, some of the classes we're working with already inherit from `NamedObject` and cannot be made subclasses of `ColoredObject`.

The question is, how can we make the `isBlue()` method work and still support contracts other than the one supported by `ColoredObject`? In Java, the answer is that we use an interface, as illustrated in Example 5-1.

Example 5-1 Defining Interfaces

```
❶ public interface ColoredObject {
      Color getColor();

      void setColor(Color newColor);
   }

❷ public interface NamedObject {
      String getName();

      void setName(String newName);
   }

   // Note the use of "implements" instead of "extends"
❸ public class NamedAndColoredObject implements
      ColoredObject, NamedObject {
      .
      .
      .
   }
```

In this example:

❶ and ❷ are now interface definitions instead of class definitions for `ColoredObject` and `NamedObject`.

❸ Is a *valid* class definition for `NamedAndColoredObject` because it implements the `ColoredObject` and `NamedObject` interfaces.

There are two things to note in this example:

- An interface provides no implementation for the methods it declares. The implementations must be provided by classes that implement the interface. `getColor()`, `setColor()`, `getName()`, and `setName()` only define method names, arguments, and return types.

- A class can extend only one other class, but it can implement any number of interfaces.

An interface is something like a shell or husk of a class—it has no inside. There is no local data associated with an interface. Table 5-1 shows the basic characteristics of variables and methods in an interface.

Table 5-1 Characteristics of an Interface

Variables are...	Methods are...
Treated like constants in an interface. They are always `final` and `static`, and they must be initialized.	Abstract. There's no implementation specified.

Any methods or variables declared in a public interface are implicitly `public`. All an interface actually does is specify a contract. That contract implicitly says that any class that implements the interface will provide a particular set of methods. [1]

The `ColoredObject` interface says that any class that implements it will provide `getColor()` and `setColor()` methods with specific arguments and return types. Given this, we can write `isBlue()` as in Example 5-2 on the next page.

1. For those familiar with Objective-C, an interface in Java is similar to a protocol in Objective-C.

Example 5-2 Passing Classes That Implement an Interface

❶ ```java
public interface ColoredObject {
   Color getColor();
   void setColor(Color newColor);
}
```

❷ ```java
public class Car extends Vehicle implements ColoredObject {
    .
    .
    .

   public Color getColor() {
     return color;
   }

   public void setColor(Color newColor) {
     color = newColor;
   }

   private Color color = Color.white;
}

public class Example {
```
❸ ```java
   public static boolean isBlue(ColoredObject o) {
     return o.getColor() == Color.blue;
   }
}

Car myAuto = new Car();
myAuto.setColor(Color.blue);
```
❹ ```java
boolean colorIsBlue = Example.isBlue(myAuto); // returns true
```

In this example:

❶ Defines the `ColoredObject` interface. It declares `getColor()` and `setColor()` methods. It is up to any class that implements this interface to define what these methods do.

❷ Is a class definition for `Car`, which implements the `ColoredObject` interface. To uphold its end of the contract, `Car` defines what the `getColor()` and `setColor()` methods actually do.

❸ Defines the `isBlue()` method. The `isBlue()` method takes a variable of type `ColoredObject` as an argument. This means that `isBlue()` can be passed any object that is an instance of a class implementing the `ColoredObject` interface.

❹ Is a class method call to `isBlue()`. The key point here is that `Example.isBlue()` can accept `myAuto` as an argument because it is of type `Car`, which implements the `ColoredObject` interface.

As long as a class provides the `getColor()` and `setColor()` methods and specifies that it implements `ColoredObject`, instances of that class can be stored in variables of type `ColoredObject` and passed as arguments to methods expecting a `ColoredObject`.

Extending Interfaces

Interfaces may be extended just like classes. Unlike classes, however, interfaces may extend any number of other interfaces, as illustrated in Example 5-3.

Example 5-3 Extending an Interface

```
interface NamedAndColoredObject extends NamedObject, ColoredObject
{
    .
    .
    .
}
```

Some languages, such as C++ and CLOS, support multiple inheritance, which allows you to extend multiple classes. However, multiple inheritance introduces complexity and problems of its own. (For a good discussion of this issue, see Alan Snyder's paper, "Inheritance and the Development of Encapsulated Software Systems," in *Research Directions in Object-Oriented Programming*, edited by Bruce Shriver and Peter Wegner.)

A Sample Program Using Interfaces

The following program illustrates several features of Java we've discussed up to this point, and it demonstrates the use of interfaces. It also shows how interesting data structures can be constructed and provides an example of enumerations in Java.

The program sorts lines from a file using a binary tree. Each line is read in and inserted into the tree. The tree is then traversed and the lines are printed in sorted order. The traversal and printing are done using an enumeration of the tree. The program relies on a class that implements the `java.util.Enumeration` interface, which provides two methods: `hasMoreElements()` and `nextElement()`.

The `hasMoreElements()` method returns a `boolean` true value as long as there are elements that have not been enumerated. The `nextElement()` method returns an `Object`—the next element in the enumeration. Built-in enumeration

classes are provided for Java classes such as `java.util.Vector`, `java.util.Hashtable`, and `java.util.Properties`. It is good practice to provide enumerations for new container classes so that Java code can be written in a consistent style.

This is the first program in which we use Java's package facility. We've grouped most of the classes into a package, which we call the `tree` package. The top-level file imports all the supporting classes in the `tree` package. The code for the tree sort program consists of five classes and one interface, as illustrated in Figure 5-1.

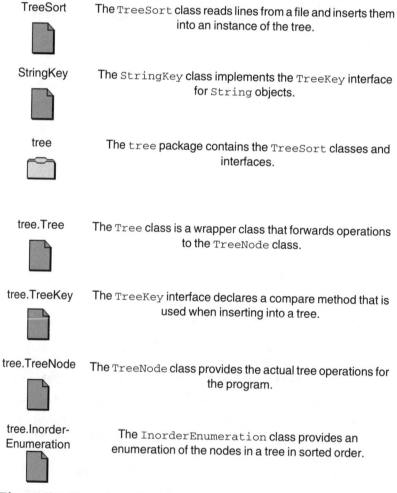

TreeSort — The `TreeSort` class reads lines from a file and inserts them into an instance of the tree.

StringKey — The `StringKey` class implements the `TreeKey` interface for `String` objects.

tree — The `tree` package contains the `TreeSort` classes and interfaces.

tree.Tree — The `Tree` class is a wrapper class that forwards operations to the `TreeNode` class.

tree.TreeKey — The `TreeKey` interface declares a compare method that is used when inserting into a tree.

tree.TreeNode — The `TreeNode` class provides the actual tree operations for the program.

tree.Inorder-Enumeration — The `InorderEnumeration` class provides an enumeration of the nodes in a tree in sorted order.

Figure 5-1 Tree Sort Class/Interface Structure

Table 5-2 shows a little more detail about the structure of these classes and interfaces.

Table 5-2 Tree Sort Program Class and Interface Summary

`TreeSort` **Class**	
Package	`null`

Imports	`java.io.*`
	`java.util.Enumeration`
	`tree.*`

Subclass of	`Object`
Interfaces	None
Description	The `TreeSort` class reads lines from a file and inserts them into an instance of the `tree.Tree` class. It then uses the `inorder()` enumeration of the tree to print sorted lines.

`StringKey` **Class**	
Package	`null`

Imports	`java.util.io*`
	`java.util.Enumeration`
	`tree.*`

Interfaces	`TreeKey`
Description	The `StringKey` class implements the `TreeKey` interface and constructs a new `StringKey` object for a given `String` object.

`Tree` **Class**	
Package	`tree`
Imports	`java.util.Enumeration` `java.util.Stack`
Interfaces	None
Description	The `Tree` class is a wrapper class that forwards operations to the `TreeNode` class. The `Tree` class exists so that empty trees can be manipulated. An empty tree has no `TreeNode` objects.

`TreeKey` **Interface**	
Package	`tree`
Imports	None
Description	The `TreeKey` interface declares a `compare()` method that is used when inserting into a tree. An instance of any class may be used as a key if its class implements the `TreeKey` interface.

Table 5-2 Tree Sort Program Class and Interface Summary (Continued)

`TreeNode` **Class**	
Package	`tree`
Imports	`java.util.Enumeration`
Subclass of	`Object`
Interfaces	None
Description	The `TreeNode` class provides the actual tree operations for the program. The `lookup()` method is not actually used in this program, but is included for completeness.

`InorderEnumeration` **Class**	
Package	`tree`
Imports	`java.util.Stack` `java.util.Enumeration`
Subclass of	`Object`
Interfaces	`Enumeration`
Description	The `InorderEnumeration` class provides an enumeration of the nodes in a tree in sorted order.

With these details in mind, we'll describe each class and interface and how they inter-relate to form a working, tree-sort program.

The TreeSort Class and the main() Method

The `TreeSort` class uses a binary tree to sort lines in a file and remove duplicated data. Each line is inserted into the tree and the tree is then enumerated to print each line. The keys for the tree must implement the `TreeKey` interface, which provides a comparison method for ordering the entries:

```
import java.io.*;
import java.util.Enumeration;
import tree.*;

public class TreeSort {
  public static void main(String[] args) {

    // Check usage.

    if (args.length < 1) {
      System.err.println("Usage: java TreeSort <file>");
      return;
    }
```

To read a line at a time, we create a `DataInputStream` object. (See *Input/Output* on page 111 for details about how this works.)

```
try {

    DataInputStream in = new DataInputStream(
        new FileInputStream(args[0]));

    // Create a new empty tree. Each line will be added to it.

    Tree        tree    = new Tree();
    String      line;
```

The `insert()` method inserts the current line into the tree. The `StringKey` class implements the `TreeKey` interface for `String` objects:

```
    while ((line = in.readLine()) != null) {
        tree.insert(new StringKey(line), line);
    }
```

The following code creates an enumeration for the tree. The enumeration will print its entries in order. An `inorder()` traversal of a tree prints the left subtree, the current node, then the right subtree:

```
    Enumeration entries = tree.inorder();

    while (entries.hasMoreElements()) {
        System.out.println(entries.nextElement());
    }

} catch (Exception e) {
    e.printStackTrace();
    return;
    }
  }
}
```

The StringKey class contains a String and implements the TreeKey interface:

```
class StringKey implements TreeKey {

  // Construct a new StringKey for a given String.

  StringKey(String val) {
    stringVal = val;
  }
```

The next method uses the compareTo() method for String objects to compare the String in this StringKey to the String in other:

```
  public int compare(TreeKey other) {
    StringKey otherStringKey = (StringKey)other;

    int compareResult =
       stringVal.compareTo(otherStringKey.stringVal);

    if (compareResult < 0) {
      return TreeKey.LESS;

    } else if (compareResult == 0) {
      return TreeKey.EQUAL;
    } else {
      return TreeKey.GREATER;
    }
  }

  // Print a StringKey by printing its String.

  public String toString() {
    return stringVal;
  }

  String stringVal;
}
```

The Tree Class

The `Tree` class stores objects in a binary tree based on the object's key. The objects in the tree may be looked up by the object's key or enumerated in sorted order. Most of the work is done by the `TreeNode` class. Operations are forwarded to the top level `TreeNode` of the tree.

```
package tree;

import java.util.Enumeration;
import java.util.Stack;

public class Tree {

    // Construct a new tree with no entries.

    public Tree() {
        topNode = null;
    }
```

The `insert()` method inserts an entry into the tree based on the `compare()` method of key:

```
    public void insert(TreeKey key, Object val) {
        if (topNode == null) {
            topNode = new TreeNode(key, val);

        } else {
            topNode.insert(key, val);
        }
    }
```

The `lookup()` method looks up an entry in the tree based on the `compare()` method of key:

```
    public Object lookup(TreeKey key) {
        if (topNode == null) {
            return null;

        } else {
            return topNode.lookup(key);
        }
    }
```

Java by Example

The `inorder()` method returns an enumeration of the tree. The enumeration returned can be used to sort the values in the tree:

```
public Enumeration inorder() {
  return new InorderEnumeration(topNode);
}

  private TreeNode topNode;
}
```

The TreeNode Class

The `TreeNode` class defines the actual `insert()` and `lookup()` operations for trees. Each instance of `TreeNode` holds a key and a value and has left and right subtrees:

```
class TreeNode {

// Construct a new TreeNode with a specific key and value.

  TreeNode(TreeKey key, Object val) {
    nodeKey   = key;
    nodeVal   = val;
    nodeLeft  = null;
    nodeRight = null;
  }
```

The `insert()` method inserts a new entry. If the `key` compares less than the `key` in this node, the method inserts the new value into the left subtree; if it compares greater than the `key` in this node, the method inserts it into the right subtree. Otherwise, `insert()` replaces the value in the current node:

```
  void insert(TreeKey key, Object val) {

    // All TreeKey objects implement the compare method.

    switch (key.compare(getKey())) {
      case TreeKey.EQUAL:
          nodeVal = val;
          break;

      case TreeKey.LESS:
          if (nodeLeft == null) {
              nodeLeft = new TreeNode(key, val);
          } else {
              nodeLeft.insert(key, val);
          }

          break;
```

```
    case TreeKey.GREATER:
        if (nodeRight == null) {
            nodeRight = new TreeNode(key, val);

        } else {
            nodeRight.insert(key, val);
        }

        break;
    }
}
```

The lookup() method looks up an entry in the tree based on the compare() function of key. The method returns null if no matching entry is found:

```
Object lookup(TreeKey key) {
    switch (key.compare(getKey())) {
        case TreeKey.EQUAL:
            return nodeVal;

        case TreeKey.LESS:
            if (nodeLeft == null) {
                return null;

            } else {
                return nodeLeft.lookup(key);
            }

        case TreeKey.GREATER:
            if (nodeRight == null) {
                return null;

            } else {
                return nodeRight.lookup(key);
            }
    }

    return null;
}
```

These methods are for the use of other classes in the package so that they do not need access to the instance variables of TreeNode objects:

```
TreeNode getLeft() {
    return nodeLeft;
}
TreeNode getRight() {
    return nodeRight;
}
```

```
TreeKey getKey() {
  return nodeKey;
}

Object getVal() {
  return nodeVal;
}

private TreeKey  nodeKey;
private Object   nodeVal;
private TreeNode nodeLeft;
private TreeNode nodeRight;
}
```

The InorderEnumeration Class

The InorderEnumeration class enumerates the entries in a tree one at a time in sorted order. The hasMoreElements() method returns false when all the entries have been enumerated. Each call to the nextElement() method returns the next entry in the tree. For each TreeNode, the left subtree, the node itself and then the right subtree are enumerated. The enumeration is performed using a stack. The stack's behavior mimics the behavior of the runtime stack in a recursive tree traversal, which might look like this:

```
void printTree(TreeNode node) {
  if (node != null) {
    printTree(node.getLeft());
    System.out.println(node.getVal());
    printTree(node.getRight());
  }
}
```

At each point where a value is printed, the state of the runtime stack will be duplicated in the enumeration. The first value to be printed will be the *leftmost* entry after the method has been called for each left subtree. At this point, all the leftmost entries will be on the runtime stack.

To initialize the enumeration, the InorderEnumeration class descends the leftmost branches of the tree, pushing each node on a stack. The top node on the stack is always the next to be enumerated. Following is the complete InorderEnumeration class:

```
class InorderEnumeration implements Enumeration {

  InorderEnumeration(TreeNode node) {
    pushLeftNodes(node);
  }

  // When the stack is empty, there are no more entries.
```

```
public boolean hasMoreElements() {
  return stack.empty() == false;
}
```

After an entry is returned, we need to enumerate the right subtree, so we set up
the stack for the right subtree just as we did at the top:

```
public Object nextElement() {
  TreeNode current = (TreeNode)stack.pop();
  pushLeftNodes(current.getRight());
  return current.getVal();
}
```

The pushLeftNodes() method descends the leftmost branches of the tree,
pushing each node:

```
private void pushLeftNodes(TreeNode node) {
  while (node != null) {
    stack.push(node);
    node = node.getLeft();
  }
}

  Stack stack = new Stack();
}
```

The TreeKey Interface

The TreeKey interface defines a compare() method that can be used to order
nodes in a tree. The compare() method should return either TreeKey.LESS,
TreeKey.EQUAL, or TreeKey.GREATER depending on how the current
TreeKey object compares to the argument TreeKey:

```
public interface TreeKey {
    public static final int LESS    = -1;
    public static final int EQUAL   =  0;
    public static final int GREATER =  1;

    public int compare(TreeKey other);
}
```

Sample Output From the Tree Sort Program

After all the classes in the tree package and the TreeSort class have been compiled, you can call the java interpreter from the command line to start the tree sorter:

```
java TreeSort file
```

Assume that the source file had the following data:

```
Z Y X W
Z Y X W
z y x w
V U T S
v u t s
Q P O N
q p o n
M L K J
m l k j
I H G F
i h g f
E D C B
e d c b
A
a
```

The interpreter will display the following sorted output:

```
A
E D C B
I H G F
M L K J
Q P O N
V U T S
Z Y X W
a
e d c b
i h g f
m l k j
q p o n
v u t s
z y x w
```

Summary

Interfaces are the fundamental mechanism in Java for approximating multiple inheritance. You can design a class that may enter into multiple contracts by specifying multiple interfaces that it supports. An interface is similar to a class definition, except that the methods in an interface are essentially stubs. Each class that `implements` an interface must specify how the interface's methods are to operate. The `TreeSort` program shows the use of interfaces to provide a generic tree facility. An inorder enumeration enables the program to process each element of the tree when it is ready to. Without the enumeration, the program structure would have to mirror the tree structure.

CHAPTER
6

- Java Array Fundamentals
- Array Initialization and Declaration
- Using Arrays of Objects
- How Arrays Fit in the Object Hierarchy

Arrays

Basics of Java Arrays

Arrays in Java are objects. As we discovered in our discussion of memory management, this means that arrays must be created with the new operator and cannot be allocated in place. For example, look at the following declaration:

```
int[] scores;
```

This declaration does not create an array. Instead, it creates a variable that can hold an array. To actually create an array of integers, it is necessary to use the new operator and create an instance, as in the following declaration:

```
scores = new int[10];
```

The size argument (in this case, 10) is required. Note that an array's size *cannot* be changed after it is created. (If you require a dynamically sized array, you can use the `java.util.Vector` class.) All the elements of the new array are initialized to the default value (0) for integers. All arrays in Java begin with element 0, so the first element is at index 0.

Array bounds are always checked in Java. If a subscript is less than 0 or greater than the array's length - 1, an `ArrayIndexOutOfBoundsException` is thrown. (We'll discuss throwing exceptions more in *Exception Handling* on page 99.)

Arrays of Objects

A common source of confusion arises when trying to create an array of objects. For example, consider the following statement:

```
String[] strings = new String[10];
```

This statement does *not* create an array of strings. Instead, it creates an array of ten `null` object references. In this respect, arrays of objects in Java are like arrays of pointers in C or C++. To populate the array with actual strings, it is necessary to store the `String` instances in the array explicitly, as in the following statement:

```
for (int i = 0; i < strings.length; i++) {
// All arrays have a public length instance variable.

❶    strings[i] = new String();
}
```

The statement in line ❶ stores a new instance of `String` in each element of the array.

The difference between declaring an array of a Java primitive type (`boolean`, `char`, `int`, `byte`, `short`, `long`, `float`, and `double`) and declaring an array of an object type is analogous to declaring a variable of a primitive type and a variable of an object type. For example, note the following two variable declarations:

```
❶ int foo;
❷ String bar;
```

In this example, line ❶ is a primitive variable declaration that creates a new integer variable, `foo`. Line ❷ is an object variable declaration (`String` is a subclass of `Object`) that creates a `null` reference to a `String`.

Multidimensional Arrays

Java does not support multidimensional arrays. You can, however, create arrays of arrays, just as you can in C and C++. This is natural since arrays in Java are objects, and it's possible to create arrays of any arbitrary object type. For example, the following declaration creates an array of null references to String arrays:

```
String[][] arrayOfStringArrays = new String[20][];
```

Note that the first dimension must be specified since the outermost array is actually being allocated. The elements of that array need to be allocated themselves, as illustrated in the following statement:

```
for (int i = 0; i < arrayOfStringArrays.length; i++) {
    // fill in each element of arrayOfStringArrays with an array of
    // strings.

    arrayOfStringArrays[i] = new String[10];
}
```

The following loop would actually fill the arrays with strings:

```
for (int i = 0; i < arrayOfStringArrays.length; i++) {
    for (int j = 0; j < arrayOfStringArrays[i].length; j++) {
        arrayOfStringArrays[i][j] = new String();
    }
}
```

A real program would probably combine the two loops like this:

```
for (int i = 0; i < arrayOfStringArrays.length; i++) {
   String[] newArray = new String[10];

   arrayOfStringArrays[i] = newArray;

   for (int j = 0; j < newArray.length; j++) {
     newArray[j] = new String();
   }
}
```

Again, the key points to remember are that Java arrays are objects that must be allocated, and arrays of Java objects are similar to arrays of pointers in C.

C++ Style Array Initialization

You can use the C++ style of enclosing an array's elements in opening and closing braces to initialize an array:

```
int[] scores = {1, 2, 3+4, 5};
```

Each element must be an expression that returns the array's component type. (Also, a comma after the last element is allowed.)

Alternative Array Declaration Syntax

Java also allows arrays to be declared in a syntax similar to C arrays. For example, the declaration:

```
int[] scores;
```

can also be written as:

```
int scores[];
```

These two forms are completely equivalent, but the latter form makes it less clear that we're just declaring a variable that can hold an array rather than the array itself. For this reason we prefer to use the former syntax.

Arrays in the Object Hierarchy

Arrays are objects in Java, but their classes are unique. Each class defined in Java (either by the system or the user) along with the primitive types has a corresponding array class. The class Object has a corresponding Object[] class that has arrays of Objects as its instances. Array classes cannot be extended directly. They are extended when their corresponding classes are extended. If class Y is a subclass of class X, then class Y[] (the class of arrays of Y) is a subclass of class X[] (the class of arrays of X).

At first glance, this seems like a reasonable arrangement. However, there is a potential problem with this type of system. Let's examine the problem with arrays so as not to fall victim to it ourselves. Consider the following scenario:

```
class X {
   int a;
}

class Y extends X {
   int b;
}

class Z {
   static void broken(X[] arrayOfX, int index, X newValue) {
     arrayOfX[index] = newValue;
   }
}
```

Class Y is a subclass of class X. Thus, Y[] (array of Y) is a subclass of X[] (array of X). Here is the problem:

```
Y[] arrayOfY = new Y[10];
X valueOfTypeX = new X();

Z.broken(arrayOfY, 0, valueOfTypeX);
```

The problem is that `Z.broken()` will try to assign `valueOfTypeX` to element 0 of `arrayOfY`. Unfortunately, `valueOfTypeX` is not a `Y`! The `Z.broken()` method will try to assign something that isn't of type `Y` to an array of type `Y`. At runtime, this will lead to an `ArrayStoreException` being thrown.

In every other case where a runtime type check is necessary to determine if an operation can be applied, the Java compiler will point it out. An explicit cast is required. In this case, however, code that is not typesafe can slip by the compiler and cause problems later at runtime. [1]

Summary

The subtle difference between creating an array and creating a variable that can hold an array sometimes confuses programmers new to Java. A simple declaration such as this:

```
int[] scores;
```

only creates a variable that can hold an array. To actually create an array of objects, you must use the `new` operator:

```
scores = new int[10];
```

This declaration initializes the 10 elements of the new array with 0, and the first element is at index 0.

Also, an array of object references is different from an array of primitive types. The elements of an array of object references must be explicitly created.

---

1. Some object-oriented languages, notably Eiffel, use this typing model (called covariance) deliberately because the Eiffel designers felt that it enhances the expressive power of the language. Other language designers consider it a bug.

CHAPTER 7

- The Java Exception Handling Model
- Exceptions in Java
- The try and catch Blocks

Exception Handling

Exceptional Conditions

Java provides an exception handling model that allows you to check for errors *only* where it is relevant to do so. This is in contrast to C, in which you have to deal with errors in the normal path of a program. A large portion of a well-written program is concerned with what to do when things go wrong. When looking at a program written in a language like C, in which you are forced to handle errors via return codes, it can be hard to see the actual algorithm being used in a procedure because there is error checking code inserted every few lines.

Problems Using Return Codes for Error Processing

Returning an error code often forces the *real* return value of a procedure to be passed back in some other way. (Real return values are commonly returned via a reference argument. Note, however, that there are no reference arguments in Java. Returning multiple values in Java requires returning an instance of a class.) A more serious flaw with using return codes for error processing is that once an error code has been issued, it must be dealt with by every procedure in the chain of calls that led to the error. As the error code ascends the call chain, it becomes more and more out of context. As a result, programmers typically re-encode the error several times on its way up the chain of calls. Even if the program does not need to do anything with the error for several levels, the program must be written to process it at each one.

Let's look at an example in C. Suppose we're working with records in a set of files and we want to look up an entry in one of the files. Table names are associated with particular file names based on context.   Errors are displayed to the user in the top level loop of the user interface:

```
/* Look up the entry for "Marianna" in the        */
/* "employee" table.                              */

/* On failure, "error" will be filled with a      */
/* structure containing details.                  */

ErrorStruct *error = NULL;
TableEntry  *entry = lookup("Marianna", "employee", &error);

if (entry == NULL) {
    return error;
}
```

In Java, we could rewrite this code to look something like this:

```
// Look up the entry for "Marianna" in the "employee"
// table.

// On failure, "error" will be filled in with details.

ErrorStruct error = new ErrorStruct();
TableEntry  entry = lookup("Marianna", "employee", error);

if (entry == NULL) {
    return error;
}
```

This version, unfortunately, requires that we allocate an `ErrorStruct` before the call—even if we don't end up using it. An alternative is to have `lookup()` return an instance of a class, as in the next example:

```
// Look up the entry for "Marianna" in the "employee" table.

// A variable of type "Result" contains a TableEntry and
// an ErrorStruct.

Result result = lookup("Marianna", "employee");

if (result.getEntry() == null) {
    return result.getError();
}
```

This version requires defining a `Result` class that is only used to return an extra value from the method. Following is another way to accomplish the same result:

```
// Look up the entry for "Marianna" in the "employee" table.

// The array returned will have a TableEntry and an ErrorStruct as
// elements 0 and 1.

Object[] result = lookup("Marianna", "employee");

if (result[0] == null) {
    return (ErrorStruct)result[1];
}
```

This version forces a type cast to be used, even though we know `result[1]` is an `ErrorStruct`.

As we can see, none of the previous three solutions are particularly satisfactory. The first version requires that we allocate an `ErrorStruct` when it isn't needed. The second version requires the definition of a `Result` class that is only used to return an extra value from the method. The third version forces an unnecessary type cast.

Catching and Throwing Exceptions

Rather than use the C-style error checking via return codes, Java recognizes that errors should *not* be dealt with in the normal path of a program. They are, in fact, *exceptional conditions*. Java implements a *catch and throw* model of exception handling similar to the one used in C++ . Using this model, you only have to pay attention to exceptional conditions where it makes sense to do so. Instead of returning errors from a method using the normal return value or parameter mechanism, Java provides an *exception handling* facility. Errors and other exceptional conditions are treated as distinct from the normal flow of control in the program, which, after all, they are. When an error occurs, an exception is *thrown*. Exceptions climb the chain of calls until they are *caught* or until the program exits.

The catch and throw method of exception handling offers two big advantages:

- An error condition can be dealt with only where it makes sense instead of dealing with it at every level between where it occurs and where it needs to be dealt with.

- Code can be written as if the operations in it will work.

Using Java's catch and throw method, we can simply rewrite the `lookup()` example as follows:

```
TableEntry entry = lookup("Marianna", "employee");
```

We can use `entry` without checking its value. This produces code that is much easier to read and modify.

try and catch

The fundamental language support for the catch and throw method of exception handling is the `try`/`catch` block. For example, at some higher level in our file database program, we could have the `try`/`catch` block in Example 7-1.

Example 7-1 `try` Block in Java

```
try {
    doFileProcessing();
    displayResults();

} catch (Exception e) {
    System.err.println("Error: " + e.getMessage());
}
```

Any error that occurred during the execution of doFileProcessing() or
displayResults() would be *caught* by the catch and processed. If an error
occurred during doFileProcessing(), displayResults() would never get
called, and execution would proceed directly to the catch block. If, instead of
having (Exception e), we had a more specific error class, such as
(LookupException e), the actual error would have to be an instance of
LookupException or one of its subclasses to be caught. Otherwise, the error
would pass through this try/catch block and continue to climb the call chain
until it reached a catch that matched it or the program exited. (Note that this
code uses the System object, which provides standard input and output streams
for reading character data and for printing output.)

You can also string multiple catches together to process different exception types
differently. For example, look at Example 7-2.

Example 7-2 Multiple Catches in try Block

```
try {
    doFileProcessing();
    displayResults();

} catch (LookupException e) {
    handleLookupException(e);

} catch (Exception e) {
    System.err.println("Error: " + e.getMessage());
}
```

In this case, a LookupException would be caught and processed by the first
catch and any other type of exception would be handled by the second catch.

The finally Statement

Exceptions can cause control to leave the current method without completing the
method's execution. If there is cleanup code such as code to close files at the end
of the method, it will never get called. To deal with this case, Java provides the
finally statement [1].

---

1. The Java finally statement is equivalent to the Common Lisp
   unwind-protect special form.

The `finally` statement can be used in conjunction with a `try` block. Basically, it ensures that if an exception occurs, any cleanup work that is necessary is taken care of because the code in a `finally` statement is guaranteed to run even if an exception occurs. For example, look at Example 7-3.

Example 7-3 Using the `finally` Statement

```
try {
    doSomethingThatMightThrowAnException();
} finally {
    cleanup();
}
```

If `doSomethingThatMightThrowAnException()` throws an exception, the `cleanup()` method will still be called, and then the exception will continue to travel up the call chain. If an exception is not thrown, `cleanup()` will get called and execution will proceed after the `finally` statement.

The throw Statement

Up to this point, we've focussed on receiving and processing errors in the `try` and `catch` block. Conversely, we need to understand how an error originates. In Java, when an error condition arises in a program, we send an exception up the call chain by using the `throw` keyword. For example, let's go back to our file lookup example. Say we want to check that `entry` is assigned an appropriate value, and if it isn't, we want to send an exception up the call chain where it will be handled by the appropriate `try` and `catch` block. Example 7-4 shows how to throw the exception.

Example 7-4 Using `throw` in Exception Handling

```
TableEntry entry = fileLookup(name, filename);

if (entry == null) {
❶   throw new FileLookupFailureException(name, filename);
}
```

In line ❶, the argument to `throw` can be any expression that returns an instance of a subclass of the `Throwable` class. (In general, this argument is almost always a subclass of `Exception`.)

The Java Exception class extends the Throwable class and represents exceptional conditions a user program may want to catch. The Throwable class provides some useful features for dealing with exceptions. Specifically, the Throwable class:

- Provides a slot for a message
- Contains a stack trace

It is often useful to create your own exception classes for special case exception handling within your program. This is normally done by creating a subclass of the Exception class.

The advantage of subclassing the Exception class is that the new exception type can be caught separately from other Throwable types, as in the LookupException example in Example 7-2 on page 104. We could simply define LookupException as in Example 7-5.

Example 7-5 Subclassing the Exception **Class**

```
public class LookupException extends Exception {
}
```

This would allow us to catch and specifically process a LookupException, without regard to other possible exceptions.

Errors

There is another high-level class in the Java runtime system that extends the Throwable class—the Error class. The runtime system uses the Error class for catastrophic failures that a program is not expected to be able to recover from.

A catch block such as the following is designed to catch all exceptions:

```
catch (Exception e) {
}
```

This catch block will not catch errors from the Error class, which is the desired behavior. If a program actually needs to trap *errors*, the following catch block will do:

```
catch (Error e) {
}
```

Declaring Exceptions

In Java, the exceptions a method can throw are considered part of its public interface. Users of a method need to know the exceptions it might throw so they can be prepared to handle them. Java requires that a method definition include a list of the exceptions the method throws. Example 7-6 shows the syntax for declaring these exceptions.

Example 7-6 Declaring Exceptions

```
public class Example {
❶    public static void exceptionExample() throws ExampleException,
     LookupException {
          .
          .
          .
     }
}
```

In line ❶, the exceptionExample() declaration includes the throws keyword, which is followed by a list of the exceptions this method might throw. In this case, that includes ExampleException and LookupException.

Defining the exceptions a method throws in the method declaration has one significant implication on the code you write. If you write a method that calls another method that can throw an exception, you must make sure the calling method does at least one of two things:

- Declares itself capable of throwing the same exception as the called method
- Includes a try/catch block to make sure the exception does not pass through to its caller

For example, the following code does both. It declares that `callExample` can throw an `ExampleException`, and it explicitly catches `LookupException`:

```
public class CallerExample {
    public static void callExample() throws ExampleException {
    try {
      Example.exceptionExample();
    } catch (LookupException e) {
      .
      .
      .
    }
}
```

Runtime Exceptions

There are a handful of common exceptions that can occur anywhere in a program. These include exceptions such as:

- `OutOfMemoryException`
- `NullPointerException`
- `ArrayIndexOutOfBoundsException`

These are referred to as *runtime exceptions*. Any exception that is a subclass of `RuntimeException` can be thrown from anywhere. Although you *can* declare them in a method declaration (and you should if you are explicitly throwing them) you do not have to explicitly declare the runtime exceptions. Doing so would introduce an unnecessary overhead in writing your programs.

It is legal to subclass `RuntimeException` and create your own exceptions that do not need to be declared. However, it's probably *not* a good idea since users of a method need to know the exceptions it might throw.

Remote Exceptions

The Java Remote Method Invocation (RMI) mechanism, described in *Remote Method Invocation* on page 175, enables the development of distributed applications. As you might expect, there are a handful of exceptional conditions particular to the execution of remote objects in distributed applications. Remote methods throw `RemoteException`, which is the superclass of all remote method exceptions. Any method calling a remote method must be written to handle `RemoteException`.

Summary

The beauty of the Java exception handling model is that it allows you to treat errors and other exceptional conditions as distinct from the normal flow of control in a program. Unlike C, in which you are forced to return errors by using return values or passing parameters, Java provides a *catch and throw* model of exception handling similar to the one used in C++ . When an error occurs, an exception is *thrown*. Exceptions climb the chain of calls until they are *caught* or until the program exits.

The fundamental language support for the catch and throw model of exception handling is the `try/catch` block. If an exception causes a method to exit before the method's cleanup code has had a chance to execute, you can use the `finally` statement to release resources. You use the `throw` keyword to send an exception up the call chain.

To define your own exceptions, you can simply subclass the `Exception` class. A method must declare any exceptions it can throw.

CHAPTER
8

- Java I/O Classes

- Standard Streams for I/O

- Printing Text Output and Reading Text Input

- File I/O

- Data I/O

Input/Output

Introduction

Input and output in Java follow the C and C++ model in which I/O support is provided by a library, not by the language itself. In Java, of course, the I/O library is a class library—the java.io package—which we'll explore in this chapter.

Like C++, Java provides typesafe I/O. There is no equivalent to the C printf() function, which can crash if the wrong type is handed to it at runtime. In fact, there is no way to pass a wrong type to an output function in Java. This is consistent with Java's primary emphasis on code safety.

Java I/O Classes and Wrappers

The Java I/O classes are designed in a layered fashion. At the bottom level, there are basic InputStream and OutputStream classes. Added facilities such as buffering, connecting to files, printing data types other than bytes, and so on are provided by what we'll call *wrapper* classes. For example, say a program created an instance of an InputStream called istream, and we wanted to buffer the input. To do that, we could use a BufferedInputStream wrapper, as in Example 8-1.

Example 8-1 Using I/O Wrappers

```
BufferedInputStream bstream = new BufferedInputStream(istream);
```

This statement creates a new `BufferedInputStream` that forwards all the normal `InputStream` operations to `istream`. By wrapping the `InputStream` object in a `BufferedInputStream`, the program can now also buffer the input. Using different types of wrappers allows a program to access arbitrarily different and useful behavior from an `InputStream` or `OutputStream` object.

It's common for Java programs that perform I/O to check the types of the streams they are passed. In this way, programs can determine if they support the operations required and, if not, wrap them appropriately. For instance, Example 8-2 shows an excerpt from the calculator program described on page 157. This code checks to see if the input is of type `DataInputStream`.

Example 8-2 Checking Types of I/O Streams Passed

```
   public Calculator(InputStream in, OutputStream out) {

      DataInputStream dataIn;
      PrintStream     printOut;

❶    if (!(in instanceof DataInputStream)) {
        dataIn = new DataInputStream(in);

❷    } else {
        dataIn = (DataInputStream)in;
      }
        .
        .
        .
   }
```

In this example, the program checks to see if it already has a `DataInputStream` in line ❶. If it doesn't, the program wraps a `DataInputStream` around the `InputStream` in. If it does have a `DataInputStream`, the program casts the `InputStream` in as in line ❷.

Type casting and the `instanceof` operator are discussed in detail in *Runtime Typing, Class Loading, and Native Methods*.

Standard Streams for a Java Program

When a Java program runs, there are three streams available by default:

- `System.in`
- `System.out`
- `System.err`

All three streams are stored in `static` variables of the `System` class. (The `System` class is in the `java.lang` package.

Table 8-1 summarizes the standard streams and their use.

Table 8-1 Standard Streams

Standard Stream	Stream Type	Use to...
`System.in`	`InputStream`	Read from user input.
`System.out`	`PrintStream`	Write user output.
`System.err`	`PrintStream`	Write user error output.

Printing Text Output in Java

The normal way of displaying output in Java is to use the `print()` and `println()` methods of the `PrintStream` class. `PrintStream.print()` sends its argument to the stream *without* a newline. `PrintStream.println()` sends its argument followed by a newline. For instance, look at the following example:

```
System.out.print("print and ");
System.out.println("println example");
```

The output from this example would look like this:

```
print and println example
```

A `PrintStream` object may not flush an output buffer until a newline is sent—unless the `PrintStream` is created with the `autoflush` option set to true. The `autoflush` option is an argument in one of the `PrintStream` constructors. In practical terms, this means that if a program needs to display a prompt, it may need to do an explicit call to `PrintStream.flush()` to make sure the prompt is displayed. For instance, look at Example 8-3.

Example 8-3 Displaying a Prompt

```
// p is a PrintStream
p.print("Please enter an integer: ");
❶ p.flush();
```

The prompt is not displayed until after the `p.flush()` in line ❶ is executed.

The standard `PrintStream` objects, `System.out` and `System.err`, are both created with `autoflush` set to true, so you do not need to explicitly call `flush()` when printing to them.

Java overloads the + operator for `String` objects, which makes printing much easier. Instead of being forced to construct long sequences of calls to `print()` and `println()`, a `String` argument may be constructed using +. In the following example, there are a series of `print()` and `println()` statements:

```
System.out.print("Ian is ");
System.out.print(8);
System.out.print(" and Drew is ");
System.out.print(6);
System.out.print(" and Li is ");
System.out.print(3);
System.out.println(" years old.");
```

Java provides the + operator to combine these statements into one statement, like this:

```
System.out.println("Ian is " + 8 + " and Drew is " + 6 + " and Li
is " + 3 + " years old. ");
```

Each argument to the + operator is converted to type `String` and then the string is converted. For primitive data types, this conversion occurs automatically. For instances of classes, the `toString()` method is called to do the conversion.

There's a default toString() method in the Object class that is called if there's no toString() method for that particular class. You can override the toString() method to define how you want your classes to be printed, as in the next example:

```
public class Person {
    public Person(String newName) {
        name = newName;
    }

    public String getName() {
        return name;
    }

❶   public String toString() {
        return "[" + getName() + "]";
    }

    private String name;
}

❷ Person kelly = new Person("Kelly");
    System.out.println(kelly);
```

In this example, line ❶ overrides the Object toString() method by defining how a Person is printed. Line ❷ prints [Kelly], using the new toString() method.

Reading Text Input in Java

There are three common ways of reading text input in Java:

- Reading some number of characters at a time
- Reading a line at a time
- Reading a token at a time

Let's look at each of these in more detail.

Reading Characters

Java supports reading some number of characters directly in the `InputStream` class. `InputStream` has `read()` methods for reading a single character and for reading an array of bytes. The following example shows how to read a single character:

```
// istream is an InputStream
int ch;

❶ while ((ch = istream.read()) != -1) {
    <... do something with ch ... >
}
```

In this example, `-1` in line ❶ indicates the end of the stream.

Reading an Array of Bytes

Example 8-4 shows how to read an array of bytes. The program is used in the following way:

```
java CopyFile file1 files2
```

Specifically, this program copies a file using `InputStream.read(byte[])`.

Example 8-4 Reading and Writing an Array of Bytes

```java
// CopyFile.java
import java.io.*;

public class CopyFile {
   public static void main(String[] args) {
      byte[] bytes = new byte[128];

      // Print usage line if no <src> or <dest> file are specified.
      if (args.length < 2) {
         System.err.println(
            "Usage: java CopyFile <src> <dest>");
         return;
      }
      try {
         InputStream istream = new FileInputStream(args[0]);
         OutputStream ostream = new FileOutputStream(args[1]);
         int count;

         while ((count = istream.read(bytes)) != -1) {
            ostream.write(bytes, 0, count);
         }

         istream.close();
         ostream.close();

      } catch (IOException e) {
         System.err.println(e);
         return;
      }
   }
}
```

❶
❷

❸
❹

❺

In this example:

❶ Opens the file named in `args[0]` and connects a `FileInputStream` object to it. (Remember that `args[0]` is the first argument and not the name of the program, as in `argv[0]` in a C `main()` declaration.)

❷ Opens the file named in `args[1]` and connects a `FileOutputStream` object to it.

❸ Reads the bytes in the input file.

❹ Writes the bytes to the output file. The 0 argument is the offset into the byte buffer, and `count` is the number of bytes to write.

❺ Closes both the input and output files.

Output of the CopyFile Program

The output of the `CopyFile` program is a duplicate file copied to the destination location. To use the `CopyFile` program, invoke the `java` interpreter from the command line and provide a source file and a destination file as arguments, as in the next example:

```
java CopyFile file newfile
```

Reading Text a Line at a Time

To read text a line at a time, you can use the `readLine()` method in the `DataInputStream` class. Example 8-5 shows an alternative to the previous program for copying a file; however, this program uses `readLine()`. The program is used in the same way as the previous program:

```
java CopyTextFile file1 files2
```

Example 8-5 Reading and Writing Text a Line at a Time

```java
// CopyTextFile.java
import java.io.*;

public class CopyTextFile {
    public static void main(String[] args) {
        if (args.length < 2) {
            System.err.println(
                "Usage: java CopyTextFile <src> <dest>");
            return;
        }

        try {
            DataInputStream istream = new DataInputStream(
                new FileInputStream(args[0]));
            PrintStream ostream = new PrintStream(
                new FileOutputStream(args[1]));
            String line;

            while ((line = istream.readLine()) != null) {
                ostream.println(line);
            }

            istream.close();
            ostream.close();

        } catch (IOException e) {
            System.err.println(e);
            return;
        }
    }
}
```

In this example:

❶ Wraps a `DataInputStream` object around a `FileInputStream`. This will allow use of the `DataInputStream` `readline()` method, which reads a line of text and returns it as a string.

❷ Wraps a `PrintStream` object around a `FileOutputStream`. This will allow use of the `PrintStream.println()` method.

❸ Reads the input file a line at a time using the `readline()` method.

❹ Prints a line at a time to the output file using the `println()` method.

Output of the CopyTextFile Program

The output of the CopyTextFile program is a duplicate file copied to the destination location. To use the CopyTextFile program, invoke the java interpreter from the command line and provide a source file and a destination file as arguments, as in the next example:

```
java CopyTextFile textfile newtext
```

Reading a Token at a Time

To read text a token at a time, you can use the StreamTokenizer class. The syntax of tokens may be specified, and then the tokenizer can be used to read each token. For example, Example 8-6 shows how to read numbers and strings separated by the ; (semi-colon) character.

The program is used in the following way:

```
java TokenizerText file
```

The important distinction between this and the previous programs is that it wraps a StreamTokenizer object around a FileInputStream in order to deal with tokens.

Example 8-6 Reading and Writing a Token at a Time

```java
// TokenizerText.java
import java.io.*;

public class TokenizerText {
   public static void main(String[] args) {
     if (args.length < 1) {
        System.err.println("Usage: java TokenizerText <src>");
        return;
     }
     try {
        StreamTokenizer stok = new StreamTokenizer(
           new FileInputStream(args[0]));

        // Treat a space as a normal character.
        stok.wordChars(0, ' ');
        // Declare ; to be the only separator char.
        stok.whitespaceChars(';', ';');
        int token;
        // token is filled with a code indicating type of item
        // just read
        while ((token = stok.nextToken()) != stok.TT_EOF) {
           switch (token) {
              case stok.TT_NUMBER:
                 // If a number is read, the value is placed in
                 // the double nval.
                 System.out.println("Number: " + stok.nval);
                 break;
              case stok.TT_WORD:

                 // If a word is read, the value is placed in
                 // the String sval.
                 System.out.println("Word: " + stok.sval);
                 break;
              default:
                 break;
           }
        }
     } catch (IOException e) {
        System.err.println(e);
        return;
     }
   }
}
```

❶

❷

In line **❶**, the program creates a `StreamTokenizer` object that returns successive tokens on each call to `nextToken()` in line **❷**. The `switch` following line **❷** is similar to a C `switch`.

Output of the TokenizerText Program

Assume we were to run the `TokenizerText` program on a file with the following data:

```
the truth; 96.8;is
out; there;
this is a; 42.5;test of
the;emergency broadcast
system
```

The output of the `TokenizerText` program is the source file, with all text separated by a semi-colon parsed according to whether it is a word or a number. Invoking the `TokenizerText` program on this file would produce the following output:

```
Word: the truth
Number: 96.8
Word: is
out
Word: there
Word: this is a
Number: 42.5
Word: test of
the
Word: emergency broadcast
system
```

File Input and Output in Java

The previous examples show simple stream-oriented file I/O in Java. Since the file classes `FileInputStream` and `FileOutputStream` are subclasses of `InputStream` and `OutputStream` respectively, they only support stream operations. However, there are often occasions when you need to be able to append to a file or treat a file as an array of bytes, which are not supported by the `InputStream` and `OutputStream` operations. The `RandomAccessFile` class provides this capability. (Note that a `RandomAccessFile` is not a stream. A `RandomAccessFile` has a file pointer associated with it that can be moved to any position within the file.)

You can open a `RandomAccessFile` in read (`r`) or read/write (`rw`) mode, and you can then change the file pointer position by using `seek()`.

Example 8-7 shows a program that appends its first file argument at the end of its second file argument.

Example 8-7 Appending Text to a File

```java
// AppendTextFile.java
import java.io.*;

public class AppendTextFile {
  public static void main(String[] args) {
    if (args.length < 2) {
      System.err.println(
          "Usage: java AppendTextFile <src> <dest>");
      return;
    }

    try {
      RandomAccessFile ifile = new RandomAccessFile(args[0],
          "r");
      RandomAccessFile ofile = new RandomAccessFile(args[1],
          "rw");

      ofile.seek(ofile.length());
      String line;

      while ((line = ifile.readLine()) != null) {
        ofile.writeBytes(line);
        ofile.writeByte('\n');
      }
      ifile.close();
      ofile.close();
    }
    catch (IOException e) {
      System.err.println(e);
      return;
    }
  }
}
```

❶
❷
❸
❹

In this example:

❶ Opens the first file argument in read (`r`) mode.

❷ Opens the second file argument in read/write (`rw`) mode.

❸ The file pointer starts at 0. Then, `ofile.seek(ofile.length()` repositions the pointer to the end of file so the program can append to it. The `RandomAccessFile` class supports the `length()` method to determine the end of the file.

❹ The `writeBytes()` method writes a string to the file, but it doesn't add a newline. (There is no `writelnBytes()`.)

Output of the AppendTextFile Program

The `AppendTextFile` program appends one file to the end of another file. Assume we were to use the `AppendTextFile` program to append a file with the following data:

```
plaid.
```

to another file with the following data:

```
Can't do
```

Running the `AppendTextFile` program on these two files would modify the second file so that it would read:

```
Can't do
plaid.
```

Data Input and Output in Java

Java also supports non-text data files. The `DataOutputStream` class has methods for writing primitive Java data types to a stream in a portable way. You can use the `DataInputStream` class to read them back in.

Java does not provide direct support for reading and printing user-defined objects. You must implement your own methods to do this.

Summary

Java stream I/O is based on the `InputStream` and `OutputStream` classes. Java also supports different types of I/O *wrappers*, which allow programs to apply a variety of useful operations to input and output streams.

Java provides three standard streams: `System.in`, `System.out`, `System.err`.

To display text output, Java provides the `print()` and `println()` methods of the `PrintStream` class. A user can specify how classes should be printed by defining `toString()` methods for them. Text input can be read using the `read()` methods of the `InputStream` class or the more specialized methods provided by the input wrapper classes.

To read and write binary data, Java provides the `DataInputStream` and `DataOutputStream` classes.

A file can be treated as an array of bytes using the `RandomAccessFile` class, which has a file pointer. Appending to a file is accomplished using the `RandomAccessFile` class by first seeking to the end of the file and then writing data to it.

CHAPTER
9

- Variable Assignments
- Casting One Type into Another
- Dynamic Class Loading
- Native Methods and Linking with C Code

Runtime Typing, Class Loading, and Native Methods

Introduction

Much of the power and flexibility of the Java language is the result of its dynamic runtime facilities. Java supports both runtime typing and runtime extensibility. In this chapter, we'll discuss those features, including how to extend Java programs by using code written in Java and by using code written in C. Note that the procedure to link Java programs with C code is fairly complex, so if you don't intend to do that, you may want to skip that section and go directly to *Multiple Threads of Execution* on page 147.

Variable Types and Their Values

Most commonly used languages such as C assign types to variables. A value stored in a variable can be assumed to be of the variable's type. In Java, however, a variable may contain a value of a different type—provided that the type is a subtype of the variable's declared type. Specifically, an object stored in a variable of type T may actually be an instance of a subclass of type T. For instance, consider the variable assignments in the next example:

```
T data;

// Assume the SubclassOfT extends T.
SubclassOfT dataItem = new SubClassOfT();

// Object in the data variable is not directly of type T.
data = dataItem;
```

The `data` variable is not of type T, but the assignment is valid because `dataItem` contains a value that is an instance of a subclass of T.

Similarly, if a variable is declared to be an interface type, that variable can hold any object whose class implements that interface:

```
// I is an Interface type.
I data;

// The ImplementsI class implements the I interface.
ImplementsI dataItem = new ImplementsI();

// Object in data implements the I interface.
data = dataItem;
```

In this case, `data` can hold the object stored in `dataItem` because the `ImplementsI` class implements the `I` interface.

The instanceof Operator

The instanceof operator provides the means to perform type comparisons. Sometimes it is necessary to determine if a reference to an object declared to be of a particular class—say class A—actually refers to an object that is an instance of a specific subclass of class A. In our discussion of *Input/Output* on page 112, we looked at this example:

```
public Calculator(InputStream in, OutputStream out) {

  DataInputStream dataIn;
  PrintStream printOut;

  // Check if we already have a DataInputStream
  if (!(in instanceof DataInputStream)) {

    // If not, wrap one around the InputStream.
    dataIn = new DataInputStream(in);

  } else {

    // If so, cast the InputStream down.
    dataIn = (DataInputStream)in;
  }
  .
  .
  .
}
```

The type of the variable in is InputStream, but we need to know if its value is actually a DataInputStream. Java makes it easy to answer this kind of question because it keeps type information with each object. An object knows its type and the interfaces it implements. (C++ did not originally have this feature—called *manifest types*—but so many people ended up creating their own runtime-type information that the designers added it to the language.)

The instanceof operator syntax looks like this:

```
<object> instanceof <type>
```

In this syntax, *<type>* can be either a class name or an interface name.

Note that the `instanceof` operator does not tell you what the most specific type for an object is. In fact, the only way to determine the specific type of an object is to use `getClass()` to obtain the object's class and then use `getName()` to return the name of the class as a string. In practice, obtaining the specific type is not generally necessary, since what you usually want to know is if a particular operation will be valid on an object; asking if the object is an instance of a type that supports the operation is all that's required.

Type Casting

Now that we can find out that an object is an instance of a particular type, what can we do with that information? The `in` variable is still of type `InputStream`. (The variable that contains the instance is still of the superclass type—that is, `in` is of type `InputStream`, but it holds a value of type `DataInputStream`, which is a subclass of `InputStream`.) If we want to apply an operation from the subclass, we can't do it through the existing variable. For instance, look at the next example:

```
in.readLine();    // Error
```

We know the value held by `in` is of type `DataInputStream`. However, `in` itself is still of type `InputStream`. We can't use the `readLine()` method on `in` because `readLine()` is defined for variables of type `DataInputStream`, not `InputStream`.

Java deals with this problem by allowing one type to be *cast* into another type. This is just like type casting in C or C++, with one notable difference. In Java, you can only cast something into a type if it is an instance of that type or a subclass of that type. If the compiler cannot prove that the cast is valid, a runtime type check is inserted. If the type check fails at the time of the cast, a `ClassCastException` is thrown.

For example, consider this line from our calculator program:

```
dataIn = (DataInputStream)in;
```

If in did not actually contain a value of type DataInputStream, an exception would be thrown. However, since in does contain a DataInputStream value, the cast succeeds and we can call DataInputStream operations (such as the readLine() method) on dataIn:

```
dataIn.readLine(); // Correct
```

Alternatively, we could perform the cast directly in the call to readLine():

```
((DataInputStream)in).readLine(); // Also correct.
```

A cast from a class to a superclass is implicit and requires no runtime check. For example, we could call the Calculator() constructor (described in *Putting the Pieces Together* on page 155) with a DataInputStream without casting it to an InputStream:

```
Calculator c = new Calculator(new DataInputStream(System.in),
    System.out);
```

Class Loading at Runtime

The runtime type information provided by Java enables one of Java's most powerful features—*dynamic class loading*. At runtime, the Java system loads classes mentioned in a Java program. These classes are loaded from directories listed in a user's CLASSPATH environment variable. This class loading facility is also available to Java programmers.

It's never necessary to explicitly load a class that is mentioned directly in your program. All mentioned classes are loaded automatically. However, dynamic class loading is useful when a program defines an interface or abstract class that may have many different implementations.

The Applet class provides an excellent example. Every applet that is executed in a web browser extends the Applet class. The class browser mentions the Applet class by name, so it is automatically loaded. However, the class browser doesn't know about the subclasses of Applet until they are loaded. It doesn't really need to know, either, since the class browser only interacts with Applet subclasses through the methods defined by Applet. An applet browser could use the

following code to load a new applet. (Note that this code would only work if the applet was available through the user's CLASSPATH. If the applet was being loaded from an http server, a class loader would be required. See *Class Loaders* on page 132 for information on how class loaders work.)

```
Class  c   = Class.forName("Ticker");
Applet app = (Applet)c.newInstance();
```

In this case, app could be manipulated using the public methods of the Applet class. (We use this technique in two of our examples: the Cellular applet described in *Putting the Pieces Together* on page 291, and the Lisp interpreter on the CD included with this book.)

Instances of the class Class contain information about particular classes that have been loaded into the Java runtime system. Each instance of Class contains information about one particular Java class. This information includes:

- The name of the class

- The name of its superclass

- The interfaces it implements

- Whether or not the class is itself an interface

All of this information is contained in the object representing the class.

static methods for a class cannot be called through the object that represents it. The only way of getting to the methods defined for a class is by creating an instance and casting the instance to the class. Each instance of Class defines a newInstance() method that calls the zero-argument constructor of the class it represents and returns the new instance. Class.newInstance() returns a value of type Object so it must be cast down to a particular class before the methods of the class can be accessed.

Class Loaders

To load classes from sources other than the paths specified in the CLASSPATH environment variable, you must define and use a class loader. A class loader has two jobs:

- Obtaining the bytes that represent a class from a source (for example, an http server)

- Installing the bytes as a class definition

Each new class loader extends the `ClassLoader` class. It defines the `loadClass()` method, which reads in class data and calls the `defineClass()` method to create an instance of the class `Class`. A `loadClass()` method for an instance of `ClassLoader` generally goes through the following steps:

```
Look up the class in a local cache (usually an instance of
java.util.Hashtable).

IF not found
  Use findSystemClass to try to locate the class using the
  standard java classpath mechanism.

  IF not found
    Try to load the bytes for the class from the source
    associated with this class loader.
    IF successful
      Call defineClass to create an instance of Class
      Install the new class in the local cache.

    ELSE
      Throw a ClassNotFoundException.

IF the class needs to be resolved (i.e. if it mentions other
classes that are not yet known)

  Call resolveClass() to resolve it.

Return the class.
```

Class loaders commonly differ in how they retrieve the bytes for a class and what, if any, security policies they enforce on classes they load.

Linking With C Code

Java also supports extending the system at runtime with code written in C. (Note that the procedure to do this is fairly complex. If you don't intend to link Java programs with C code, you may want to skip over this section.) You can declare methods in classes to be `native` (see *Native Methods* on page 31). You can then implement the bodies of these methods in C. This can be useful when you require machine-specific code or you need extremely high performance.

Using methods written in C is a five-step process. You need to:

1. Declare native methods.

2. Generate .h files that your C files can include. These .h files describe the structure of the Java classes used by the native methods.

3. Generate the *stub* functions that the Java runtime will use to call your native methods.

4. Build a dynamic library with the generated stub functions and your C functions.

5. Link the library into the Java runtime system.

Before showing some examples of native methods, let's go through each of these steps in detail for a UNIX environment.

Declaring Native Methods

A native method is declared exactly like an abstract method, except the keyword `abstract` is replaced with the keyword `native`. Instead of defining the method body, you must terminate the declaration with a semi-colon. Following is the native declaration we'll use in our example (on page 139):

```
public native Object fetch(LispSymbol sym) throws
    UnboundSymbolException;
```

That's all there is to declaring a native method.

Generating Include Files

In order to implement a native method, you must have C declarations for all the Java classes you use. You have to use the `javah` program to generate these C declarations. This `javah` program will generate the relevant information for a set of classes specified on the command line. For instance, following is the `javah` command used for our examples:

```
javah -o lisp/java_structs.h java.lang.String java.util.Vector
lisp.LispSymbol lisp.LispEnv
```

The native method in our examples uses two classes from the `lisp` package, along with the `String` and `Vector` classes. `javah` will create the structure declarations needed and place them in `lisp/java_structs.h`. Here is what the `lisp/java_structs.h` file looks like after being created by `javah`:

```
/* DO NOT EDIT THIS FILE - it is machine generated */
#include <native.h>
/* Header for class java_lang_String */

#ifndef _Included_java_lang_String
#define _Included_java_lang_String

typedef struct Classjava_lang_String {
  struct HArrayOfChar *value;
  long offset;
  long count;
/* Inaccessible static: InternSet */
} Classjava_lang_String;
HandleTo(java_lang_String);

#endif
/* Header for class java_util_Vector */

#ifndef _Included_java_util_Vector
#define _Included_java_util_Vector
struct Hjava_lang_Object;

typedef struct Classjava_util_Vector {
  struct HArrayOfObject *elementData;
  long elementCount;
  long capacityIncrement;
} Classjava_util_Vector;
HandleTo(java_util_Vector);

#endif
/* Header for class lisp_LispSymbol */

#ifndef _Included_lisp_LispSymbol
#define _Included_lisp_LispSymbol
struct Hjava_lang_String;

typedef struct Classlisp_LispSymbol {
  struct Hjava_lang_Object *localVal;
  struct Hjava_lang_String *name;
}Classlisp_LispSymbol;
HandleTo(lisp_LispSymbol);
```

```
#endif
/* Header for class lisp_LispEnv */

#ifndef _Included_lisp_LispEnv
#define _Included_lisp_LispEnv
struct Hlisp_LispEnv;
struct Hjava_util_Vector;

typedef struct Classlisp_LispEnv {
   struct Hlisp_LispEnv *parent;
   struct Hjava_util_Vector *localVars;
   struct Hjava_util_Vector *localVals;
} Classlisp_LispEnv;
HandleTo(lisp_LispEnv);

struct Hlisp_LispSymbol;
extern struct Hjava_lang_Object *lisp_LispEnv_fetch(struct
Hlisp_LispEnv *,struct Hlisp_LispSymbol *);
#endif
```

In the file, there are declarations for all the classes we asked for and a declaration for a function at the end of the file. This is the function that must be defined to implement the native method. Note that in the class and function declarations, each period (.) in a class name is replaced by an underscore (_).

It's important to understand the structure of a Java object in memory before writing native methods. Each object referenced in a Java program consists of a structure with two fields:

- A pointer to its data slots

- A pointer to its methods

Collectively, these are called the *handle* on the object. Figure 9-1 shows how the LispEnv class we use in our example would look in memory.

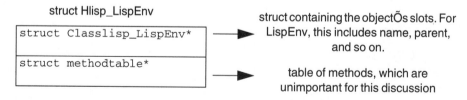

Figure 9-1 Structure of a Java Object in Memory

To make manipulating the slots of a Java instance more convenient, the C
unhand(x) macro will return the particular structure with slots, given a pointer
to a handle. So the following would be valid:

```
struct Hlisp_LispEnv* henv = ....;
Classlisp_LispEnv*    env  = unhand(henv);
```

Then, the following would be a correct reference:

```
env->localVars
```

We'll explore the manipulation of these objects shortly in our examples.

Generating Stub Functions

Java needs to embed the functions we write for our native methods into the
runtime system. It does this via stub functions that are also generated by the
javah program. To create stubs, it is necessary to use javah with the -stubs
option, as in the following:

```
javah -stubs -o lisp/stubs.c lisp.LispEnv
```

This command would create a file named lisp/stubs.c, which looks like this:

```
/* DO NOT EDIT THIS FILE - it is machine generated */
#include <StubPreamble.h>

/* Stubs for class lisp_LispEnv */
/* SYMBOL: "lisp_LispEnv/fetch(Llisp/LispSymbol;)Ljava/lang/Objec
t;", Java_lisp_LispEnv_fetch_stub */
stack_item *Java_lisp_LispEnv_fetch_stub(stack_item *_P_,struct
execenv *_EE_)
{
   extern void* lisp_LispEnv_fetch(void *,void *);
   _P_[0].p = lisp_LispEnv_fetch(_P_[0].p,((_P_[1].p)));
   return _P_ + 1;
}
```

The only thing you need to do with this file is link it in to your dynamic library later.

Building a Library

Let's assume that you've written the C functions for your native methods. (We'll see how this works in our examples). Now you need to create a dynamic library. On a Solaris UNIX system, you would use the following compiler command:

```
cc -I<path to jdk>/jdk-1.0/include -I<path to jdk>/jdk-
1.0/include/solaris -G -o env.so <C file1> ... <C fileN> stubs.c
```

This command line assumes that the include files generated by `javah` are in the current directory. The `-G` flag says to create a dynamic library. Note that we link in the `stubs.c` file generated by `javah`.

We now have a library we can link into a Java system.

Linking a Library Into Java

To link a dynamic library containing native methods into Java, you create a `static` initializer for a class. The `static` initializer uses either `System.load(<pathname>)` or `System.loadLibrary(<library name>)`. If the library is located within your dynamic library search path, you can use `loadLibrary()`; otherwise you must specify a full path name. Here is the `static` initializer we use in the example on page 139.

```
public class LispEnv implements LispPrintable {
   static {
     System.load("<path to Lisp>/Lisp/lisp/env.so");
   }
   .
   .
   .
}
```

When the `LispEnv` class is loaded into the runtime system, the `env.so` dynamic library will be automatically linked in.

Examples

Following are three versions of a native method, each digging progressively deeper into the internals of Java structures. This native method is used to look up the value of a variable in a Lisp interpreter. Assume that the bottleneck in the interpreter is the speed of variable lookup, and we hope to improve performance by using a native method. The environment structure containing our variables consists of a set of linked frames, each containing a vector of names and a vector of values. When a variable name is looked up, a search is done on the name vector of the current frame. If a match is found, the corresponding element of the value vector is returned. If no match is found, the search is repeated with the frame contained in the parent link of the current frame. If there is no match at the end of the frame, we check an immediate value slot in the symbol itself. If is empty, we throw an UnboundSymbol exception.

The only thing that will change in the three examples is the index_of() function, which looks up a LispSymbol in a frame.

Using Native Methods, Example 1

In the first example, we will compare variable names by using the Java dynamic invocation interface to call the String.equals() method:

```
#include "java_structs.h"

/* look up a variable in a frame. If found, return the index;
   otherwise, return -1
*/

int
index_of(
    ClassArrayOfObject*     vec,    /* Vector of names */
    long                    len,    /* Length of the name vector */
    Classlisp_LispSymbol*   sym     /* Lisp symbol to look up */
)
{
  long i;

  /* Fetch the actual array of object pointers from the
     java.util.Vector */

  struct Hjava_lang_Object** oarray = vec->body;

  /* step through the array of objects and call String.equals to
     compare the entries with the argument symbol */

  for (i = 0; i < len; i++) {

    /* use "unhand" to get to the actual symbol object */

    Classlisp_LispSymbol* other_sym =
      unhand((Hlisp_LispSymbol*)oarray[i]);
```

```
    /* Call execute_java_dynamic_method to invoke String.equals.
       Arguments are:
       1) execution context (0 means current context).
       2) object to call method on.
       3) method name.
       4) method signature
          Translation:

          (                 - beginning of arguments
          L                 - argument is an instance of a class
          java/lang/Object  - the name of the argument's class
          ;                 - end of class description
          )                 - end of arguments
          Z                 - returns a boolean.

       5) method argument   */

    int result = execute_java_dynamic_method(
       0,
       (Hjava_lang_Object*)sym->name,
       "equals",
       "(Ljava/lang/Object;)Z",
       (Hjava_lang_Object*)other_sym->name);

    /* If the boolean result is true, return the index */

    if (result) {
      return i;
    }
  }

  /* The name was not found in the current frame */
  return -1;
}

/* The function that implements the native "fetch" method */

struct Hjava_lang_Object*
lisp_LispEnv_fetch(
  struct Hlisp_LispEnv*   env,
  struct Hlisp_LispSymbol* sym
)
{
  int                  var_index;
  Classlisp_LispEnv*   lenv;
  Classlisp_LispSymbol*lsym;

  /* If we were passed a null object, throw an exception. Note that
```

calling SignalError does not cause control to leave the
function. The third argument to SignalError is a char* which
can be passed a message string. */

```
if (env == 0 || sym == 0) {
  SignalError(0, "java/lang/NullPointerException", 0);
  return 0;
}

/* Extract the symbol and environment from the handles */

lenv = unhand((struct Hlisp_LispEnv*)env);
lsym = unhand((struct Hlisp_LispSymbol*)sym);

/* Call index_of to see if the symbol is located in the current
   frame */

var_index = index_of(
  unhand(unhand(lenv->localVars)->elementData),
  unhand(lenv->localVars)->elementCount,
  lsym);

/* If the symbol was not found, repeat the lookup in the parent
   frame; if there is no parent frame, check the symbol's
   localValue. If there is no local value, throw an
   UnboundSymbolException */

if (var_index == -1) {
  if (lenv->parent == 0) {
    if (lsym->localVal == 0) {
      SignalError(0, "lisp/UnboundSymbolException", 0);
      return 0;
    } else {
      return lsym->localVal;
    }
  }

  return lisp_LispEnv_fetch(lenv->parent, sym);
}

/* return the value from the frame */

return unhand(unhand(lenv->localVals)->elementData)-
  >body[var_index];}
```

Using Native Methods, Example 2

For the next two examples, we'll only show `index_of()` since everything else is the same.

In this version, we extract C strings from Java strings and compare them using the `strcmp()` function. `makeCString` returns a pointer to garbage collected memory containing a C version of a Java string. To obtain a pointer to a C string allocated with `malloc()`, you would use `allocCString()`:

```
int
index_of(
  ClassArrayOfObject*  vec,
  long                 len,
  Classlisp_LispSymbol* sym
)
{
  long                 i;

  /* Extract a C string from the argument symbol */

  char*                      s       = makeCString(sym->name);
  struct Hjava_lang_Object**  oarray = vec->body;

  for (i = 0; i < len; i++) {

    /* Extract a C string from the current frame entry */

    Classlisp_LispSymbol* other_sym =
      unhand((Hlisp_LispSymbol*)oarray[i]);

    /* Compare them the old fashioned way */

    if (strcmp(s, makeCString(other_sym->name)) == 0) {
      return i;
    }
  }

  /* not found */

  return -1;
}
```

Using Native Methods, Example 3

The final version compares Java strings directly, avoiding the overhead of a method call as well as the overhead of copying strings:

```
int
```

```
index_of(
    ClassArrayOfObject*        vec,
    long                       len,
    Classlisp_LispSymbol*      sym
)
{
    long                         i;
    struct Hjava_lang_Object** oarray = vec->body;

    for (i = 0; i < len; i++) {
        struct Classlisp_LispSymbol* other_sym =
            unhand((struct Hlisp_LispSymbol*)oarray[i]);

        /* Get the actual string structures from the handles */

        Classjava_lang_String* symstring   =
            unhand(sym->name);
        Classjava_lang_String* otherstring =
            unhand(other_sym->name);

        /* A Java String contains a count of characters --
           If the counts differ, they don't match */

        if (symstring->count == otherstring->count) {
            long count = symstring->count;
            long j;

            /* Extract the unicode arrays from the strings. Since
               Java Strings are immutable, the implementation shares
               them and a particular String object may start at
               some offset into a unicode array */

            unicode* symchars   = unhand(symstring->value)->body +
                symstring->offset;
            unicode* otherchars = unhand(otherstring->value)->body +
                otherstring->offset;

            /* Compare the unicode arrays */

            for (j = 0; j < count; j++) {
                if (symchars[j] != otherchars[j]) {
                    break;
                }
            }

            if (j == count) {
                return i;
            }
```

```
      }
    }

    return -1;
}
```

Summary

This chapter highlights how Java variables can hold values of types other than the variable's type. Java provides extensive support for dynamic type operations and dynamic extension of the system. The type of an object may be determined at runtime and all casting between types is checked. An invalid cast will cause an exception to be thrown. New classes may be added to the system during operation and can include code written in C. Class loaders are used to install classes obtained from external sources. The Java development environment provides tools to assist in writing extensions in C.

CHAPTER
10

- Creating Multiple Threads with the Thread Class

- Locking Resources and How They Work

Multiple Threads of Execution

Introduction

Until recently, the only programmers who had to worry about concurrent execution were those writing operating systems and embedded control software. Most application programmers wrote programs that just ran from start to finish. Some exceptions include multiuser applications that allocate a process to each user and process control programs like the UNIX shell, the sole purpose of which is to create multiple processes. Though these count as applications, they have a strong systems programming flavor.

This has changed with the advent of graphical user interfaces (GUIs). Prior to the use of GUIs, when a program interacted with a user, it was usually because it needed an input before it could continue. There wasn't much point to having multiple threads of control. Now a program's user interface often has its own state that the user can manipulate while the program underneath is doing something else. This is probably the most common use of *threads*. (For a complete discussion of the use of threads, see *Threads Primer: a Guide to Multithreaded Programming*, Bill Lewis and Daniel Berg, SunSoft Press.)

Java has exceptionally good support for programming with multiple threads of execution. Unlike most languages in which support for threads is only available at the library level, Java builds thread support directly into the language. This includes built-in support for creating threads and for locking resources necessary for proper execution of multiple threads.

Creating Threads

You create multiple threads of control in a Java program via the `Thread` class. You can do this in two different ways:

- Define a class that *extends* the `Thread` class
- Define a class that `implements` the `Runnable` interface

Extending the Thread Class

The first way to create a thread is to define a new subclass of `Thread`. This is a simple matter of using the `extends` keyword, as in Example 10-1.

Example 10-1 Creating Multiple Threads With the `Thread` Class

```
❶ public class ExampleThread extends Thread {
❷    public void run() {
    < ... call synchronized methods and do whatever the thread needs to do ... >
      }
  }
```

In this example, line ❶ defines a class that `extends` the `Thread` class. Line ❷ defines a `run()` method. Every class that extends the `Thread` class needs to have a `run()` method that specifies whatever tasks are required when this thread is executed.

Now, to start a new thread, you use the `start()` method, which is defined in the `Thread` class. Example 10-2 shows how this works.

Example 10-2 Starting a Thread

```
ExampleThread ethread = new ExampleThread();
ethread.start();
```

When the new class is instantiated and its `start()` method is called, a new thread of control is created. The new thread then calls the `run()` method, which in this case is defined in the `ExampleThread` class.

Implementing the Runnable Interface

The second way to create a thread is to define a class that *implements* the Runnable interface. Any class can represent a thread if it implements the Runnable interface and defines a run() method, as in Example 10-3.

Example 10-3 Implementing Threads With the Runnable Interface

```
❶ public class ExampleRunnable implements Runnable {
❷    public void run() {
         <... perform tasks ... >
      }
   }
   ExampleRunnable er = new ExampleRunnable();
❸ new Thread(er).start();
```

In this example:

❶ Defines a new class that implements the Runnable interface.

❷ Defines a run() method that performs whatever tasks are required when this thread is executed.

❸ Creates a new Thread instance with a Runnable object (in this case, er) as an argument. The start() method of the new instance is then called. This starts a new thread of control.

This method of creating threads of control is very useful if the class we want to run in a thread already extends some other class. We can't extend Thread if we're already extending another class. By using the Runnable interface, we can still create multiple threads even when we're already extending another class.

We'll discuss the methods and attributes of the Thread class in more detail in *Part 2—Writing Java Applets*. Applets rely heavily on the use of threads, as we'll show in several examples.

Resource Locking

The most complicated area of programming with threads arises when multiple threads must access a shared resource. The problems that arise can be surprisingly subtle. Consider the following example:

```
public class BrokenThreadExample {
  public int nextCounter() {
    return counter++;
  }

  private int counter = 0;
}
```

This example looks innocent enough. You might think we could use it to supply an increasing counter to multiple threads. Unfortunately, it's broken. The problem can be hard to see because many programmers tend to think of the built-in operations in a language like Java as atomic units. The line:

```
return counter++;
```

is actually a compound operation. The current value of the counter is read, it is incremented by one, and the value is written back. What happens if another thread writes its value back between the read and the write? Here's a scenario that illustrates the problem:

Thread 1 reads `counter` and finds the value 0.
Thread 2 reads `counter` and finds the value 0.
Thread 1 adds one and writes 1 into `counter`.
Thread 2 adds one and writes 1 into `counter`.

Now, the `counter` value is set to 1, even though both threads incremented it.

Using the synchronized Modifier

To avoid this problem, we *lock* a resource (like the `counter` in our example) while a thread is accessing it. In Java, locking resources is extremely simple. Each object in Java has a lock associated with it. A method that uses the `synchronized` modifier automatically acquires the lock on its instance before proceeding. If the instance's lock is already held by another thread, the method will block until it can obtain the lock. So all that is needed to fix our example is to add synchronized to the nextCounter() method, as illustrated in Example 10-4.

Example 10-4 Locking Resources With synchronized **Modifier**

```
public class FixedThreadExample {
   public synchronized int nextCounter() {
     return counter++;
   }

   private int counter = 0;
}
```

Now, before Thread 1 reads the counter, it acquires the lock on the shared FixedThreadExample instance. It reads counter, increments it, and writes it back. Any other threads waiting to access the shared FixedThreadExample wait their turn.

Class methods may also need to be synchronized. If this is necessary, you can also use the synchronized modifier with these static methods. Each class has its own lock on resources just as instances do.

Using synchronized Blocks

It is possible for a method to acquire the lock on an object other than its own. This is done using a synchronized block, as in Example 10-5.

Example 10-5 Using a `synchronized` Block

```java
public class SynchronizedBlockExample {
    public int getCounter() {
      return counter;
    }

    public void setCounter(int newValue) {
      counter = newValue;
    }

    private int counter = 0;
}

SynchronizedBlockExample myCounter =
  new SynchronizedBlockExample();

synchronized (myCounter) {
    int currentCounter = myCounter.getCounter();
    myCounter.setCounter(currentCounter + 1);
}
```

❶

In line ❶, we lock a specific instance of a `SynchronizedBlockExample` rather than the current object. Within the `synchronized` block, we use the `getCounter()` method to read the counter and the `setCounter()` method to write a new value while holding the lock on `myCounter`. In this way, no other thread can access `myCounter`.

Summary

Unlike many other languages, Java builds thread support directly into the language. There is built-in support for creating threads and for locking resources necessary for proper execution of multiple threads.

You can create multiple threads of control by using the `Thread` class, in one of two ways: define a class that *extends* the `Thread` class or define a class that *implements* the `Runnable` interface. The latter method is particularly useful when a class already extends another class, but you still want it to run multithreaded.

Java also provides a simple way to lock resources necessary for the proper execution of multiple threads. By using the `synchronized` modifier, a method automatically acquires the lock on its class or instance before proceeding. If the object's lock is already held by another thread, the method will block until it can obtain the lock.

CHAPTER 11

- Developing a Java Calculator
- Calculator Classes
- Calculator Interfaces

Putting the Language Pieces Together

Four-Function Calculator

We've now covered enough of Java to work through a larger example. We'll implement a stack-based calculator showing how to use Java features such as interfaces and exception handling to make it elegant and extensible. Commands for the calculator will be single non-numeric characters, and operands will be of type `double`.

The program is used in the following way:

```
java RunCalculator
calc>
```

At the prompt, you can enter functions for the calculator to perform.

The classes that comprise the calculator are grouped together into a `calc` package. This package consists of six classes and three interfaces, as illustrated in Figure 11-1.

calc	The `calc` package, which contains the calculator classes and interfaces.
calc.Calculator	The primary `Calculator` class. Contains the `calculate()` method.
calc.CalcStack	The `CalcStack` class is a wrapper around the `java.util.Stack` class. `CalcStack` supports typesafe stack operations on `CalcStackItem` objects.
calc.Reader	The `Reader` class performs the input parsing for the calculator.
calc.Processable-Character	The `ProcessableCharacter` class holds a character value and implements the `Processable` interface.
calc.Processable-Double	The `ProcessableDouble` class holds a double value and implements the `Processable` interface.
calc.ExitException	The `ExitException` class is a subclass of the `Exception` class and is used to signal the userÕs desire to exit the calculator.
calc.Displayable	The `Displayable` interface provides a `display()` method used to print the results of a calculation.
calc.Processable	The `Processable` interface Provides the `process()` method that gets called for each item returned by the reader.
calc.CalcStackItem	The `CalcStackItem` interface provides the methods required by operands of the calculator. `CalcStackItem` extends both `Displayable` and `Processable` and adds the `doubleValue()` method to return a `double` corresponding to the operand.

Figure 11-1 Calculator Class Structure

With this picture in mind, we'll describe each class and interface and how they inter-relate to form a working, four-function calculator program.

The Calculator main() Method

At the top of the calculator is the RunCalculator class that includes a main() method. The RunCalculator class imports the calc package, which has all the classes and interfaces necessary to implement the calculator. The RunCalculator class looks like this:

```
import calc.*;

public class RunCalculator {
    public static void main(String[] args) {
    new Calculator().calculate();
    }
}
```

The Calculator Class

The top-level class in the calc package is the Calculator class. It provides constructors for creating calculators and a calculate() method called in the main() method of RunCalculator. Table 11-1 summarizes the constructors and instance method provided by the Calculator class.

Table 11-1 Calculator Program Class Summary

Package		calc
Imports		java.io
Constructors		public Calculator() public Calculator(DataInputStream in, PrintStream out)
Instance **Methods**	**Name:**	calculate()
	Returns:	void
	Throws:	None

The `Calculator` class starts out with package commands. All the classes for the calculator are in package `calc`. The `Calculator` class imports a few classes from `java.io`:

```
package calc;

import java.io.InputStream;
import java.io.OutputStream;
import java.io.DataInputStream;
import java.io.PrintStream;
```

The `Calculator` class has two constructors. The first one is for creating an interactive calculator that uses `System.in` and `System.out`:

```
public class Calculator {

  public Calculator() {
    this(System.in, System.out);
  }
```

The second constructor connects the calculator to arbitrary input and output streams. This constructor ensures that the input and output streams are of type `DataInputStream` and `PrintStream`, respectively, so that all the operations the calculator needs are available. The `Calculator` class reads a line at a time, so it uses a `DataInputStream` for input. The `DataInputStream` class provides a `readline()` method:

```
  public Calculator(InputStream in, OutputStream out) {

    DataInputStream dataIn;
    PrintStream     printOut;

    if (!(in instanceof DataInputStream)) {
      dataIn = new DataInputStream(in);
    } else {
      dataIn = (DataInputStream)in;
    }

    if (!(out instanceof PrintStream)) {
      printOut = new PrintStream(out);
    } else {
      printOut = (PrintStream)out;
    }
```

The instance variables for the `Calculator` class contain a `Reader` object that parses input, a `CalcStack` that holds operands, and an output stream to display results:

```
reader= new Reader(dataIn); // Object that handles all input.
stack = new CalcStack();    // Operand stack.
output= printOut;           // Output stream.
}
```

The `calculate()` method runs a loop, taking user input and printing results until the exit command `e` is entered. The main loop is then exited:

```
public void calculate() {

boolean finished = false;

while (!finished) {

    // First, display a prompt. Use flush() to force the
    // prompt to be displayed, even though no newline is
    // printed.

     output.println();
     output.print("calc> ");
     output.flush();

    // Read a line at a time so extra prompts aren't
    // inserted between the processing of multiple items
    // in a line. The continue goes back to print another
    // prompt if the input is blank. If we just read the
    // next item and processed it, an input line like
    // 3 4 + = would cause a prompt to be displayed four
    // times, once for each item processed.

    if (!reader.readLine()) {
        continue;
    }
```

At this point, the reader has a new line waiting to be parsed. Note that this `try` block contains the first use of an interface in the program. The `Processable` interface provides one method, `process()`. By using this interface, it would be easy to add new types of items to the calculator without the main class needing to change:

```
    try {
        // item is declared to be of type Processable,
        // which is an interface with a process() method.
        Processable item;
        // Process each item in the current input line.
        // reader.hasInput() returns true as long as there
        // is something other than spaces in its buffer.
```

```
        while (reader.hasInput()) {
            // reader.read() returns a Processable instance

            item = reader.read();

            if (item != null) {

                // Here, call the process() method of item.
                // The Calculator class does not need to know
                // anything about the kind of object item is.
                // It only needs to know that item provides
                // a process() method

                item.process(stack, output);
            }
        }
```

We have defined a special exception called ExitException that can be thrown by any Processable. When it is caught by the calculator, the calculate() method exits.

If any exception other than an ExitException is thrown (such as an invalid operator), the program displays a stack trace and continues after re-initializing the calculator:

```
    } catch (ExitException e) {
        System.err.println("Exiting.");
        finished = true;

    } catch (Exception e) {

        // If any exception other than an ExitException
        // occurs, print a stack trace and reset the
        // calculator state.
        // The reader will automatically read a fresh line
        // and needn't be reset.

        System.err.println("An exception occurred:");
        e.printStackTrace();
        stack = new CalcStack();
    }
  }
}

private Reader          reader;
private CalcStack       stack;
private PrintStream     output;
}
```

The Reader Class

The calculator encapsulates all input handling in the `Reader` class. Each calculator has its own `reader` object (created in the constructor for the `Calculator` class). The `Reader` class uses several methods, which are summarized in Table 11-2.

Table 11-2 `Reader` **Class Summary**

Package			`calc`
Imports			`java.io.DataInputStream;` `java.io.IOException;`
Constructors			`public Reader(DataInputStream in)`
`public` **Instance** **Methods**	**Name:**		`readline()`
	Returns:		`boolean`
	Throws:		None
	Use:		Reads a line from a `DataInputStream` object.
	Name:		`read()`
	Returns:		`Processable`
	Throws:		None
	Use:		Uses a the `private` method `readInternal()` to read input, if there is any.
	Name:		`hasInput()`
	Returns:		`boolean`
	Throws:		None
	Use:		Skips whitespace and checks if the buffer is empty.
`private` **Instance** **Methods**	**Name:**		`readInternal()`
	Returns:		`Processable`
	Throws:		None
	Use:		Reads the next `Processable` object.
	Name:		`readNumber()`
	Returns:		`Processable`
	Throws:		None
	Use:		Gathers all the input characters that could be a `double`.

Table 11-2 Reader Class Summary (Continued)

Name:	`peekCh()`
Returns:	`char`
Throws:	None
Use:	Returns the next character in the line buffer without consuming it.
Name:	`peekCh(int n)`
Returns:	`char`
Throws:	None
Use:	Returns the *nth* character remaining in the line buffer without consuming any characters.
Name:	`getCh()`
Returns:	`char`
Throws:	None
Use:	Consumes and returns the next character in the line buffer.
Name:	`bufferExhausted()`
Returns:	`boolean`
Throws:	None
Use:	Returns true if the line buffer is empty.
Name:	`skipWhite()`
Returns:	`void`
Throws:	None
Use:	Consumes spaces, tabs, and newlines in the line buffer.

The `Reader` class handles all input for a calculator. It supports reading a line, reading the next entry, and checking if the current line is exhausted. Note that the class definition is followed by use of the `static final` idiom, which is used to define constants for all the special characters that might be entered:

```
class Reader {

  // Constants
  // Whitespace

    private static final char SPACE   = ' ';
    private static final char TAB     = '\t';
    private static final char NEWLINE = '\n';

    // '.' and '-' for numeric input.

    private static final char DOT     = '.';
    private static final char MINUS   = '-';

  // A special value for end of input when looking ahead
  // in an exhausted buffer.

    private static final char EOI     = (char)-1;
```

The `Reader` class has only one constructor. All it does is save the `DataInputStream` the reader will take input from. The reader holds on to the input stream for the calculator:

```
public Reader(DataInputStream in) {
  inputStream = in;
}
```

The `readLine()` method reads a line from the `DataInputStream`. Here, the class must catch `IOException` since `DataInputStream.readLine()` can throw it:

```
// Read a line from the DataInputStream. If the line
// is not empty, return true; otherwise return false.

public boolean readLine() {
  try {
    buffer = inputStream.readLine();

  } catch (IOException e) {
    return false;
  }

  bufferLength = buffer.length();
  if (bufferLength == 0) {
    return false;
  }
```

```
index = 0;    // Initialize the offset into the
              // buffer.
return true;
}
```

The `read()` method uses a private method, `readInternal()`, to read input if there is any input available; otherwise the `read()` method returns `null`:

```
// Skip over any whitespace and read the next number or operator.

public Processable read() {
  if (hasInput()) {
    return readInternal();
  } else {
    return null;
  }
}
```

The `hasInput()` method skips whitespace and checks if the buffer is empty:

```
public boolean hasInput() {
  skipWhite();
  return !bufferExhausted();
}
```

The `readInternal()` method returns a `Processable` type. In this simple calculator, a `Processable` is either a `ProcessableCharacter` or a `ProcessableDouble`. Note that here we use the constants previously defined with the `static final` modifiers:

```
// Read either a Double or a Character depending on the first few
// characters of the next item.

private Processable readInternal() {
  char ch = peekCh();

  // A number starts with a digit, a '.', or a '-'.

  if (Character.isDigit(ch) ||
    ch == DOT ||
    (ch == MINUS && (Character.isDigit(peekCh(1)) ||
    peekCh(1) == DOT))) {
    return readNumber();
  } else {
    return new ProcessableCharacter(getCh());
  }
}
```

`Reader.readNumber()` gathers all the characters that could make up a `double` and uses `Double.valueOf()` to try to parse the result as a `double`. If `Double.valueOf()` fails to parse the characters as a `double`, it will throw a `NumberFormatException`:

```
// Read and return a Double.

private Processable readNumber() {
  StringBuffer buf = new StringBuffer();

  char ch = peekCh();

  if (ch == MINUS) {
    buf.append(getCh());
    ch = peekCh();
  }

  while (Character.isDigit(ch) || ch == DOT) {
    buf.append(getCh());
    ch = peekCh();
  }

  // Double.valueOf will throw an exception if the
  // input has more than one DOT.

  Double doubleObj = Double.valueOf(buf.toString());

  return new ProcessableDouble(doubleObj.doubleValue());
}

// Skip whitespace.

private void skipWhite() {
  while (!bufferExhausted()) {
    char ch = buffer.charAt(index);

    if (ch != SPACE &&
        ch != TAB &&
        ch != NEWLINE) {
      break;
    }

    index++;
  }
}
```

```
// Return the next character from the buffer and advance the
```

```
    // buffer offset.

  private char getCh() {
    return buffer.charAt(index++);
  }
```

The peekCh() and peekCh(int n) are overloaded methods. Note how peekCh() is simply implemented in terms of peekCh(int n):

```
  // Skip over any whitespace and read the next number or operator.
  // Look ahead at the next character in the buffer without
  // advancing the buffer offset.

  private char peekCh() {
    return peekCh(0);
  }


  // Look ahead numAhead characters into the buffer. Return EOI if
  // there are not numAhead characters left.

  private char peekCh(int numAhead) {
    if (index + numAhead >= bufferLength) {
      return EOI;
    }

    return buffer.charAt(index + numAhead);
  }

    // Return whether or not the buffer has been emptied.

  private boolean bufferExhausted() {
    return index == bufferLength;
  }
  private DataInputStream inputStream;
  private int            index;
  private int            bufferLength;
  private String         buffer;
}
```

The ExitException Class

The ExitException class exists only to have a unique exception class that Calculator.calculate() can check for:

```
package calc;

// The exception thrown when the user wants to exit the program.
class ExitException extends Exception {
}
```

The Displayable Interface

The Displayable interface is implemented by any object that can be printed on a PrintStream. For the calculator, this is only CalcStackItem objects:

```
package calc;

import java.io.PrintStream;

public interface Displayable {
    void display(PrintStream output);
}
```

The Processable Interface

All calculator tokens implement the Processable interface. In this calculator, both ProcessableCharacter and ProcessableDouble implement the Processable interface. ProcessableCharacter represents operators, and ProcessableDouble represents operands:

```
package calc;

import java.io.PrintStream;

public interface Processable {
    void process(CalcStack stack, PrintStream output)
    throws ExitException;
}
```

The ProcessableCharacter Class

The `ProcessableCharacter` class represents operators for the calculator. The `process()` method for `ProcessableCharacter` determines the operation to perform based on the character input and makes the appropriate changes to the calculator stack:

```java
package calc;

import java.io.PrintStream;

public class ProcessableCharacter implements Processable {

  // Create a new ProcessableCharacter.
  public ProcessableCharacter(char val) {
    characterVal = val;
}
```

`ProcessableCharacter.process` pops values off of the calculator stack and performs operations on them, pushing the results. If an invalid operator is found, an error message is printed. If the user enters the exit command e, an instance of `ExitException` is thrown that will cause the calculator to quit its `calculate()` method:

```java
public void process(CalcStack stack, PrintStream
  output) throws ExitException {

  double tempArg;

  switch (characterVal) {
    case '+':
       stack.pushDouble(stack.popDouble() +
       stack.popDouble());
       break;
    case '-':
       tempArg = stack.popDouble();
       stack.pushDouble(stack.popDouble() -
       tempArg);
       break;
    case '*':
       stack.pushDouble(stack.popDouble() *
       stack.popDouble());
       break;
    case '/':
       tempArg = stack.popDouble();
       stack.pushDouble(stack.popDouble() /
       tempArg);
       break;
```

```
        case '=':
            stack.pop().display(output);
            break;
        case 'e':
            throw new ExitException();
        default:
            System.err.println("Unknown operator: " +
                characterVal);
            break;
        }
    }

    private char characterVal;
}
```

The ProcessableDouble Class

The `ProcessableDouble` class holds a `double` value and implements `CalcStackItem` so it knows how to push it on the stack when `process()` is called or print it out when `display()` is called:

```
package calc;

import java.io.PrintStream;

public class ProcessableDouble implements CalcStackItem {

    // Create a new ProcessableDouble

    public ProcessableDouble(double val) {
        doubleVal = val;
    }

    // Push a ProcessableDouble onto a CalcStack.

    public void process(CalcStack stack, PrintStream output) {
        stack.push(this);
    }

    // Print the double value of a ProcessableDouble on a
    // PrintStream.

    public void display(PrintStream output) {
        output.println(doubleVal);
    }

    // Return the double value of the ProcessableDouble.
```

```
public double doubleValue() {
  return doubleVal;
}

private double doubleVal;
}
```

The CalcStack Class

The CalcStack class provides a typesafe Stack that requires no casting. The Stack class in java.util holds instances of Object, so when values are popped they must be cast down to their actual classes. CalcStack uses a java.util.Stack in its implementation. Since CalcStack is not a subclass of Stack, users may not push arbitrary objects onto a CalcStack. The only push() method requires a CalcStackItem argument. Note how popDouble() uses the fact that the CalcStackItem interface provides a doubleValue() method to return a double without casting:

```
package calc;

import java.util.Stack;

public class CalcStack {

  // Create a new CalcStack.

  public CalcStack() {
    stack = new Stack();
  }

  // Push an instance of CalcStackItem onto the CalcStack.

  public void push(CalcStackItem item) {
    stack.push(item);
  }

  // Pop an instance of CalcStackItem from the CalcStack.

  public CalcStackItem pop() {
    return (CalcStackItem)stack.pop();
  }

  // Return true if the CalcStack is empty, false otherwise.

  public boolean empty() {
    return stack.empty();
  }
```

```
// Return the top item from the CalcStack without popping it.

public CalcStackItem peek() {
  return (CalcStackItem)stack.peek();
}

// Wrap a double in a ProcessableDouble and push it on the stack.

public void pushDouble(double item) {
  stack.push(new ProcessableDouble(item));
}

// Pop the top item off a CalcStack and return its double value.

public double popDouble() {
  return pop().doubleValue();
}

  private Stack stack;
}
```

The CalcStackItem Interface

The `CalcStackItem` interface represents values on a `CalcStack`. A class that
implements it must support `process()`, `display()`, and `doubleValue()`
methods:

```
package calc;

import java.io.PrintStream;

public interface CalcStackItem extends Displayable, Processable {
  double doubleValue();
}
```

Output From the Calculator Program

After all the classes in the `calc` package and the `RunCalculator` class have been compiled, you can call the `java` interpreter from the command line to start the calculator:

```
java RunCalculator
```

The interpreter will display the calculator prompt on the screen, and you can begin using it:

```
calc>

calc> 3 5 + =
8
```

Summary

Many of Java's features come together in this chapter to illustrate a simple, elegant calculator program that can easily be adapted to include new functions. In particular, the calculator program illustrates how Java interfaces, exception handling, I/O, and packages work.

In *Part 2—Writing Java Applets*, we'll expand on some of these topics and also address the specific issues of managing keyboard and mouse events, using animation, images, sound, and other graphical elements you may want to use in Java programs that will run in a web browser.

But for now, it's on to the conclusion of Part I.

CHAPTER
12

Remote Method Invocation

What is Remote Method Invocation?

The Java Remote Method Invocation (RMI) mechanism, as its name suggests, provides the means to invoke methods remotely. Practically speaking, this ability enables the development of distributed applications. By using the Java RMI, applications can communicate and execute across multiple systems on a network.

The Java RMI system is Java's mechanism for doing distributed programming. As such, it is extremely flexible and is much easier to use than other distributed programming approaches such as RPC. Using RMI, methods can be invoked on remote objects as easily as they can on local ones. Sending sets of argument objects across the network is handled automatically.

The Java RMI mechanism is supported in the language by the `java.rmi`, `java.rmi.server`, and `java.rmi.registry` packages.

Before getting into the details of these packages, let's take a look at how RMI works.

How RMI Works

An application using RMI makes initial contact with a remote object by looking it up in a registry. The registry returns a stub object that can be used to manipulate its remote counterpart. For example, take a look at Figure 12-1.

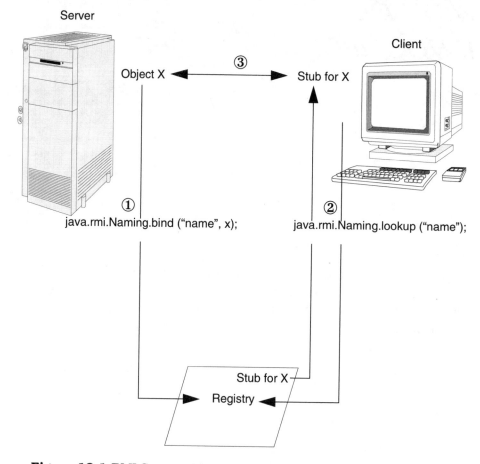

Server

Client

Object X ③ Stub for X

① java.rmi.Naming.bind ("name", x);

② java.rmi.Naming.lookup ("name");

Stub for X
Registry

Figure 12-1 RMI Server, Client, and Registry Relationship
① The server process registers the remote object X with the
registry using the `Naming.bind()` method.
② The client calls `Naming.lookup()`, which contacts the registry
and obtains a stub object for X.
③ The client then uses the stub as if it is a local object, but

When a remote method is executed, the `java.rmi` runtime encodes the
arguments and sends them over the network to a server that decodes them. The
server then invokes the method, encodes the result and sends it back. Finally, the
client-side `java.rmi` runtime decodes the result.

To set this picture in motion, let's look at a test program that utilizes RMI.

Calling Remote Methods

Example 12-1 demonstrates the simplest form of an RMI application—a remote object registers itself with a registry and one of its methods is called remotely by another process. The OpTest class looks up a remote object registered as "operator" and invokes the call operation on it. The java.rmi.Naming class is used to perform the lookup. The call operation will be performed in a remote process.

Example 12-1 Calling Remote Methods

```
    package rmi1;

    import java.rmi.*;
    import java.rmi.server.*;

    public class OpTest {

      public static void main(String[] args) {

❶        System.setSecurityManager(new StubSecurityManager());

          try {

❷            RemOp ro = (RemOp)Naming.lookup("operator");

❸            ro.call();

          } catch (Exception x) {
              x.printStackTrace();
              System.exit(-1);
          }
      }
    }
```

The purpose of the main() method in this test program is to look up a remote object (operator) and invoke call(). Notice in the call in line ❶ to System.setSecurityManager(). A Java process can have a SecurityManager that specifies security policies related to reading and writing files, making socket connections to other hosts, and so on. By default, no SecurityManager is present; however, Java RMI applications will not run without a SecurityManager. Once a SecurityManager has been set for a Java process, it cannot be changed. A simple, highly restrictive SecurityManager called java.rmi.server.StubSecurityManager is provided with the RMI distribution.

The object `ro` in line ❷ is an RMI stub that acts as a proxy for a remote object in another process. This is the simplest case for a remote call since no arguments are being passed and no value is returned. The type `RemOp` in the cast is an interface. (*All* remote objects are referenced through interfaces.)

The `Naming.lookup()` method searches for a name in an RMI registry and returns a stub reference to the object stored under that name. (We'll describe registries in more detail shortly.)

Line ❸ invokes the call operation remotely. The remote side of the example consists of two parts: an interface that defines the `call()` operation and a class that implements it. First, let's look at the interface.

The RemOp Interface

The `RemOp` interface in Example 12-2 is a remote interface for an object that supports the call operation.

Example 12-2 Extending the `Remote` Interface

```
package rmi1;

import java.rmi.*;

public interface RemOp extends Remote {
  public void call() throws RemoteException;
}
```

All interfaces for remote operations must extend the `Remote` interface. The `Remote` interface does not define any operations. It merely serves to identify remote objects. Note that all remote operations must declare themselves capable of throwing `RemoteException`.

Now let's look at the class that implements the `RemOp` interface.

The RemImpl Class

The `RemImpl` class in Example 12-3 implements the `RemOp` interface and supports remote invocation of the call operation. The `getName()` method returns a unique string identifying a particular instance of `RemImpl`.

Example 12-3 Implementing the `RemOp` Interface

```
package rmi1;

import java.rmi.*;
import java.rmi.server.*;
```

```
    public class RemImpl extends UnicastRemoteServer
    implements RemOp {

❶   public static void main(String[] args) {
        System.setSecurityManager(new StubSecurityManager());

        try {

            // Register an instance of RemImpl.

            Naming.rebind("operator", new RemImpl());

        } catch (Exception x) {
            x.printStackTrace();
            return;
        }
    }

❷   public RemImpl() throws RemoteException {
    }

❸   public void call() throws RemoteException {
        System.out.println(getName());
        System.out.println("Location: " +
                        System.getProperty("LOCATION"));
    }

    // Return a unique name for a RemImpl object.

    public String getName() {
        return "Remote operation: " + hashCode();
    }

}
```

The main() method in line ❶ registers a new instance of RemImpl with the registry on the local host.

Note that in line ❷, a remote implementation class must have a zero-argument constructor that declares itself capable of throwing RemoteException. (We'll see this in a number of our examples in this chapter.)

The call() method in line ❸ prints the name of the RemImpl instance and the value of the LOCATION property. We set the LOCATION property when running the examples to distinguish between server and client processes. The property will be set to "server" in the server process and "client" in the client process.

Running the rmi1 Example

All of the examples in this chapter assume that each process is running on a separate system. You can, however, run these processes in the background on one system to emulate the behavior of the test application in a distributed, networked environment. (This is true of all the examples in this chapter.) Specifically, to run this example:

1. Set your CLASSPATH to include the applications/RMI directory and the java.rmi directory from the CD.

2. From the applications/RMI/rmi1 directory, use the following command to start a registry:

```
java java.rmi.registry.RegistryImpl
```

3. From the applications/RMI/rmi1 directory, use the following command to start the server for the application:

```
java -DLOCATION=server rmi1.RemImpl
```

4. Use the following command to run the example:

```
java -DLOCATION=client rmi1.OpTest
```

Note that the operation is performed on the server. The interpreter will display output similar to the following:

```
Remote operation: 841549921
Location: server
```

Building RMI Applications

Now that we've seen an introductory example, let's take a closer look at how to build an RMI application. Constructing an RMI application consists of three steps:

• Defining remote interfaces

• Creating classes that implement the interfaces

• Creating stub and skeleton classes for the implementation classes

Let's look at what is involved at each step.

Defining Interfaces

All methods that can be run remotely must be declared as part of an interface that extends `Remote`. In our first example, the `RemOp` interface extends `Remote` and declares the method `call()`. As we mentioned in the introduction, the `Remote` interface does not declare any methods of its own. It is only used to identify remote objects:

```
public interface RemOp extends Remote {
  public void call() throws RemoteException;
}
```

A class may implement any number of remote interfaces. It may also define methods that are not included in a remote interface, but these other methods will not be available remotely.

Creating Classes That Implement the Interfaces

Classes that implement remote interfaces must be defined. They must be subclasses of the `RemoteObject` class. `RemoteObject` provides support for the `hashCode()`, `equals()`, and `toString()` methods as applied to remote instances. `hashCode()` and `equals()` are redefined so that remote references to an object may be used as keys in hash tables. In practice, implementation classes extend a subclass of `RemoteObject`.

Example 12-4 shows the class structure.

Example 12-4 `Object` and `RemoteObject` Class Structure

```
java.lang.Object
    java.rmi.server.RemoteObject
        java.rmi.server.RemoteServer
            java.rmi.server.UnicastRemoteServer
```

Subclasses of `RemoteServer`, such as `UnicastRemoteServer`, define the semantics of remote requests. It is possible to define different subclasses of `RemoteServer` to create replicated remote objects, persistent remote objects, and so on. The only subclass currently defined is `UnicastRemoteServer`, which provides a non-replicated point-to-point remote object model. Individual instances reside in processes and can be contacted in order to run methods. All the remote object classes we will look at extend `UnicastRemoteServer`.

Every method defined in an implementation class that will be made available remotely must declare itself capable of throwing `RemoteException`. In addition, a zero-argument constructor must be defined that can throw `RemoteException`, as in this example:

```
public RemImpl() throws RemoteException {
}
```

The important things to remember when writing a remote implementation class are:

- Extend `UnicastRemoteServer`

- Implement one or more remote interfaces

- Declare all remote methods capable of throwing `RemoteException`

- Define a zero-argument constructor that throws `RemoteException`

Creating Stub and Skeleton Classes

RMI uses classes called *stub* and *skeleton* to provide the interface to application programs. Stub classes are the client-side images of remote object classes. They implement the same interfaces as the remote classes and forward methods invoked on their instances to the corresponding remote instances.

Conversely, skeleton classes reside on the server. When a remote method request arrives, a skeleton instance calls the actual method on an implementation instance and then returns the results to the client.

Stubs and skeletons are generated from an implementation class using the `rmic` (RMI compiler) program. For our `RemImpl` class, the following command will generate a stub and skeleton class in the current directory:

```
rmic rmi1.RemImpl
```

The two files produced are:

```
RemImpl_Stub.class
RemImpl_Skel.class
```

Passing Arguments to Remote Methods

To invoke methods on remote objects, the arguments to the methods and the return values must be sent across the network. The Java RMI handles this in one of two ways, depending on whether an argument or return value is an instance of `RemoteObject` or not. For arguments and return values that *are* remote objects, a reference is passed over the network and a stub that refers to the remote object is created on the other side.

Arguments and return values that are *not* remote objects are copied over the network. Other objects referred to by an argument object are copied as well. In fact, all the non-remote objects that can be reached by a chain of references from an argument are copied. (The remote ones are passed by reference).

Let's assume that we have two classes, NR and R, which stand for non-remote and remote. R is a subclass of RemoteObject. In Figure 12-2 and Figure 12-3, arg, nr1, nr2, and nr3 are instances of NR; r1 is an instance of R.

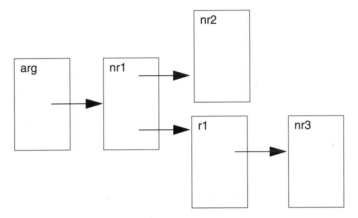

Figure 12-2 Passing Arguments to Remote Methods on Client Side

If a remote method was invoked with arg as an argument, the following would happen:

1. arg would be copied.
2. The reference from arg to nr1 would be followed, and nr1 would be copied.
3. The reference from nr1 to nr2 would be followed, and nr2 would be copied.
4. The reference from nr1 to r1 would be followed, but since r1 is a remote object, a reference would be passed. On the server side, the copy of nr1 would contain a reference to a stub for r1.

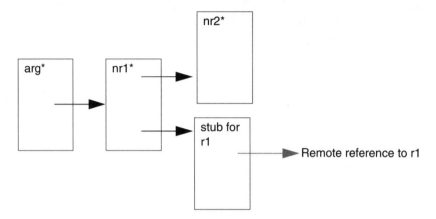

Figure 12-3 Passing Arguments to Remote Methods on Server Side

The process of encoding arguments for network transmission is known as *marshaling*. The inverse process is *unmarshaling*. Marshaling and unmarshaling of objects for RMI is handled by the Java Object Serialization system. Object serialization in Java is automatic and in most cases need not be a concern of RMI application writers, even though support is available for special-purpose serialization routines if necessary.

The notions of client and server for an RMI application are only meaningful in the context of a single remote method call. For instance, after the call that caused `arg` in our diagram to be copied to the server, a method on the server side could be invoked on the stub for `r1`. This would cause a remote call back to the originating process, reversing the roles of client and server.

The next example demonstrates RMI arguments passed both by copying and by reference. It also demonstrates client/server role reversal. The first call made by the test program passes a remote object. When its `execute()` method is called, the method runs in the same process as the test program. The second call passes a non-remote object. When its `execute()` method is called, it runs in the server process.

Figure 12-4 shows the package overview for the next test application that uses the Java RMI.

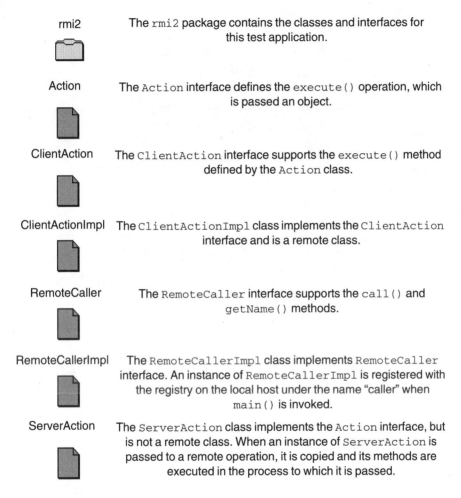

rmi2
  The rmi2 package contains the classes and interfaces for this test application.

Action
  The Action interface defines the execute() operation, which is passed an object.

ClientAction
  The ClientAction interface supports the execute() method defined by the Action class.

ClientActionImpl
  The ClientActionImpl class implements the ClientAction interface and is a remote class.

RemoteCaller
  The RemoteCaller interface supports the call() and getName() methods.

RemoteCallerImpl
  The RemoteCallerImpl class implements RemoteCaller interface. An instance of RemoteCallerImpl is registered with the registry on the local host under the name "caller" when main() is invoked.

ServerAction
  The ServerAction class implements the Action interface, but is not a remote class. When an instance of ServerAction is passed to a remote operation, it is copied and its methods are executed in the process to which it is passed.

Figure 12-4 Classes for Passing Arguments to Remote Arguments

ActionTest in Example 12-5 creates two objects that implement the Action interface (see page 187). One is a remote object of type ClientActionImpl. The other is a non-remote object of type ServerAction. When the ClientActionImpl instance is passed to a RemoteCaller, its execute() method will run in the same process as the ActionTest main() method. When the ServerAction instance is passed, its execute() method will run in the same process as the RemoteCaller call method.

Example 12-5 rmi2.ActionTest **Class**

```
package rmi2;

import java.rmi.*;
import java.rmi.server.*;

public class ActionTest {
  public static void main(String[] args) {
      System.setSecurityManager(new StubSecurityManager());

      try {

          // Create a new remote action object.

          ClientActionImpl cai = new ClientActionImpl();

          // Create a new non-remote action object.

          ServerAction    sa  = new ServerAction();

          // Find an instance of RemoteCaller in the local
          // registry.

          RemoteCaller    rc =
            (RemoteCaller)Naming.lookup("caller");

          // Pass the remote action object to the remote caller.

          rc.call(cai);

          // Pass the non-remote action object to the remote
          // caller.

          rc.call(sa);

      } catch (Exception x) {
          x.printStackTrace();
          System.exit(-1);
      }
  }
}
```

The Action Interface

The `Action` interface in Example 12-6 defines the `execute()` operation that is passed an object. The argument is typically the object that invoked `execute()`.

Example 12-6 `rmi2.Action` **Interface**

```
package rmi2;

import java.rmi.*;

public interface Action {
  public void execute(Object o) throws RemoteException;
}
```

The ServerAction Class

The `ServerAction` class in Example 12-7 implements the `Action` interface but is not a remote class. When an instance of `ServerAction` is passed to a remote operation, it is copied and its methods are executed in the process it is passed to.

Example 12-7 `rmi2.ServerAction` **Class**

```
package rmi2;

import java.rmi.*;
import java.rmi.server.*;

public class ServerAction implements Action {

❶   public void execute(Object o) throws RemoteException {
        if (o instanceof RemoteCaller) {
            System.out.println(((RemoteCaller)o).getName());
        } else {
            System.out.println(o);
        }

        System.out.println("Location: " +
                        System.getProperty("LOCATION"));
    }
}
```

The `execute()` method in line ❶ displays the name and location of the object `o`. The location will be either "server" or "client" depending on whether `execute()` runs in the server or client process. (You'll notice that we use this convention in examples throughout this chapter.)

The ClientAction Interface

The ClientAction interface in Example 12-8 supports the execute() method defined by Action and is implemented by remote objects. When an instance of a class that implements ClientAction is passed to a remote operation, a stub is passed as a proxy. Methods invoked on the stub are executed in the process that passed the stub, not the process that received it.

Example 12-8 rmi2.ClientAction Interface

```
package rmi2;

import java.rmi.*;

public interface ClientAction extends Remote, Action {
  public void execute(Object o) throws RemoteException;
}
```

The RemoteCaller Interface

The RemoteCaller interface in Example 12-9 supports two methods: call() and getName(). The call() method takes an Action as an argument and is intended to call execute() on the action. The getName() method returns the unique name of a particular RemoteCaller.

Example 12-9 rmi2.RemoteCaller Interface

```
package rmi2;

import java.rmi.*;

public interface RemoteCaller extends Remote {

  // Execute the Action "a".

  public void call(Action a) throws RemoteException;

  // Return a unique name for a RemoteCaller.

  public String getName() throws RemoteException;
}
```

The RemoteCallerImpl Class

The RemoteCallerImpl class in Example 12-10 implements the
RemoteCaller interface. An instance of RemoteCallerImpl is registered with
the registry on the local host under the name "caller" when main() is invoked.

Example 12-10 rmi2.RemoteCallerImpl **Class**

```
package rmi2;

import java.rmi.*;
import java.rmi.server.*;

public class RemoteCallerImpl extends UnicastRemoteServer
implements RemoteCaller {

  public static void main(String[] args) {
      System.setSecurityManager(new StubSecurityManager());

      try {
❶         Naming.rebind("caller", new RemoteCallerImpl());
      } catch (Exception x) {
          x.printStackTrace();
          return;
      }
  }

❷  public RemoteCallerImpl() throws RemoteException {
   }

❸  public String getName() throws RemoteException {
      return "Remote operation: " + hashCode();
   }

❹  public void call(Action a) throws RemoteException {
      a.execute(this);
   }
 }
```

Line ❶ registers an instance of RemoteCallerImpl with the local registry under
the name "caller."

As we've already seen in our first RMI example, all remote implementation
classes must have a zero-argument constructor that declares itself capable of
throwing RemoteException, which we do in line ❷.

The getName() method in line ❸ returns the unique name of a RemoteCallerImpl. The call() method in line ❹ invokes the Action object passed as an argument.

The ClientActionImpl Class

The ClientActionImpl class in Example 12-11 implements the ClientAction interface and is a remote class. When an instance of ClientActionImpl is passed to a remote operation, a stub is passed as a proxy. Methods invoked on the stub are executed in the process that passed the stub.

Example 12-11 rmi2.ClientActionImpl **Class**

```
package rmi2;

import java.rmi.*;
import java.rmi.server.*;

public class ClientActionImpl extends UnicastRemoteServer
implements ClientAction {

    // All remote implementation classes must have a
    // zero-argument constructor that declares itself
    // capable of throwing RemoteException.

    public ClientActionImpl() throws RemoteException {
    }

    // Display the name and location of the object "o". The
    // location will be either "server" or "client" depending
    // on whether execute() runs in the server or client
    // process.

    public void execute(Object o) throws RemoteException {
        if (o instanceof RemoteCaller) {
            System.out.println(((RemoteCaller)o).getName());
        } else {
            System.out.println(o);
        }

        System.out.println("Location: " +
                        System.getProperty("LOCATION"));
    }
}
```

Running the rmi2 Example

This example assumes that each process is running on a separate system. To run this example follow these four steps.

1. Set your CLASSPATH to include the applications/RMI directory and the java.rmi directory from the CD.

2. From the applications/RMI/rmi2 directory, use the following command to start a registry:

    ```
    java java.rmi.registry.RegistryImpl
    ```

3. From the applications/RMI/rmi2 directory, use the following command to initialize a remote action:

    ```
    java -DLOCATION=server rmi2.RemoteCallerImpl
    ```

4. Use the following command to run the example:

    ```
    java -DLOCATION=client rmi2.ActionTest
    ```

The first call runs on the client, and the second on the server. The interpreter will display output similar to the following:

```
Remote operation: 841550278
Location: client
Remote operation: 841550278
Location: server
```

Managing Multiple RMI Client Processes

The next example demonstrates cooperation between multiple RMI client processes. References to remote objects can be freely passed between any number of processes and methods can be invoked that will run in the process containing the actual implementation object. In the next example, one process sends a remote reference to another process, which then becomes the target of a method invocation from a third process. To make things a little more interesting, the initial method invocation by the third process changes the action that will be executed on the second invocation.

The next test application has the same set of classes as the one in Figure 12-4, only some of the implementations are different. The two test classes in this example are ActionTestSet and the ActionTestCall. The ActionTestSet class sends a remote object to the server process that is then invoked by the ActionTestCall class.

The `ActionTestCall` class in Example 12-12 looks up a `RemoteCaller` in line ❶ and invokes its `call()` method twice. If the `RemoteCaller` was initialized with a `ClientActionImpl` object, the second time `call()` is invoked, and it will execute an instance of `ServerAction` that the `ClientActionImpl` object associated with the `RemoteCaller`.

Example 12-12 rmi3.`ActionTestCall` **Class**

```
package rmi3;

import java.rmi.*;
import java.rmi.server.*;

public class ActionTestCall {
  public static void main(String[] args) {
      System.setSecurityManager(new StubSecurityManager());

      try {

          // Look up a RemoteCaller and invoke its call() method
          // twice.
❶
          RemoteCaller rc = (RemoteCaller)Naming.lookup("caller");
          rc.call();
          rc.call();

      } catch (Exception x) {
          x.printStackTrace();
          return;
      }
   }
}
```

The ActionTestSet Class

The `ActionTestSet` class in Example 12-13 initializes the action associated with a `RemoteCaller` object (line ❷). The initial value is an instance of `clientActionImpl` that will reset the action when its `execute()` method is invoked. Notice in line ❶ that the `ClientActionImpl` instance cai will set the action for a `RemoteCaller` to a copy of the `ServerAction` instance sa when its `execute()` method is invoked.

Example 12-13 rmi3.ActionTestSet Class

```
package rmi3;

import java.rmi.*;
```

```
import java.rmi.server.*;

public class ActionTestSet {

  public static void main(String[] args) {
      System.setSecurityManager(new StubSecurityManager());

      try {

          ServerAction     sa  = new ServerAction();
          ClientActionImpl cai = new ClientActionImpl();

❶        cai.setServerAction(sa);

          RemoteCaller     rc =
❷        (RemoteCaller)Naming.lookup("caller");

          // Initialize the action for "rc" to an instance
          // of ClientActionImpl.

          rc.setAction(cai);

      } catch (Exception x) {
          x.printStackTrace();
          return;
      }
   }
 }
```

The ClientActionImpl Class

The ClientActionImpl class in Example 12-14 implements the
ClientAction interface and is a remote class. When an instance of
ClientActionImpl is passed to a remote operation, a stub is passed as a proxy.
Methods invoked on the stub are executed in the process that passed the stub. An
instance of ClientActionImpl will change the saved action object associated
with a RemoteCaller when the RemoteCaller invokes its execute()
method.

Example 12-14 `rmi3.ClientActionImpl` **Class**

```java
package rmi3;

import java.rmi.*;
import java.rmi.server.*;

public class ClientActionImpl extends UnicastRemoteServer
implements ClientAction {

    public ClientActionImpl() throws RemoteException {
    }

    public void setServerAction(ServerAction sa) {
        serverAction = sa;
    }

    public void execute(Object o) throws RemoteException {
        if (o instanceof RemoteCaller) {
            RemoteCaller rc = (RemoteCaller)o;
            System.out.println(rc.getName());
            rc.setAction(serverAction);

        } else {
            System.out.println(o);
        }

        System.out.println("Location: " +
                            System.getProperty("LOCATION"));
    }

    ServerAction serverAction;
}
```

❶ `public void execute(Object o) throws RemoteException {`

❷ `            rc.setAction(serverAction);`

Notice that the `execute()` method in line ❶ displays the name and location of the object o, and the location will be either "server" or "client" depending on whether `execute()` runs in the server or client process. This is the same as in the previous examples. However, this implementation of the `execute()` method also replaces the action associated with the argument with an instance of `ServerAction` (line ❷).

The RemoteCaller Interface

The `RemoteCaller` interface in Example 12-15 supports three methods:

- `setAction()` — Stores a reference to an action object in the RemoteCaller
- `call()` — Is intended to call `execute()` on the action
- `getName()` — Returns the unique name of a particular RemoteCaller

Example 12-15 `rmi3.RemoteCaller` **Interface**

```
package rmi3;

import java.rmi.*;

public interface RemoteCaller extends Remote {

    // Store an instance of Action in the RemoteCaller.

    public  void setAction(Action a) throws RemoteException;

    // Execute the action stored in the RemoteCaller.

    public void call() throws RemoteException;

    // Return a unique name for a RemoteCaller.

    public String getName() throws RemoteException;
}
```

The RemoteCallerImpl Class

The `RemoteCallerImpl` class in Example 12-16 implements the `RemoteCaller` interface. An instance of `RemoteCallerImpl` is registered with the registry on the local host under the name "caller" when `main()` is invoked.

Example 12-16 `rmi3.RemoteCallerImpl` **Class**

```
package rmi3;

import java.rmi.*;
import java.rmi.server.*;

public class RemoteCallerImpl extends UnicastRemoteServer
implements RemoteCaller {
```

```
// Register an instance of RemoteCallerImpl with the
// local registry under the name "caller".

public static void main(String[] args) {
    System.setSecurityManager(new StubSecurityManager());

    try {
        Naming.rebind("caller", new RemoteCallerImpl());
    } catch (Exception x) {
        x.printStackTrace();
        return;
    }
}

public RemoteCallerImpl() throws RemoteException {
}

// Return the unique name of a RemoteCallerImpl.

public String getName() throws RemoteException {
    return "Remote operation: " + hashCode();
}

// Set the local action object for a RemoteCallerImpl.

public void setAction(Action a) throws RemoteException {
    action = a;
}

// Invoke execute() on a stored Action object.

public void call() throws RemoteException {
    action.execute(this);
}

    private Action action;
}
```

Running the rmi3 Example

To run this example:

1. Set your CLASSPATH to include the applications/RMI directory and the java.rmi directory from the CD.

2. From the applications/RMI/rmi3 directory, use the following command to start a registry:

```
java java.rmi.registry.RegistryImpl
```

3. From the `applications/RMI/rmi3` directory, use the following command to start the server for the application:

```
java -DLOCATION=server rmi3.RemoteCallerImpl
```

4. From the `applications/RMI/rmi3` directory, use the following command to initialize a remote action:

```
java -DLOCATION=client rmi3.ActionTestSet
```

5. Use the following command to run the example:

```
java -DLOCATION=client2 rmi3.ActionTestCall
```

The two operations run in the client and server process, but not in the client2 process. The interpreter will display output similar to the following:

```
Remote operation: 841550479
Location: server
Remote operation: 841550479
Location: client
```

RMI and Threads

When an RMI application makes a remote method call, a thread is spawned on the remote server to process the request. Since Java threads are not guaranteed to be preemptive, it's possible for a remote call to hang waiting for an opportunity to execute in the remote process. In the next example, the remote call back to the `ActionTestSet` process cannot complete until the computation thread calls `Thread.yield()`. Without the call to `Thread.yield()`, the remote call could hang indefinitely.

This test application relies on the classes in interfaces shown in Figure 12-5.

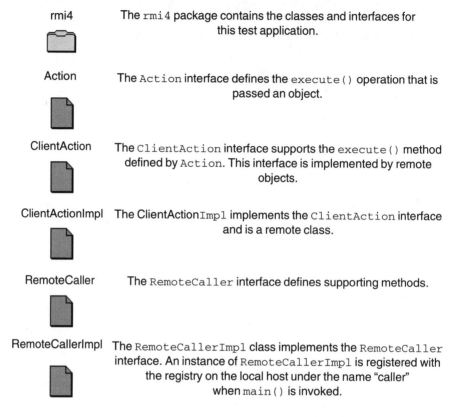

rmi4	The rmi4 package contains the classes and interfaces for this test application.
Action	The Action interface defines the execute() operation that is passed an object.
ClientAction	The ClientAction interface supports the execute() method defined by Action. This interface is implemented by remote objects.
ClientActionImpl	The ClientActionImpl implements the ClientAction interface and is a remote class.
RemoteCaller	The RemoteCaller interface defines supporting methods.
RemoteCallerImpl	The RemoteCallerImpl class implements the RemoteCaller interface. An instance of RemoteCallerImpl is registered with the registry on the local host under the name "caller" when main() is invoked.

Figure 12-5 Classes for the RMI Threads Example

The next example shows the interaction between threads and RMI. Like the previous rmi3 example, one process sends a remote object to a server, which is invoked by another process. In this case, the original process goes into a busy loop after sending the object. The remote call initiated by the second process cannot be completed until the thread containing the busy loop in the first process yields.

The ActionTestCall class in Example 12-17 looks up a RemoteCaller and invokes its call() method.

Example 12-17 rmi4.ActionTestCall **Class**

```
package rmi4;

import java.rmi.*;
import java.rmi.server.*;

public class ActionTestCall {
  public static void main(String[] args) {
      System.setSecurityManager(new StubSecurityManager());

      try {
         RemoteCaller rc = (RemoteCaller)Naming.lookup("caller");
         rc.call();

      } catch (Exception x) {
         x.printStackTrace();
         return;
      }
   }
}
```

The ActionTestSet Class

The ActionTestSet class in Example 12-18 initializes the action associated with a RemoteCaller object. The initial value is an instance of ClientActionImpl. ActionTestSet then enters a loop that yields() periodically. Remote operation requests may only be serviced when the main thread yields.

Example 12-18 rmi4.ActionTestSet

```
package rmi4;

import java.rmi.*;
import java.rmi.server.*;

public class ActionTestSet {
  public static void main(String[] args) {
       System.setSecurityManager(new StubSecurityManager());

      try {

          // Initialize the action object for a RemoteCaller.

          ClientActionImpl cai = new ClientActionImpl();
          RemoteCaller    rc  =
                     (RemoteCaller)Naming.lookup("caller");
          rc.setAction(cai);
```

```
                    // Go into a loop waiting for a remote request.

                    int bigNumber = (int)(Math.random() * 10) + 1000000;

                    for (int i = 0; i < bigNumber; i++) {
                        for (int j = 0; j < bigNumber; j++) {
                            k = k + 1;
                        }

                        System.out.println(i);

                        // Yield so other threads can run. A remote request
                        // can only be handled here.

                        Thread.yield();
                    }

                    System.out.println(k);

                } catch (Exception x) {
                    x.printStackTrace();
                    return;
                }
            }

        private static long k;
    }
```

The ClientActionImpl Class

The `ClientActionImpl` class in Example 12-19 implements the `ClientAction` interface and is a remote class. When an instance of `ClientActionImpl` is passed to a remote operation, a stub is passed as a proxy. Methods invoked on the stub are executed in the process that passed the stub.

Example 12-19 `rmi4.ClientActionImpl` **Class**

```
    package rmi4;

    import java.rmi.*;
    import java.rmi.server.*;

    public class ClientActionImpl extends UnicastRemoteServer
    implements ClientAction {

        public ClientActionImpl() throws RemoteException {
        }
```

```
public void execute(Object o) throws RemoteException {
    if (o instanceof RemoteCaller) {
        RemoteCaller rc = (RemoteCaller)o;
        System.out.println(rc.getName());

    } else {
        System.out.println(o);
    }

    System.out.println("Location: " +
                        System.getProperty("LOCATION"));
    }
}
```

Running the rmi4 Example

As we've mentioned in the previous examples, in a true RMI application, each Java process would be running on a separate system. You can, however, run these processes in the background on one system to emulate the behavior of the test application in a distributed, networked environment. Specifically, to run this example follow these steps:

1. Set your CLASSPATH to include the applications/RMI directory and the java.rmi directory from the CD.

2. From the applications/RMI/rmi4 directory, use the following command to start a registry:

   java java.rmi.registry.RegistryImpl

3. From the applications/RMI/rmi4 directory, use the following command to start the server for the application:

   java -DLOCATION=server rmi4.RemoteCallerImpl

4. From the applications/RMI/rmi4 directory, use the following command to initialize a remote action:

   java -DLOCATION=client rmi4.ActionTestSet

5. Use the following command to run the example:

```
java -DLOCATION=client2 rmi4.ActionTestCall
```

The message from the remote operation is not printed until immediately after a number is printed (i.e., when the client process calls `Thread.yield()`). The interpreter will display output similar to the following:

```
0
1
2
3
4
5
6
7
Remote operation: 841551282
Location: server
8
9
10
11
12
```

Registries

To begin a remote interaction via RMI, an initial connection to a remote object must be obtained. This is done via a *registry*. Registries are objects associated with a particular host and port that provide dictionaries of remote objects referenced by name.

Finding Objects in a Registry

A typical RMI session begins with a client contacting a registry and obtaining a reference to a remote object. A registry may be contacted directly or by using the URL based `java.rmi.Naming` interface.

Example 12-20 shows sample code that uses the `Registry` interface directly.

Example 12-20 Using the `Registry` Interface Directly

```
Registry registry = LocateRegistry.getRegistry();
Builder  builder1 = (Builder)registry.lookup(args[1]);
Builder  builder2 = (Builder)registry.lookup(args[2]);
```

Example 12-21 shows a sample call using the `Naming` class to look up a registry.

Example 12-21 Contacting a Registry Using the `Naming` **Class**

```
RemoteCaller rc = (RemoteCaller)Naming.lookup("caller");
```

In both these examples, the host and port for the registry have been set by default to the local host and the standard default registry port.

To specify a different host and/or port, the `getRegistry()` call may take any of the following forms (where *host* is a string and *port* is an `int`), as in Example 12-22.

Example 12-22 Specifying a Host or Port With `getRegistry()` **Method**

```
Registry registry = LocateRegistry.getRegistry(host);
Registry registry = LocateRegistry.getRegistry(port);
Registry registry = LocateRegistry.getRegistry(host, port);
```

To specify host and port information to the `Naming` interface, URLs are used as in Example 12-23.

Example 12-23 Specifying a Host or Port With the `Naming` **Interface**

```
Remote o = Naming.lookup("rmi://host/object_name");
Remote o = Naming.lookup("rmi://host:port/object_name");
```

Both the `Registry` interface and the `Naming` interface also support listing the entries in the registry, as in Example 12-24.

Example 12-24 Listing Registry Entries

```
String[] entries = registry.list();
String[] entries = Naming.list(URL);
```

Changing the Contents of a Registry

Objects can be added to a registry using the `bind()` and `rebind()` methods (Example 12-25). `rebind()` is just like `bind()`, except that `bind()` throws an `AlreadyBoundException` if an object is already stored in the registry under the specified name.

Example 12-25 Adding Contents to a Registry

```
Registry registry = LocateRegistry.getRegistry();
registry.rebind("a name", new BuildImp()); // or registry.bind()
Naming.bind("another name", new RemImpl()); // or Naming.rebind()
```

Objects are removed from a registry either via an unbind() call or by having a different object attached to the same name with rebind(), as in Example 12-26.

Example 12-26 Removing Contents From a Registry

```
registry.unbind("a name");
Naming.unbind("another name");
```

Not all remote objects need to be stored in a registry. It's only necessary that an object be there to make initial contact. After that, remote references to other objects may be created and passed back and forth as arguments and return values.

Garbage Collection of Remote References

The RMI runtime keeps track of every remote reference to a remote object. When all remote references have been dropped, the object behaves like a normal object and may be garbage collected when there are no more references to it. The RMI runtime maintains *weak* references to remote objects. A weak reference is one that is ignored by the garbage collector. If an object has only weak references referring to it, the garbage collector is free to collect it.

If a remote object needs to be notified when it is no longer referred to remotely, it can implement the java.rmi.server.Unreferenced interface. When the last remote reference is dropped, unreferenced() will be called on the object. It is possible for unreferenced() to be called multiple times. If other remote references to the object are generated before it is garbage collected, unreferenced() will be called when those references are dropped.

Maintaining Object References Across Multiple Processes

Our final example shows just how easy it is to deal with remote objects using RMI. The program will construct a remote linked list in which every other node is in a different process and none of them are in the main process. The list will then be traversed just as if it were local.

This test application relies on the classes and interfaces shown in Figure 12-6.

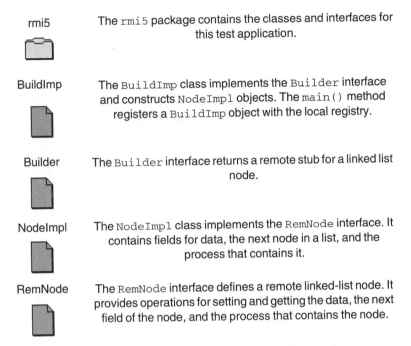

rmi5 — The rmi5 package contains the classes and interfaces for this test application.

BuildImp — The BuildImp class implements the Builder interface and constructs NodeImpl objects. The main() method registers a BuildImp object with the local registry.

Builder — The Builder interface returns a remote stub for a linked list node.

NodeImpl — The NodeImpl class implements the RemNode interface. It contains fields for data, the next node in a list, and the process that contains it.

RemNode — The RemNode interface defines a remote linked-list node. It provides operations for setting and getting the data, the next field of the node, and the process that contains the node.

Figure 12-6 Classes for the RMI Linked List Example

This test application relies on the Builder interface, which constructs new remote nodes. Two processes containing BuildImp objects will construct nodes and hand them back to the top-level ListTest program. The ListTest program will alternately create list nodes in either of two BuildImp processes. It will then traverse the list twice, first printing the list contents and then printing the locations of each list node.

The ListTest class in Example 12-27 creates a linked list that is spread across two remote processes. The nodes in the list alternate between the two processes. First the data elements, and then the process locations of the list cells are printed.

As you look through the code, notice how we create node builders in two different processes in lines ❶ and ❷.

Example 12-27 rmi5.ListTest **Class**

```
package rmi5;

import java.rmi.*;
import java.rmi.server.*;
import java.rmi.registry.*;

public class ListTest {
  public static void main(String[] args) {
      if (args.length != 3) {
        System.err.println(
         "Usage: java rmi5.ListTest <count> <server1> <server2>");
        System.exit(-1);
      }

      System.setSecurityManager(new StubSecurityManager());

      try {

          // Find the local registry.

          Registry registry = LocateRegistry.getRegistry();

          // Read in the length of the list.

          int      count    = Integer.parseInt(args[0]);

          // Create node builders in two different processes.
          // The processes should be registered under the
          // names found in arguments 1 and 2.

          Builder  builder1 = (Builder)registry.lookup(args[1]);
          Builder  builder2 = (Builder)registry.lookup(args[2]);

          // The head of the list.

          RemNode  list     = null;

          // Create "count" list nodes, alternating between
          // processes and attach them to the list.
```

❶
❷

```java
            for (int i = 0; i < count; i++) {
                RemNode node = builder1.newNode();
                node.setNext(list);
                node.setData(i);
                list          = node;

                // Swap the two node builders so that the
                // next time around the other one will be used.

                Builder temp = builder2;
                builder2      = builder1;
                builder1      = temp;
            }

            // Print the data elements in the list.

            RemNode listptr = list;
            System.out.print("[ ");

            while (listptr != null) {
                System.out.print(listptr.getData() + " ");
                listptr = listptr.getNext();
            }

            System.out.println("]");

            // Print the process locations of each node
            // in the list.

            listptr = list;
            System.out.print("[ ");

            while (listptr != null) {
                System.out.print(listptr.getLocation() + " ");
                listptr = listptr.getNext();
            }

            System.out.println("]");

        } catch (Exception x) {
            x.printStackTrace();
            System.exit(-1);
        }
    }
}
```

The Builder Interface

The `Builder` interface in Example 12-28 defines the `newNode()` method that returns a remote stub for a linked list node.

Example 12-28 `rmi5.Builder` **Interface**

```
package rmi5;

import java.rmi.*;

public interface Builder extends Remote {
  public RemNode newNode() throws RemoteException;
}
```

The BuildImp Class

The `BuildImp` class in Example 12-29 implements the `Builder` interface and constructs `NodeImpl` objects. The `main()` method registers a `BuildImp` object with the local registry.

Example 12-29 `rmi5.BuildImp` **Class**

```
package rmi5;

import java.rmi.*;
import java.rmi.server.*;
import java.rmi.registry.*;

public class BuildImp extends UnicastRemoteServer
implements Builder {
  public static void main(String[] args) {
     if (args.length != 1) {
         System.err.println(
           "Usage: java rmi5.BuildImp <binding name>");
         System.exit(-1);
     }

     System.setSecurityManager(new StubSecurityManager());

     try {

         // Register a BuildImp object in the local registry
         // under the name in argument zero.

         location        = args[0];
         Registry registry = LocateRegistry.getRegistry();
         registry.rebind(location, new BuildImp());
```

```
        } catch (Exception x) {
            x.printStackTrace();
            System.exit(-1);
        }
    }

    public BuildImp() throws RemoteException {
    }

❶   public RemNode newNode() throws RemoteException {
        NodeImpl node = new NodeImpl();
        node.setLocation(location);
        return node;
    }

    private static String location;
}
```

Notice that the newNode() method (line ❶) returns an instance of the remote class NodeImpl. Its location field will contain the same value as the BuildImp object's location field.

The RemNode Interface

The RemNode interface in Example 12-30 defines a remote linked-list node. Operations are provided to set and get the data and the next and location fields of the node. The location field refers to the process that contains the node.

Example 12-30 rmi5.RemNode **Interface**

```
package rmi5;

import java.rmi.*;

public interface RemNode extends Remote {
  public RemNode getNext() throws RemoteException;
  public void    setNext(RemNode next) throws RemoteException;

  public int     getData() throws RemoteException;
  public void    setData(int data) throws RemoteException;
```

```
    public String getLocation() throws RemoteException;
    public void setLocation(String location) throws RemoteException;

}
```

The NodeImpl Class

The `NodeImpl` class implements the `RemNode` interface. It contains instance variables for data, the next node in a list, and the process that contains it. Notice while looking through the code that the `getLocation()` method in line ❶ obtains the name under which this node's builder is registered. Each process containing a node builder should have it registered under a distinct name. Also, note that line ❷ sets the process location for this node. This is used by the node builder that creates a node. The name under which the builder is registered is stored in the node's location instance variable.

Example 12-31 `rmi5.NodeImpl` **Class**

```
package rmi5;

import java.rmi.*;
import java.rmi.server.*;
import java.rmi.registry.*;

public class NodeImpl extends UnicastRemoteServer
implements RemNode {

  public NodeImpl() throws RemoteException {
  }

  // Return the next node in a list.

  public RemNode getNext() throws RemoteException {
      return next;
  }

  // Set the next node in a list.

  public void setNext(RemNode next) throws RemoteException {
      this.next = next;
  }
```

```
    // Return the data value for this node.

    public int getData() throws RemoteException {
        return data;
    }

    // Set the data value for this node.

    public void setData(int data) throws RemoteException {
        this.data = data;
    }

❶  public String getLocation() throws RemoteException {
        return location;
    }

❷  public void setLocation(String location) throws RemoteException {
        this.location = location;
    }

    private RemNode next;
    private int     data;
    private String  location;
}
```

Running the rmi5 Example

To run this example:

1. Set your CLASSPATH to include the applications/RMI directory and the java.rmi directory from the CD.

2. From the applications/RMI/rmi5 directory, use the following command to start a registry:

   java java.rmi.registry.RegistryImpl

3. From the applications/RMI/rmi5 directory, use the following commands to start two servers for the application:

   java rmi5.BuildImp *name1*
   java rmi5.BuildImp *name2*

4. Use the following command to run the example:

   java rmi5.ListTest *length_of_list name1 name2*

The two outputs are:

- The contents of the list
- The process locations of each node

Assuming the length of the list were 8 and the two servers were named `name1` and `name2`, the Java interpreter would display output similar to the following:

```
[ 7 6 5 4 3 2 1 0 ]
[ name2 name1 name2 name1 name2 name1 name2 name1 ]
```

Summary

The `java.rmi` package supports the creation of distributed, networked applications. In the Java RMI implementation, a server process registers a remote object with a registry. A client, in turn, contacts the registry and obtains a stub for the named remote object. The client then uses that stub as if it were a local object, but methods are actually executed on the remote object.

Building an RMI application involves three primary steps: defining remote interfaces, creating classes that implement those interfaces, and creating stub and skeleton classes for the implementation classes. Stub and skeleton classes are generated by the `rmic` compiler, and they are the client-side images of remote object classes.

CHAPTER 13

- Learning About JDBC

- Basics of Developing JDBC Applications

- Implementing an Employee Lookup in JDBC

Java
Database
Connectivity

What is Java Database Connectivity?

It was clear very early in the development of Java that access to databases would become important. Many business applications depend on databases but, more importantly for Java, a very large number of Internet applications include some form of data retrieval.

Most of the programming languages (Perl, for example) that compete with Java in the world of web applications already provide support for database access in one form or another. Any Java solution, however, must be generic and platform-independent. As it turns out, there already exists a relational database API that meets these criteria: the X/Open SQL Call Level Interface (CLI). The X/Open SQL CLI is the basis for the Microsoft Open Database Connectivity (ODBC) interface. Unfortunately, since ODBC is a C-based interface, using it directly from Java would introduce a variety of problems associated with native method interfaces. Instead of a direct connection to ODBC, JavaSoft is specifying a similar interface called Java Database Connectivity (JDBC), which is a Java-based counterpart to ODBC. Database vendors will supply JDBC *drivers* for their databases so that Java programs may access them transparently. (The need for a driver and a database to use JDBC means that most of you reading this book will not be able to run the examples in this chapter.)

In this chapter, we will show how to use JDBC by implementing the back end of an example we used in our chapter on *Exception Handling*—a hypothetical `lookup()` method to retrieve employee information.

Structure of a JDBC Application

A JDBC application consists of at least these four parts:

- The application code
- The JDBC runtime
- A JDBC driver
- A relational database

Figure 13-1 shows how the four parts communicate.

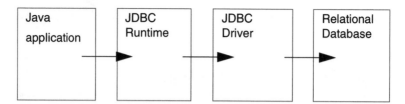

Figure 13-1 JDBC Structure

A fifth part may be added if a JDBC driver is not available for a particular database. A component called the JDBC-ODBC bridge can be used to implement JDBC on top of an ODBC driver for a database, as illustrated in Figure 13-2.

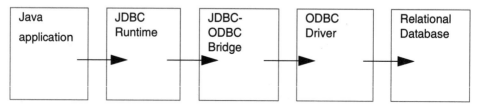

Figure 13-2 JDBC-ODBC Bridge in JDBC Structure

In either case, the application uses the standard JDBC interface to communicate with the database.

Any number of JDBC drivers may be loaded into a Java runtime. The actual driver selected for a particular interaction is determined at database connection time.

Database Connections

A JDBC application begins by requesting a database connection. It does this by calling one of the `java.sql.DriverManager.getConnection()` methods, as in Example 13-1. The most general version takes a URL and a set of properties as arguments. The URL specifies the protocol used to connect to the database and the particular database to connect to. The set of properties is encoded as an instance of `java.util.Properties` which is a subclass of `java.util.Hashtable`. The properties usually include at least a user and a password.

Example 13-1 Connecting to a Database

```
import java.sql.*;
import java.util.*;
   .
   .
   .
Properties props = new Properties();
props.put("user", "Judy");
props.put("password", "Argyle");

Connection conn =
  DriverManager.getConnection("jdbc:myprotocol:employee", props);
```

The JDBC runtime searches its list of drivers until it finds one that understands the `myprotocol` protocol. It then asks that driver for a connection. The syntax of the URL argument is:

jdbc : *subprotocol* : *subname*

It is recommended that a *subname* that includes a network address be in the following form:

/ / *hostname* : *port* / *subsubname*

where *subsubname* can have any desired syntax. Here's an example of a network JDBC URL:

```
jdbc:myprotocol://empserver:9876/employee
```

The set of drivers included in a JDBC runtime is derived from two sources:

- The `jdbc.drivers` property specified on the Java command line

- Calls to `Class.forName` (*driver class name*)

In the first case, the `jdbc.drivers` property contains a colon-separated list of driver class names:

```
java -Djdbc.drivers=empdb.Driver:custdb.Driver
localclasses.jdbcServer
```

In the second case, an application class can explicitly load a driver via:

```
Class.forName("empdb.Driver");
```

The static initializer for a driver class creates an instance of itself and registers it with the `DriverManager`.

Interacting With a Database

Once a connection has been established to a database, an application can use the methods defined by `java.sql.Connection` to construct SQL statements that can be applied to the database.

This is done by creating instances of `java.sql.Statement` and executing them. For instance, we can create an employee table, as in Example 13-3.

Example 13-2 Interacting With a Database

```
Statement s = conn.createStatement();
s.executeUpdate("create table employee " +
                "(name char(30), age integer, salary integer)");
```

`Statement.executeUpdate()` is used to execute statements without results such as updates, insertions, deletes, creates, or drop calls for tables and indexes. Queries that return results are executed with `Statement.executeQuery()`.

Now, Example 13-3 shows how to return all employees with last name *Grindstaff*.

Example 13-3 Returning Entries From a Table

```
ResultSet rs =
  s.executeQuery("select * from employee where name like '%
                Grindstaff'");
```

`Statement.executeQuery()` returns an instance of `java.sql.ResultSet`, which can be iterated through to obtain individual rows.

Enquiring minds may want to print information about the Grindstaffs, which can be accomplished as in Example 13-4.

Example 13-4 Printing a Query Result

```
while (rs.next()) {// ResultSet.next() returns false when there
                   // are no more results.

  String name   = rs.getString(1);  // "name" will be padded
                                     // to 30 chars
  int    age    = rs.getInt(2);
  int    salary = rs.getInt(3);

  System.out.println(name + " " + age + " " + salary);
}
```

As you can see, fetching individual fields from a row is done using type specific
`get*` methods.

SQL/Java Type Correspondence

Table 13-1 shows the type correspondence between SQL and Java.

Table 13-1 SQL/Java Type Correspondence

SQL Type	Java Type
BIGINT	long
BINARY	byte[]
BIT	boolean
CHAR	String
DATE	Date (java.sql.Date)
DECIMAL	Numeric (java.sql.Numeric)
DOUBLE	double
FLOAT	double
INTEGER	int
LONGVARBINARY	byte[]
LONGVARCHAR	String
NUMERIC	Numeric (java.sql.Numeric)
REAL	float
SMALLINT	short
TIME	Time (java.sql.Time)
TIMESTAMP	Timestamp (java.sql.Timestamp)

Table 13-1 SQL/Java Type Correspondence (Continued)

SQL Type	Java Type
TINYINT	byte
VARBINARY	byte[]
VARCHAR	String

Each Java type that corresponds to an SQL type has a `get` method for `ResultSet`, as shown in Table 13-2.

Table 13-2 `ResultSet.get` Methods

Java Type	Corresponding get Methods
boolean	getBoolean()
byte	getByte()
byte[]	getBytes()
double	getDouble()
float	getFloat()
int	getInt()
Date (java.sql.Date)	getDate()
Numeric (java.sql.Numeric)	getNumeric()
String	getString()
Time (java.sql.Time)	getTime()
Timestamp (java.sql.Timestamp)	getTimestamp()

All of these `get` methods may be passed either the integer index of the column (starting at 1) or the name of the column. So, for Example 13-4 on page 219, `rs.getInt(2)` and `rs.getInt("age")` would be equivalent.

To determine if the value of a column is SQL null, it is necessary to first fetch it and then call `ResultSet.wasNull()`. The `wasNull()` method returns true if the last column fetched was null.

Executing Precompiled SQL

It is often useful when writing database applications to *precompile* an SQL statement and then execute it multiple times with different parameters. This is accomplished in JDBC using the `java.sql.PreparedStatement` class, as in Example 13-5.

Example 13-5 Executing Precompiled SQL

```
PreparedStatement ps =
  conn.prepareStatement("update employee set salary = ?
                          where name = ?");
```

Each "?" must be replaced by a parameter value before executing the statement. For instance:

```
ps.setInt(1, 150000);
ps.setString(2, "Myrnie");
ps.executeUpdate();
```

Table 13-3 shows the type correspondence between Java and SQL.

Table 13-3 Java/SQL Type Correspondence

Java Type	SQL Type
boolean	BIT
byte	TINYINT
byte[]	VARBINARY
double	DOUBLE
float	FLOAT
int	INTEGER
Date (java.sql.Date)	DATE
Numeric (java.sql.Numeric)	NUMERIC
String	VARCHAR
Time (java.sql.Time)	TIME
Timestamp (java.sql.Timestamp)	TIMESTAMP

In the cases of byte[] and String, if the values are too large for VARBINARY and VARCHAR, they are mapped onto LONGVARBINARY and LONGVARCHAR.

The `PreparedStatement` class includes `set*` methods that correspond to Java types, as shown in Table 13-4.

Table 13-4 `PreparedStatement.set` Methods

Java Type	Corresponding set Methods
`boolean`	`setBoolean()`
`byte`	`setByte()`
`byte[]`	`setBytes()`
`double`	`setDouble()`
`float`	`setFloat()`
`int`	`setInt()`
`Date (java.sql.Date)`	`setDate()`
`Numeric (java.sql.Numeric)`	`setNumeric()`
`String`	`setString()`
`Time (java.sql.Time)`	`setTime()`
`Timestamp (java.sql.Timestamp)`	`setTimestamp()`

There is also a `PreparedStatement.setNull()` call to set a parameter to SQL null.

Generic get and set Methods

Both `ResultSet.get` methods and `PreparedStatement.set` methods have generic counterparts. `ResultSet.getObject()` will return an instance of the Java class that matches the SQL type of a column. If the SQL type were `INTEGER`, an instance of `java.lang.Integer` would be returned. `PreparedStatement.setObject()` sets a database column to the SQL type that corresponds to its Java instance argument.

Resources

Both the `ResultSet` and `Statement` classes provide `close()` methods that will free any resources associated with them. It is a good idea to call `close()` explicitly when instances of `ResultSet` and `Statement` are no longer needed because their resources will not be freed automatically until they are garbage collected. (This means that potentially, they may *never* be freed because Java objects are not guaranteed to be collected.)

Metadata

JDBC allows users to determine what facilities are provided by a database or a driver using methods defined in the `java.sql.DatabaseMetaData` class. Many specifics including whether or not a database or driver supports outer joins, stored procedures, unions, or a particular transaction isolation level can be queried by using these methods.

Transactions

A JDBC user can choose between two styles of transaction support. A connection can be in *auto-commit* mode, in which case every statement is committed immediately, or an ongoing transaction can be maintained that is ended with a call to `Connection.commit()` or `Connection.abort()`. Instances of `PreparedStatement` and `ResultSet` are closed on either call. Switching between the two styles is done via a call to `Connection.setAutoCommit(boolean)`.

The actual semantics of transactions are based on the underlying database support. `DatabaseMetaData` methods are available to determine support.

Cursors

Limited cursor support is provided by JDBC. The cursor associated with a result set can be obtained and used in positioned update and delete statements. The cursor is returned by the `ResultSet.getCursorName()` method. It remains valid until the `ResultSet` resources are freed either by the closing of the `ResultSet` or its parent `Statement`.

Exercising the JDBC

Now let's revisit our employee lookup example we introduced in our chapter on *Exception Handling*. To implement this type of lookup with JDBC, we need to support the call:

```
TableEntry entry = lookup("Marianna", "employee");
```

Example 13-6 on page 224 shows how we would go about doing this. First, however, look at Figure 13-3, which shows the classes supporting our JDBC lookup implementation.

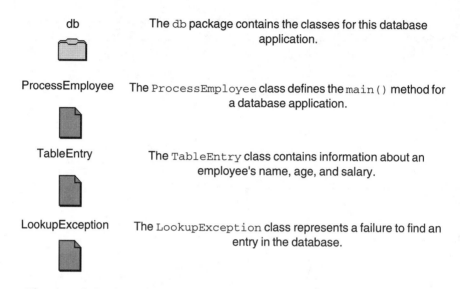

db	The db package contains the classes for this database application.
ProcessEmployee	The ProcessEmployee class defines the main() method for a database application.
TableEntry	The TableEntry class contains information about an employee's name, age, and salary.
LookupException	The LookupException class represents a failure to find an entry in the database.

Figure 13-3 Classes Supporting JDBC Employee Lookup

As you look through the example, notice that the ProcessEmployee class provides a main() method that takes an employee's first name, looks up the employee, and prints his or her information. If there are multiple entries with the same first name, only the first one is processed. Note that the lookup() method itself (line ❶) executes an SQL select statement and retrieves its results. The results are returned in a TableEntry instance. You might also pay attention to the initDatabase() method in line ❷. It establishes a connection to a database using the java.sql.DriverManager.getConnection() method.

Example 13-6 Employee Lookup Example

```
package db;

import java.sql.*;
import java.util.*;

public class ProcessEmployee {

    // The main() method initializes the database, looks up an
    // employee, and processes the results.

    public static void main(String[] args) {
        if (args.length != 1) {
```

```
        System.err.println("Usage: java db.ProcessEmployee
                        <name>");
        System.exit(-1);
    }

    try {
        // Set up a connection to the database.

        initDatabase();

        // look up the command line argument in "employee" table.

        TableEntry entry = lookup(args[0], "employee");

        // Process the result from the lookup. If the lookup failed
        // an exception would have been thrown and we would not
        // have arrived at this point.

        process(entry);

    } catch (LookupException e) {
        e.printStackTrace();
        System.exit(-1);
    }
}

// The lookup() method executes an SQL select statement and
// retrieves its results. The results are returned in a
// TableEntry instance.

private static TableEntry lookup(String name, String table)
throws LookupException {
    try {
        // Create an instance of java.sql.Statement associated
        // with a particular database connection.

        Statement s = getConnection().createStatement();

        // Execute the query statement and capture the results.

        ResultSet rs = s.executeQuery("select * from " + table +
                                " where name like '" +
                                name + " %'");

        // Check to make sure there is at least one row.

        if (!rs.next()) {
            throw new LookupException();
```

❶

```
        }

            // Fetch the columns out of the returned row.

            String fullName = rs.getString(1);
            int    age      = rs.getInt(2);
            int    salary   = rs.getInt(3);

          // Free up any resources associated with the statement and
          // result set.

            s.close();

            // Return the entry.

            return new TableEntry(fullName, age, salary);

        } catch (SQLException e) {
            e.printStackTrace();
            System.exit(-1);
        }

        return null;
    }

    // initDatabase() establishes a connection to a database using
    // the java.sql.DriverManager.getConnection() method.

❷   private static void initDatabase() {
        try {
            Properties props = new Properties();
            props.put("user", "hr");
            props.put("password", "eyesonly");

        connection =
          DriverManager.getConnection("jdbc:myprotocol:db",
                                                  props);

        } catch (SQLException e) {
            e.printStackTrace();
            System.exit(-1);
        }
    }

    // Print the results of a query.

    private static void process(TableEntry entry) {
        System.out.println(entry);
```

```
   }

  private static Connection getConnection() {
      return connection;
  }

 private static Connection connection; // the database connection.
}

// The TableEntry class contains information about employees. An
// employee's name, age, and salary are stored.

class TableEntry {

  // Construct a new TableEntry instance.
  TableEntry(String entryName, int entryAge, int entrySalary) {
      name   = entryName;
      age    = entryAge;
      salary = entrySalary;
  }

  // Return an employee's name.

  String getName() {
      return name;
  }

  // Return an employee's age.

  int getAge() {
      return age;
  }

  // Return an employee's salary.

  int getSalary() {
      return salary;
  }
```

```
        // Display the information about an employee in a nice format.

        public String toString() {
            return "EMPLOYEE:\n" + "  NAME:    " + name   + "\n" +
                                   "  AGE:     " + age    + "\n" +
                                   "  SALARY: " + salary + "\n";
        }

        private String name;
        private int    age;
        private int    salary;
    }

    // The LookupException class represents a failure to find an entry
    // in the database.

    class LookupException extends Exception {
    }
```

The Java interpreter will display output similar to the following:

```
> java db.ProcessEmployee Marianna
EMPLOYEE:
  NAME:   Marianna Gaudaur
  AGE:    39
  SALARY: 200000
>
```

Summary

The Java JDBC interface provides an easy-to-use platform independent means of working with relational databases. JDBC is largely derived from ODBC, but is completely Java based. An application may talk to multiple databases using different JDBC drivers. Drivers are installed either via the `jdbc.drivers` property or via explicit loading by an application. JDBC operations are invoked through `Connection`, `Statement`, and `ResultSet` classes. There are `get` and `set` methods provided that correspond between Java types and SQL types.

Writing Java Applets

PART TWO

CHAPTER 14

- Applet Tools and Class Support

- Displaying Applet Output

- Creating Configurable Applets

- Creating Active Applets

Introduction to Applets

Introduction

Applets are simple Java programs that run in web browsers. The ways applets differ from standalone Java programs are largely a result of the environment in which they run. Applets are invoked through a different interface than a `main()` method. Applets are also different in that they are not allowed to make changes to the machine on which they are running. This security is enforced by the Java runtime system.

In this part of the book, we'll describe several applets, highlighting different programming techniques along the way. Note that all the applets we discuss are available on the CD accompanying this book. We encourage you to try them out to see how they work before reading about how they are constructed.

Java's Applet Tools and Class Support

Applets are almost always graphical applications. As such, they use the Java Abstract Window Toolkit, otherwise known as the *awt*. The awt (actually, it's the `java.awt` class library) allows you to write graphics code that is independent of the target platform. The awt avoids potential inconsistencies with the behavior of native windowing systems by actually using components from the native system. These components are called *peers*. You don't generally need to deal directly with peers when writing Java applets, but their presence is evident when writing event handling routines, as will be seen in *Events and Threads in Applets* on page 247.

227

In Java parlance, graphics objects such as panels, scrollbars, containers, labels, buttons, and so on are generically referred to as *components*. That is because most graphic objects are derived from the Component class in the awt. The awt.Component class includes some of the most commonly used methods in applets. These include the paint(), repaint(), and update() methods. Table 14-1 summarizes their use.

Table 14-1 Commonly Used awt.Component **Methods**

Common awt.Component Methods	Description
paint()	The paint() method paints the component.
repaint()	The repaint() method schedules a call to the component's update() method as soon as possible.
update()	The update() method is responsible for redrawing the applet. The default version redraws the background and calls the paint() method.

The Java Applet class (in the applet package) provides another set of methods particularly important when writing applets. Chief among these are the init(), start(), stop(), and destroy() methods. Table 14-2 summarizes their use.

Table 14-2 Commonly Used applet.Applet **Methods**

Common applet.Applet Methods	Description
init()	When a document with an applet is opened, the init() method is automatically called to initialize the applet. You do not need to explicitly call this method in an applet, although you can override it if an applet needs to initialize state. The init() method is called only once for an applet.
start()	When a document with an applet is opened, the start() method is automatically called to start the applet. You do not need to explicitly call this method in the applet, although you can override it if necessary. The start() method is called every time the document is opened.
stop()	When a document with an applet is no longer displayed, the stop() method is automatically called. This method is always called before the destroy() method is called.
destroy()	After the stop() method has been called, the destroy() method may be called to clean up any resources that are being held.

Displaying Applet Output

For consistency and ease of illustration, all of the applets in this part of the book are used in the following way:

```
appletviewer applet_name.html
```

In this syntax, *applet_name*.html is a minimal HTML file that can be used as an argument to the appletviewer. The HTML file looks like this:

```
<title>
<hr>
<applet code="applet_name.class" width=200 height=80>
</applet>
<hr>
```

Each applet on the CD included with this book has a corresponding HTML file that can be used as an argument to the appletviewer. Of course, these applets could also be displayed within a Java-enabled web browser, as long as the web page includes the appropriate HTML applet tag to call the applet.

A Simple Applet

To begin with applets, recall from the first chapter the HelloWorldApplet. This is one of the simplest possible applets:

```
import java.applet.Applet;
import java.awt.Graphics;

public class HelloWorldApplet extends Applet {
    public void paint(Graphics g) {
        g.drawString("Hello Brave New World!", 50, 25);
    }
}
```

The only thing an applet really *has* to do is define a paint() method. The paint() method will be called automatically when the applet is displayed or resized. The argument to paint() is a Graphics object. Graphics objects store the current color, font, and other information used when performing graphics operations. They also provide methods for drawing objects such as lines, images, and strings.

A simple applet like this one is pretty easy to put together. However, applets that can be configured with HTML tags and applets that perform dynamic actions on the screen need to do more than simply define a `paint()` method. We'll examine what it takes to develop more sophisticated applets in the following sections.

Configurable Applets

Applets can be written so that they can be configured with HTML code. In effect, the applet makes a set of parameters *configurable*, and if those parameters are specified in the HTML code, they override the default settings specified in the applet. In this section, we'll show exactly how to do this.

Displaying a Static Label

In the next applet, we create a `StaticLabel` class. It displays a label (that is, a text string). It also includes parameters for the label and for the font, which the user can specify in the HTML file to override the default values. This applet will also center the label, which will show some other useful features.

The most important things to note in the example are the `init()` method and the use of `getParameter()`. If an applet needs to initialize state, it can override the default `init()` method that is normally called when a document with an applet is opened. The `init()` method is called automatically before the applet is started.

This example uses the `init()` method to read the user-defined parameters specified in the HTML code and set the label and font. The `getParameter()` method takes a `String` argument and returns the value of the user-specified parameter with that name in the source HTML file. If no value has been specified for the parameter, `getParameter()` returns `null`. The applet supplies default values for `label`, `fontname`, `fontsize`, `fontslant`, and `fontweight`. These default values will be used if the user doesn't specify these parameters in the HTML file.

Other points to note are the use of the `size()` method to return the width and height of the applet and the use of the `FontMetrics` class to examine features of a font. Here's the code for the `StaticLabel` class:

```
import java.awt.*;

// The StaticLabel class takes a text string and displays it centered
// in an applet. The font and label can be passed as parameters from
// HTML.

public class StaticLabel extends java.applet.Applet {

  public void init() {
```

```
// Read in parameters and set values for textValue and
// textFont. The label parameter holds the text you want to
// be displayed.

String param = getParameter("label");
if (param != null) {
   textValue = param;
}
```

The four parameters, fontname, fontslant, fontweight, and fontsize are used to select a font for the label. In the Java font model, fontslant and fontweight are combined into fontStyle:

```
String fontName = FONTNAME;
int    fontStyle = FONTSTYLE;
int    fontSize = FONTSIZE;

param = getParameter("fontname");

if (param != null) {
   fontName = param;
}

param = getParameter("fontslant");

if (param != null && (param.equals("italic") ||
   param.equals("ITALIC"))) {
      fontStyle |= Font.ITALIC;
}

param = getParameter("fontweight");

if (param != null && (param.equals("bold") ||
   param.equals("BOLD"))) {
   fontStyle |= Font.BOLD;
}

param = getParameter("fontsize");

if (param != null) {
   fontSize = Integer.parseInt(param);
}

// Create a font object named textFont from the font
// parameters.

textFont = new Font(fontName, fontStyle, fontSize);
}
```

The `paint()` method paints the label. Dimensions are recomputed every time, in case the applet is resized. `dim` is the applet width and height. `metrics` is the set of font parameters for the font we have chosen. `textWidth` is the width of the label in the chosen font. `x` is the horizontal position of the beginning of the label. `y` is the vertical position of the baseline of the label. The baseline is the position of the bottom of a line of text, not counting the descending tails of lower case g, y, etc. The extra space taken up by the tails is called the *descent* of the font:

```java
public void paint(Graphics g) {

    Dimension    dim       = size();
    FontMetrics  metrics   = getFontMetrics(textFont);
    int          textWidth = metrics.stringWidth(textValue);

    // The label will be clipped if x and y are outside the applet.

    int x = (dim.width - textWidth) / 2;
    int y = (dim.height - metrics.getHeight()) / 2 +
            metrics.getHeight() - metrics.getDescent();

    // Draw the label.

    g.setFont(textFont);
    g.setColor(textColor);
    g.drawString(textValue, x, y);
}

// Private state variables and constants.

private String textValue = LABEL;
private Font   textFont   = null;
private Color  textColor = Color.black;

// Default values for applet parameters. These values will be
// used if the user leaves label, fontname, fontsize, fontslant,
// or fontweight unspecified.

private static final String LABEL     = "Hello, world.";
private static final String FONTNAME  = "TimesRoman";
private static final int    FONTSIZE  = 24;
private static final int    FONTSTYLE = Font.PLAIN;
}
```

Output From the Static Label Applet

Assume an HTML file with the following parameters set in it:

```
<title>Static Label</title>
<hr>
<applet code="StaticLabel.class" width=200 height=80>
<param name=label value="Hello, World.">
<param name=fontname value="Courier">
<param name=fontslant value="italic">
<param name=fontweight value="bold">
<param name=fontsize value="24">
</applet>
<hr>
```

Figure 14-1 shows sample output from the StaticLabel applet.

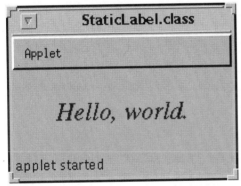

Figure 14-1 A Configurable Applet
The Hello World display is defined in the HTML file, which
overrides the default values defined in the applet code.

The HTML applet parameters take precedence over the default font
characteristics defined in the StaticLabel applet. (See *The HTML applet and
param Tags* on page 380 for more information.)

Incorporating Images and Sound

Including images, sound, or both in an applet is easy. However, doing interesting
things with them can be tricky. We'll look at animation and active images a little later,
but first let's see how to read in and display images and sounds. The next example
adds a definition for the start() method that will override the default start()
method. The start() method is called when the applet's document is visited.

The `ImageWithSound` class reads in a `.gif` image and a `.au` audio file. (These files reside in the `Image` and the `Audio` directory on the CD included with this book.) The applet displays the image and plays the sound. The `IMAGE` and `AUDIO` `static final` variables hold default values for the image and sound file names. Following is the code for the `ImageWithSound` class:

```java
import java.awt.*;
import java.applet.*;

public class ImageWithSound extends Applet {

  public void init() {

    // Read in an image and an audio clip.

    String imageName = IMAGE;
    String audioName = AUDIO;

    String param = getParameter("image");

    if (param != null) {
      imageName = param;
    }

    param = getParameter("audio");

    if (param != null) {
      audioName = param;
    }

    // Create a MediaTracker to inform us when the image has
    // been completely loaded.

    tracker = new MediaTracker(this);
```

The `getCodeBase()` method returns the URL of the applet's directory. These calls will read in image and sound files relative to the applet's directory:

```java
    sound = getAudioClip(getCodeBase(), audioName);
```

The `getImage()` method returns immediately. The image is not actually loaded until it is first used. By using a `MediaTracker`, we make sure the image is loaded before we try to display it.

```java
    image = getImage(getCodeBase(), imageName);

    // Add the image to the MediaTracker so that we can wait
    // for it.
```

```
    tracker.addImage(image, 0);
  }
```

Here, we display the image. The `this` argument to the `drawImage()` method is there because `drawImage()` expects an `ImageObserver`. An image may not be complete when `drawImage()` returns. If so, the `ImageObserver` argument is notified later. The `ImageObserver` is notified via its `imageUpdate()` method. Applets that do elaborate image processing can override `imageUpdate()` to get information about the state of images.

```
  public void paint(Graphics g) {
    g.drawImage(image, 0, 0, this);
  }

  // Play the audio clip.

  public void start() {

    // Load the image and wait until it's done.

    try {
      tracker.waitForID(0);
    } catch (InterruptedException e) {
    }

    repaint();
    sound.play();
  }

  // Default values for the image and sound file names.
  private static final String IMAGE= "Images/onbeach.gif";
  private static final String AUDIO= "Audio/gong.au";
  // Private state variables.

  private Image      image;
  private AudioClip sound;
  private MediaTracker tracker;
}
```

Output From the ImageWithSound Applet

Figure 14-2 shows sample output from the `ImageWithSound` applet. (You'll have to imagine the gong.)

Figure 14-2 An Applet With Image and Sound
A gong rings when the applet starts.

Active Applets

An applet that runs continuously introduces a new requirement. It needs to provide a separate thread of control so that it doesn't interfere with the operation of the rest of the system. In most cases, the applet's `start()` method starts the thread and its `stop()` method stops the thread. We haven't seen a `stop()` method yet, but it gets called when the applet's document is no longer displayed.

The next applet relies heavily on the `repaint()` method, so before looking at the applet, let's look at how `repaint()`, `update()` and `paint()` work together to redraw an applet. The `repaint()` method is called when an applet is resized or exposed, and can be called directly by an applet. Despite its name, `repaint()` does not immediately redraw the applet; instead, it schedules a redraw as soon as possible. When the redraw occurs, the applet's `update()` method is called. There is a default `update()` method defined in `awt.Component` that redraws the background of the applet and then calls `paint()`. Although this is generally sufficient, it is sometimes necessary to override `update()` to avoid redrawing the background. (We'll show this in some of our later applet examples.)

The `repaint()` method has four different signatures, as shown in Table 14-3.

Table 14-3 Forms of the `repaint()` Method

Signature	Description
`repaint()`	Repaint the entire applet as soon as possible.
`repaint(long maxTime)`	Repaints the entire applet within `maxTime` milliseconds.
`repaint(int x,int y,int width, int height)`	Repaint just the area of the applet specified by the arguments.
`repaint(long maxTime,int x,int y, int width,int height))`	Repaint the specified area within the specified maximum time.

We'll use the first and third forms of `repaint()` in our applet examples.

Now, with that as background, let's look at an applet that displays a label that blinks on and off at a user-specifiable rate.

Displaying a Flashing Label

The `FlashingLabel` class is based on the `StaticLabel` class previously described. The `FlashingLabel` class takes a text string and displays it in the center of an applet. When displayed, the text will blink on and off at a rate determined by the `sleepTime` parameter. The `font`, `label`, and `sleepTime` parameters can be passed from the HTML file. The applet supplies default values which will be used if the user fails to specify them in the HTML file. Here's the code for the `FlashingLabel` class:

```
import java.awt.*;

public class FlashingLabel extends java.applet.Applet implements
    Runnable {

    public void init() {

        // Read in parameters and set values for sleepValue,
        // textValue, and textFont. The sleeptime parameter tells how
        // long to pause between flashes. (in milliseconds).

        String param = getParameter("sleeptime");
```

```
if (param != null) {
    sleepValue = Integer.parseInt(param);
}

// The label parameter holds the text to be displayed.
param = getParameter("label");
if (param != null) {
    textValue = param;
}
```

As we saw in the `StaticLabel` example, the four parameters: `fontname`, `fontslant`, `fontweight`, and `fontsize` are used to select a font for the label. The `fontslant` and `fontweight` are combined into `fontStyle`:

```
String fontName  = FONTNAME;
int    fontStyle = FONTSTYLE;
int    fontSize  = FONTSIZE;

param = getParameter("fontname");

if (param != null) {
    fontName = param;
}

param = getParameter("fontslant");

if (param != null && (param.equals("italic") ||
   param.equals("ITALIC"))) {
   fontStyle |= Font.ITALIC;
    }

param = getParameter("fontweight");
if (param != null && (param.equals("bold") ||
   param.equals("BOLD"))) {
   fontStyle |= Font.BOLD;
}

param = getParameter("fontsize");

if (param != null) {
    fontSize = Integer.parseInt(param);
}

// Create a font object named textFont from the font
// parameters.

textFont = new Font(fontName, fontStyle, fontSize);
}
```

```
public void paint(Graphics g) {

// Paint the label every other time the paint() method is called.

  paintThisTime = !paintThisTime;

  if (paintThisTime == false) {
     return;
  }
```

As in the StaticLabel applet, the paint() method recomputes the dimensions every time it paints the label, in case the applet is resized. dim is the applet width and height. metrics is the set of font parameters for the font we have chosen. textWidth is the width of the label in the chosen font. x is the horizontal position of the beginning of the label. y is the vertical position of the baseline of the label. The baseline is the position of bottom of a line of text, not counting the descending tails of lowercase g, y, etc. The extra space taken up by the tails is called the descent of the font:

```
   Dimension    dim         = size();
   FontMetrics  metrics     = getFontMetrics(textFont);
   int          textWidth   = metrics.stringWidth(textValue);

   // The label will be clipped if x and y are outside the applet.

   int    x      = (dim.width  - textWidth) / 2;
   int    y      = (dim.height - metrics.getHeight()) /2 +
                     metrics.getHeight() - metrics.getDescent();

   // Draw the label. First, set the font first so that the
   // FontMetrics() method will return a correct value for the
   // width of the label.

   g.setFont(textFont);
   g.setColor(textColor);
   g.drawString(textValue, x, y);
   }

// Create a thread for this applet and start it.

public void start() {
  flashThread = new Thread(this);
  flashThread.start();
}

// Stop the applet's thread.

public void stop() {
```

```
    flashThread.stop();
  }
```

Between each repaint, the `sleep()` method pauses the thread for the number of milliseconds in the `sleepValue` parameter:

```
public void run() {
  while (true) {
    try {
        flashThread.sleep(sleepValue);
    } catch (InterruptedException e) {
    }
    repaint();
  }
}
// Private state variables and constants.

  private String        textValue       = LABEL;
  private int           sleepValue      = SLEEPTIME;
  private Font          textFont        = null;
  private Thread        flashThread     = null;
  private boolean       paintThisTime   = false;
  private Color         textColor       = Color.black;
  private static finalStringLABEL       = "Hello, world.";
  private static finalStringFONTNAME    = "TimesRoman";
  private static finalint  FONTSIZE     = 24;
  private static finalint  FONTSTYLE    = Font.PLAIN;
  private static finalint  SLEEPTIME    = 650;
}
```

Output From the Flashing Label Applet

Figure 14-3 shows sample output from the FlashingLabel applet, with some HTML parameters overriding the default text values.

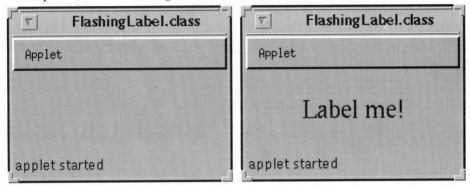

Figure 14-3 A Flashing Applet
The first display shows the text flashing off, and the second shows the text flashing on.

Summary

This chapter provides a brief introduction to applets. It highlights the use of the basic methods from the Applet class and the awt, and illustrates circumstances when you would override those methods. The applets themselves show how to read applet parameters specified in HTML code and how to create multiple threads.

We haven't yet shown any graphics programming, form creation, or event handling. These will be discussed in the following chapters. Understanding how Java deals with these areas is necessary for writing interesting applets, but at this point you at least understand the basics of the applet model.

CHAPTER
15

- Demonstrating Simple Event Handling

- Events and Threads

- Sample Event Handling Applets

Events and Threads in Applets

Introduction

Graphical user interfaces in Java are based on the processing of events, such as mouse clicks or keyboard key sequences. A programmer defines the actions to be taken when various events occur. In this chapter we'll describe two applets, the first of which simply responds to user events, and the second of which introduces an independent thread of control that interacts with the event processing.

In all the examples, the event handling methods return `boolean` values. When a method returns a `true` value, it means that the method has handled the event and no further processing is required. If an event handling method returns a `false` value, the event is forwarded to the current component's peer. This mechanism allows programmers to override the default behavior of native windowing components when necessary and rely on the built-in behaviors otherwise.

Simple Event Handling

The first event handling applet is a simple puzzle that demonstrates how to respond to events generated by the user. We'll define how the puzzle operates by creating a `Puzzle` class.

243

Puzzle Applet

This applet is a simple puzzle in which the goal is to change all the squares on the board to black. Figure 15-1 shows the puzzle applet display.

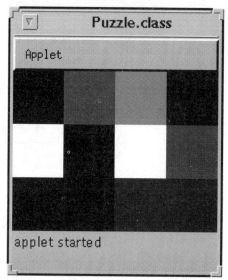

Figure 15-1 Puzzle Applet Display

Each time the mouse changes squares, the new square is advanced one step through the color sequence. To make the game a little bit harder, moving the mouse directly back to the previous square doesn't change anything. The only events monitored in the example are the mouseMove and mouseDrag events.

Here's the code to the Puzzle class:

```java
import java.applet.*;
import java.awt.*;

// The Puzzle class implements a simple puzzle in which the goal is
// to change all the squares on the board to black. Each mouse move
// is checked to see if the mouse has changed squares. If the mouse
// has moved to a square other than the one it was in one move
// earlier, the new square is advanced one step through the color
// sequence.

public class Puzzle extends Applet {
```

The `init()` method initializes the applet and creates a board, which has the dimensions `appletWidth/50` and `appletHeight/50`:

```
public void init() {

  scale = 50;   // Each square is 50 pixels on a side.

  // Make sure the height and width are multiples of scale.

  appletWidth = Math.max(size().width, scale) / scale * scale;
  appletHeight =
    Math.max(size().height, scale) / scale * scale;
```

These variables record the previous square and the previous square once removed.

```
  lastX        = -1;
  lastY        = -1;
  nextToLastX  = -1;
  nextToLastY  = -1;

  // The dimensions of the board.

  cellWidth    = appletWidth  / scale;
  cellHeight   = appletHeight / scale;

  board = new char[cellWidth][cellHeight];

  // Determine the length of the puzzle's color sequence. A
  // longer sequence is harder. If the parameter value is
  // greater than the number of colors, use the total number of
  // colors. If the value is less than 2, use 2. If the number
  // of colors is unspecified, use DEFAULT_NUM_COLORS.

  String param = getParameter("numcolors");

  if (param != null) {
    numColors = Integer.parseInt(param);

    if (numColors > colors.length) {
      numColors = colors.length;

    } else if (numColors < 2) {
      numColors = 2;
    }

  } else {
    numColors = DEFAULT_NUM_COLORS;
  }
```

```
// Resize to a multiple of the scale value.

resize(appletWidth, appletHeight);

// Initialize the colors of the board to random values and
// draw the board.

reset();
}
```

The `reset()` method is called at the start of the applet and every time the puzzle is successfully completed. It sets the colors of the board to random values. The board is an array of chars to save space. Each cell of the board holds an index into the array of colors:

```
private void reset() {
   for (int i = 0; i < cellWidth; i++) {
      for (int j = 0; j < cellHeight; j++) {

         // Initialize the cell to a random value between 0 and
         // the number of colors - 1.

         board[i][j] = (char)((Math.random() * 10) %
            numColors);
      }
   }
   repaint();
}
```

The `testWin()` method tests for the solution of the puzzle. If all the cells contain the index of the first color, the puzzle is solved. When the puzzle is solved, the method plays the *winning* sound and resets the board:

```
private void testWin() {
   for (int i = 0; i < cellWidth; i++) {
      for (int j = 0; j < cellHeight; j++) {
         if (board[i][j] != 0) {
            return;
         }
      }
   }
   getAudioClip(getCodeBase(), "Audio/gong.au").play();
   reset();
}
```

The `paint()` method repaints the board. This method could be made more efficient by only repainting the changed square. We'll make this optimization in later examples:

```
public void paint(Graphics g) {
   for (int i = 0; i < cellWidth; i++) {
```

```
    for (int j = 0; j < cellHeight; j++) {
        g.setColor(colors[board[i][j]]);
        g.fillRect(i * scale, j * scale, scale, scale);
    }
  }
}
```

These are the methods that handle the mouseMove and mouseDrag events. Anytime the mouse moves without a button being pressed, mouseMove is called. If a button is being held down, mouseDrag is called. We want to do the same thing in either case so mouseMove and mouseDrag can both call the same routine:

```
public boolean mouseMove(Event evt, int pixelX, int pixelY) {
  return processMovement(evt, pixelX, pixelY);
}

public boolean mouseDrag(Event evt, int pixelX, int pixelY) {
  return processMovement(evt, pixelX, pixelY);
}
```

The processMovement() method does all event handling for the applet. The event location is scaled into cell coordinates and the scaled x and y values are compared to the last two cells. If the new cell is distinct from either of the previous two cells, the color of the new cell is updated. A special version of repaint() is called, which tells Java to clip changes that fall outside the current square:

```
private boolean processMovement(Event evt, int pixelX, int
  pixelY) {

  // Scale the pixel coordinates to cell coordinates.

  int cellX = pixelX / scale;
  int cellY = pixelY / scale;

  // If the new cell is the same as the last one or the next to
  // last one, don't do anything.

  if ((cellX == lastX && cellY == lastY) ||
      cellX == nextToLastX && cellY == nextToLastY) {
    return true;
  }

  // If the new cell coordinates fall outside the board, do
  // nothing.

  if (cellX >= cellWidth || cellY >= cellHeight) {
    return true;
  }
```

```
        // Update the color index of the current cell.

        board[cellX][cellY] = (char)((board[cellX][cellY] + 1) %
            numColors);

        // Save the previous two cells.

        nextToLastX  = lastX;
        nextToLastY  = lastY;
        lastX        = cellX;
        lastY        = cellY;

        // Repaint the applet, clipping the painted region to the
        // the changed square.

        repaint(0, cellX * scale, cellY * scale, scale, scale);

        // Check if the puzzle is solved.

        testWin();

        // Return true so the event is not forwarded to this
        // component's peer.

        return true;
    }

    // If the number of colors is not specified, default to 4.

    private static final int DEFAULT_NUM_COLORS = 4;

    private int     appletHeight;// Height of the applet.
    private int     appletWidth;// Width of the applet.
    private int     numColors;  // Number of colors in the puzzle.
    private int     scale;      // One side of a square in pixels.
    private char    board[][];  // Game board.
    private int     lastX;      // X index of previous cell.
    private int     lastY;      // Y index of previous cell.
    private int     nextToLastX;// X index of next to last cell.
    private int     nextToLastY;// Y index of next to last cell.
    private int     cellWidth;  // Width of game board in cells.
    private int     cellHeight; // Height of game board in cells.

    // The maximum number of colors in the puzzle is 6.

    private Color   colors[]= { Color.black,
                                Color.white,
                                Color.red,
```

```
        Color.green,
        Color.blue,
        Color.yellow };
}
```

Output From the Puzzle Applet

It's hard to show a graphical puzzle game being played in a book, but Figure 15-2 shows the Puzzle applet, as displayed by the `appletviewer`.

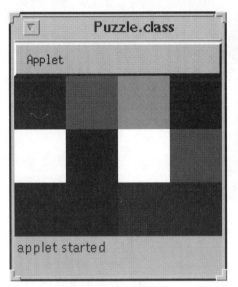
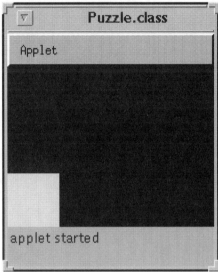

Figure 15-2 An Applet That Manages Mouse Movements
The first frame shows the Puzzle applet after being started, and the second frame shows the game nearly completed. One more move and the remaining square changes to black and the gong sounds.

Managing Events and Threads

Now that we've seen simple handling of mouse events, let's look at a little more complicated example. In the next example, we'll introduce a separate thread of control.

Memory Game Applet

This next applet is a memory game in which a pattern is displayed that the user must try to remember and duplicate. The display thread uses calls to the `Thread.sleep()` method to pause between squares. Selected squares are highlighted by changing their colors using the `Color.brighter()` method.

The `Memory` class implements a game in which the user uses the mouse to duplicate a sequence of squares that have been highlighted. Each time the user successfully duplicates the pattern, the pattern display speeds up. Eventually, the pattern slows back down, increases in number by one square, and starts speeding up again. If the user fails in reproducing the sequence, the game starts over. Here's the code for the `Memory` class:

```java
import java.applet.*;
import java.awt.*;
import java.lang.Math;   // For generating random numbers.


// This class implements a memory game. A sequence of squares is
// highlighted that the user must remember and reproduce. If
// successful,the sequence display gets faster and then longer. If
// the user fails in reproducing the sequence, the game starts over.
```

To initialize the applet, this code scales the height and width by the number of colors. This sets the display time and pattern length to easy values—that is, long for the display time and short for the pattern length:

```java
public class Memory extends Applet implements Runnable {

  public void init() {

    // Each row and column has one cell of each color.

    numCellsOnSide = colors.length;

    // Scale width and height to multiples of the number of cells
    // on a side.

    int appletHeight= Math.max(size().width, numCellsOnSide) /
      numCellsOnSide * numCellsOnSide;
    int appletWidth = Math.max(size().height, numCellsOnSide) /
      numCellsOnSide * numCellsOnSide;

    // Set the width and height of the cells for painting.
```

```
cellWidth    = appletWidth  / numCellsOnSide;
cellHeight   = appletHeight / numCellsOnSide;

// Initialize the display time and the pattern length to
// easy values.
getReallyEasy();

// Resize to our new width and height.

resize(appletWidth, appletHeight);
}
```

The `start()` method creates a thread for the pattern display. We start the game by immediately displaying a pattern, so we call `Thread.start()` right away:

```
public void start() {
  memoryThread = new Thread(this);
  memoryThread.start();
}
```

The `stop()` method stops the display thread. This is only called when the page displaying the applet is exited:

```
public void stop() {
  memoryThread.stop();
}
```

This applet implements the `Runnable` interface, so it must define a `run()` method. This method will be called when the `memoryThread start()` method is called. The call to `reset()` creates a new pattern and displays it. The display thread is then suspended until a new pattern is needed:

```
public void run() {
  while (true) {
    reset();
    memoryThread.suspend();
  }
}
```

We redefine the `update()` method derived from `java.awt.Component`, because the default version redraws the background each time. This applet completely covers the background, so redrawing the background is unnecessary:

```
public void update(Graphics g) {
  paint(g);
}
```

In this `paint()` method, we optimize for the painting of single cells. When a method makes a change to a single cell, it sets `fullPaint` to `false` and sets `paintColor`, `paintX`, and `paintY` before calling `repaint()`. If `fullPaint` is `false`, we just redraw the cell at (`paintX`, `paintY`); otherwise we redraw the entire grid:

```
public void paint(Graphics g) {
  if (fullPaint) {
    for (int i = 0; i < numCellsOnSide; i++) {
      for (int j = 0; j < numCellsOnSide; j++) {
        g.setColor(colors[i][j]);
        g.fillRect(i * cellWidth, j * cellHeight,
          cellWidth, cellHeight);
      }
    }

  } else {

    // paintColor, paintX, and paintY must be set before this
    // method is called with fullPaint == false.

    g.setColor(paintColor);
    g.fillRect(paintX, paintY, cellWidth, cellHeight);
    fullPaint = true;
  }
}
```

All the following event handling routines check the value of the `resetting` flag and do nothing if it is set. The `resetting` flag is set while the current pattern is being displayed.

When the user presses a button down in a square, we highlight the square and begin to watch the mouse movement. If the user releases the button in the same square, we consider the square selected and process the move. If the mouse leaves the square we just unhighlight the square and proceed as if nothing had happened:

```
public boolean mouseDown(Event evt, int x, int y) {

  // If the pattern is being displayed, don't do anything.

  if (resetting) {
    return true;
  }

  // Scale the pixel coordinates to cell coordinates.

  int cellX = x / cellWidth;
  int cellY = y / cellHeight;
```

```
// Set paintX, paintY and paintColor so the paint() method
// will know which square to redraw and what color to paint it.

paintX       = cellX * cellWidth;
paintY       = cellY * cellHeight;
paintColor   = colors[cellX][cellY].brighter();

// Tell the paint method to only paint a single square.

fullPaint  = false;

// Schedule an update.

repaint();

// Set the current cell X and Y coordinates so we can determine
// if the user releases the mouse in the same cell.

currentX  = cellX;
currentY  = cellY;

// Set the checkMove flag so that we pay attention to drag
// and mouseUp events.

checkMove = true;
return true;
}
```

When a mouse drag occurs, we check if a mouse-down event has occurred and if
the mouse is now in the same square. If the mouse has left the square in which the
mouse-down event occurred, we unhighlight the mouse-down square and return
to the default state:

```
public boolean mouseDrag(Event evt, int x, int y) {

// If we're currently displaying the pattern or no mouse down
// occurred within the applet, do not do anything.

if (resetting || !checkMove) {
    return true;
}

// Scale the pixel coordinates to cell coordinates.

int cellX  = x / cellWidth;
int cellY  = y / cellHeight;

// If the mouse has not left the mouse down square, do not do
```

```
  // anything.

  if (cellX == currentX && cellY == currentY) {
     return true;
  }

  // Set paintX, paintY and paintColor so the paint method
  // will know which square to redraw and what color to paint it.
  // Note that we don't repaint the square the mouse is now in
  // but, instead, the square the mouse just left.

  paintX = currentX * cellWidth;
  paintY = currentY * cellHeight;

  paintColor = colors[currentX][currentY];

  // Tell the paint method to only paint a single square.

  fullPaint  = false;

  // Schedule an update.

  repaint();

  // Return to the default state.

  checkMove = false;
  return true;
}

// If the mouse button is released and the button had been pressed
// within the applet, unhighlight the square and add the square
// to the user's pattern. Check if the user has completed the
// pattern or selected the wrong square.

public boolean mouseUp(Event evt, int x, int y) {

  // If we're currently displaying the pattern or no mouse down
  // occurred within the applet, do nothing.

  if (resetting || !checkMove) {
     return true;
  }

  // Scale the pixel coordinates to cell coordinates.

  int cellX  = x / cellWidth;
  int cellY  = y / cellHeight;
```

```
// Set paintX, paintY and paintColor so the paint method
// will know which square to redraw and what color to paint it.

paintX       = cellX * cellWidth;
paintY       = cellY * cellHeight;
paintColor   = colors[cellX][cellY];

// Tell the paint method to only paint a single square.

fullPaint  = false;

// Schedule an update.

repaint();
```

The `testPattern()` method will try to match the user's selection with the next cell in the pattern. If it matches, the pattern index is advanced and a check is made to see if the user has completed the pattern. If the selection doesn't match, the current game ends and a new game starts:

```
testPattern(cellX, cellY);

checkMove = false;
return true;
}
```

This method compares a cell with the next cell in the stored pattern. If it matches, a check is made for the pattern being complete. If it fails, the game ends and a new game is started. Each time a pattern is completed, the pattern display speed increases or the pattern is lengthened:

```
private void testPattern(int x, int y) {
    int[] nextMatch = pattern[next++];
    if (nextMatch[0] == x && nextMatch[1] == y) {

        // If the current cell matched, check if we're at the
        // end of the pattern.

        if (next == patternLength) {

            // If the pattern is complete, play a winning sound and
            // make the next pattern harder. Resume the pattern
            // display thread to display a new pattern.

            win();
            getHarder();
            memoryThread.resume();
        }
```

```
    } else {

        // If the user failed to match the current cell, play a
        // losing sound and make the next pattern really easy.
        // Resume the pattern display thread to display a new
        // pattern.

        lose();
        getReallyEasy();
        memoryThread.resume();
    }
}
// Play a winning sound.

private void win() {
    getAudioClip(getCodeBase(), "Audio/gong.au").play();
}

// Play a losing sound.

private void lose() {
    getAudioClip(getCodeBase(), "Audio/beep.au").play();
}

// Make the pattern harder. Decrement the display time until it
// gets too fast then slow it down and make the pattern longer.

private void getHarder() {
    if (sleepTime > minimumSleepTime) {
        sleepTime -= sleepTimeDecrement;
    } else {
        patternLength++;
        sleepTime = resetSleepTime / 2;
    }
}

// Make the pattern really easy. Make the display time very long
// and the pattern very short. This is used to start a new game.

private void getReallyEasy() {
    sleepTime    = resetSleepTime / 2;
    patternLength= initialPatternLength;
}
```

The `reset()` method starts a new pattern. It generates the pattern, and displays it to the user. The pattern sequence is generated using the `Math.random()` method and each square in the pattern is displayed as it is generated:

```
private void reset() {

    // Set resetting to true so events will be ignored while the
    // pattern is displayed.

    resetting = true;

    checkMove = false;
    fullPaint = true;

    // Display a flashy color rolling effect to signal the start
    // of a new pattern.

    loopColors();

    // Initialize the current index into the pattern to 0. This
    // is used to keep track of where the user is in duplicating
    // the pattern.

    next = 0;

    // Create a new pattern array. Each element is a pair of
    // X and Y coordinates. We could save space using chars or
    // shorts but this is always a small array so it doesn't
    // really matter.

    pattern = new int[patternLength][2];

    for (int i = 0; i < patternLength; i++) {

        // Select random X and Y coordinates.

        int randomX = (int)((Math.random() * 10) %
            numCellsOnSide);
        int randomY = (int)((Math.random() * 10) %
            numCellsOnSide);

        // Set the next pattern entry to the new coordinates.

        pattern[i][0] = randomX;
        pattern[i][1] = randomY;

        // Display the pattern square by redrawing it briefly in a
        // brighter version of its current color.
```

```
        paintColor    = colors[randomX][randomY].brighter();
        paintX        = randomX * cellWidth;
        paintY        = randomY * cellHeight;
        fullPaint     = false;
        repaint();

        // Sleep so the user can see the bright color before we
        // darken it again. The sleep time decreases as patterns
        // are successfully duplicated.

        goToSleep(sleepTime);

        // Redraw the square in its original color before going to
        // the next square.

        paintColor = colors[randomX][randomY];
        fullPaint = false;
        repaint();

        // Sleep between squares.

        goToSleep(repaintSleepTime);
    }

    // Allow mouse events to be processed.

    resetting = false;
}

// Rotate the colors of the grid to signal a new pattern. Sleep
// between each rotation so the user can see it.

private void loopColors() {

    // Rotate as many times as there are colors so we return to
    // our initial color pattern.

    for (int i = 0; i < colors.length; i++) {
        rotateColors();
        repaint();
        goToSleep(rotateSleepTime);
    }
}

// Rotate the entries in the color array.

private void rotateColors() {
    Color[] temp = colors[0];
```

```
  for (int i = 0; i < colors.length - 1; i++) {
     colors[i] = colors[i + 1];
  }

  colors[colors.length - 1] = temp;
}
```

In this applet we don't care if a sleep is interrupted, so we don't do anything with an InterruptedException:

```
private void goToSleep(int n) {
  try {
     Thread.currentThread().sleep(n);
  } catch (InterruptedException e) {
  }
}


// Constants.

private static final int resetSleepTime    = 1500;
private static final int repaintSleepTime   = 30;
private static final int rotateSleepTime    = 300;
private static final int minimumSleepTime   = 150;
private static final int sleepTimeDecrement = 100;
private static final int initialPatternLength= 4;


private Thread memoryThread;     // The thread for displaying
                                 // patterns.
private int    cellWidth;        // The pixel width of a cell.
private int    cellHeight;       // The pixel height of a cell.
private int    numCellsOnSide;   // The number of cells on one
                                 // side of the grid.
private int    sleepTime;        // How long to sleep while
                                 // displaying a pattern square.
private int    next;             // The current index into the
                                 // pattern.
private int    currentX;         // The X coordinate of the
                                 // square in which a mouse down
                                 // occurred.
private int    currentY;         // The Y coordinate of the
                                 // square in which a mouse down
                                 // occurred.
private int    paintX;           // The X coordinate of the
                                 // square to paint.
private int    paintY;           // The Y coordinate of the
                                 // square to paint.
private int[][]pattern;          // The current pattern.
private int    patternLength;    // The length of the current
                                 // pattern.
```

```
    private booleanfullPaint;          // Whether or not to paint a
                                       // single cell.
    private booleancheckMove;          // Whether or not a mouse down
                                       // occurred.
    private booleanresetting;          // Whether or not the pattern
                                       // is currently being
                                       // displayed.
    private Color  paintColor;         // Color of the single cell to
                                       // paint.
    private Color[][]colors =          // The colors in the grid.
      {
        {  Color.blue.darker(),
           Color.yellow.darker(),
           Color.red.darker(),
           Color.green.darker() },

        {  Color.yellow.darker(),
           Color.red.darker(),
           Color.green.darker(),
           Color.blue.darker() },

        {  Color.red.darker(),
           Color.green.darker(),
           Color.blue.darker(),
           Color.yellow.darker() },

        { Color.green.darker(),
           Color.blue.darker(),
           Color.yellow.darker(),
           Color.red.darker() }
      };
    }
```

Output From the Memory Game Applet

Figure 15-3 shows the output from the Memory game applet.

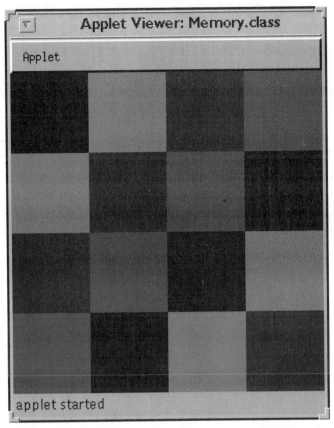

Figure 15-3 Applet Managing Events and Threads
The applet flashes a color pattern. The user must duplicate the

Summary

Developing interesting applets most likely requires managing events such as mouse and keyboard actions. Also, many applets are manipulated by the user, so the applet needs to perform ongoing operations at the same time it is interacting with the user. This requires multiple threads of execution in the applet. In this chapter, we've illustrated event handling and threads in applets. Next, we'll develop these concepts and illustrate applets that combine these with forms to see how to create a Java graphical user interface.

CHAPTER
16

- Using Containers
- Standard Layout Managers
- Using GridBagLayout
- Custom Layout Managers

Forms in Applets

Introduction

Many applications that interact with users display forms of one kind or another. The applets we've seen so far have been composed of single components. However, Java supports developing applets composed of multiple components. There are some special classes in the awt package that support this. In particular, the Container class and LayoutManager interface are useful for developing applets with multiple components. In this chapter, we'll describe these classes and illustrate their use to create a forms-based, multicomponent applet.

Containers

Instances of the Container class group other components. Applets themselves are containers since the Applet class extends the Panel class which extends the Container class. All containers provide operations to add, remove, and paint their components. Containers also provide methods to determine which component is under the mouse and to deliver an event to a particular component.

Using containers, you can group related components together and treat them as a unit. In general, this simplifies the program, and it is particularly useful in arranging components on the display.

Layout Managers

Containers do not do the whole job of grouping components. You need some way to arrange components on the screen. This is accomplished by instances of the `LayoutManager` interface. Each container has an associated layout manager that arranges its components within the container. (Java provides several types of layout managers.) Components are arranged according to a plan that is specific to each particular type of layout manager.

The `Panel` class uses an instance of `FlowLayout` for its default `LayoutManager`. That means that `FlowLayout` is the default layout manager for applets, since the `Applet` class extends the `Panel` class. (All the applets discussed up to this point have implicitly used `FlowLayout`.) The `FlowLayout` manager adds components to a row until the row is full, and then it moves to the next row. This is much like the way an HTML page is formatted by default.

The Java environment provides the following set of layout managers:

- `BorderLayout` — Lays out the components around the sides and in the center of the container in north, east, west, south, and center positions. The gaps between components can be specified.

- `CardLayout` — Only one component is visible at a time. The user can switch between different components. The components can themselves be containers, which allows switching between multiple layouts.

- `FlowLayout` — Places components left to right until there is no more room, then moves to the next line. The lines can be aligned to the left, center, or right.

- `GridBagLayout` — Arranges components both vertically and horizontally using an elaborate set of constraints to determine how much space is allocated to each component and how it should be placed relative to previous components. (We use `GridBagLayout` in the next example.)

- `GridLayout` — Lays out grids of identically sized components. The horizontal and vertical gaps between components may be specified.

A Forms-based Applet

Using most of these layouts is straightforward. The next applet example, however, uses the most complicated layout manager provided by default in the Java environment—the `GridBagLayout`.

This applet attempts to determine a person's occupation (within an engineering organization) based on certain traits such as coffee consumption, fashion sense, and a few others. The values are entered using a simple form, as illustrated in Figure 16-1.

```
┌─────────────────────────────────────────────────────────┐
│ ▽      Applet Viewer: OccupationOracle.class              │
├─────────────────────────────────────────────────────────┤
│ Applet                                                    │
│                                                           │
│ Name:              ┌──────────────────────────────────┐  │
│                    │ I                                │  │
│                    └──────────────────────────────────┘  │
│                                                           │
│ Age:               ┌────┐                                │
│                    │    │                                │
│                    └────┘                                │
│ Binary World View:  □                                    │
│                                                           │
│ Coffee consumption: ┌────┐                               │
│                    │    │                                │
│                    └────┘                                │
│ Fashion sense:                                           │
│  ◇ Low                                                    │
│  ◆ Medium                                                 │
│  ◇ High                                                   │
│                    ┌──────────────────────────────────┐  │
│ Occupation:        │ Unknown                          │  │
│                    └──────────────────────────────────┘  │
│ applet started                                            │
└─────────────────────────────────────────────────────────┘
```

Figure 16-1 A Sample Form

The following code is for the multiple component applet.

```
import java.applet.Applet;
import java.awt.*;

// The OccupationOracle class makes a guess at a person's occupation
// within an engineering organization based on a few key traits.
// Invalid entries in numeric fields result in an Unknown occupation.
// This applet uses the awt.GridBagLayout class to structure the
// occupation form. The awt.GridBagLayout class allows fields to
// be placed in rows and columns within a form. Each component
// is given a display area based on the constraints in effect
// when it is added to the layout.
```

```
public class OccupationOracle extends Applet {

   // Construct the form. Create each component of the form and
   // add it to the layout. Initialize the occupation to Unknown.

   public void init() {

      // Use the GridBagLayout layout to construct rows and
      // columns.

      GridBagLayout    gridbag   =   new GridBagLayout();
```

This creates a new set of `constraints` to use when adding a component to the layout. The constraint values in effect when a component is added to the layout are cloned and stored in conjunction with the component by the layout:

```
      GridBagConstraints constraints = new GridBagConstraints();

      // Set the font for the form.

      setFont(new Font("TimesRoman", Font.BOLD, 18));

      // Associate the GridBagLayout object with the applet.

      setLayout(gridbag);

      // The anchor constraint determines how a component
      // is justified within its display area.

      constraints.anchor   = GridBagConstraints.WEST;
```

The `weighty` constraint determines how much vertical space should be given to this component. If left at 0.0, all components clump up in the middle as the padding is applied to the outside as shown in Listing 16-1:

Listing 16-1 The weighty constraint determines space

```
      constraints.weighty = 1.0;
      // Create a name label and text field.

      makeNameField();

      // Setting the gridwidth constraint to 1 causes the component
      // to take up the minimum horizontal space in its row.

      constraints.gridwidth = 1;

      // addFormComponent() will associate the current constraints
      // with a component and add the component to the form.
```

```
addFormComponent(gridbag, nameLabel, constraints);

// Setting the gridwidth constraint to REMAINDER will
// cause the component to fill up the remainder of its row:
// i.e. it will be the last entry in the row.

constraints.gridwidth  =  GridBagConstraints.REMAINDER;

// The fill constraint tells what to do if the item is in
// an area larger than it is. In this case we want to fill
// any extra horizontal space.

constraints.fill       =  GridBagConstraints.HORIZONTAL;

addFormComponent(gridbag, nameField, constraints);

// Create and add an age label and text field.

makeAgeField();

constraints.gridwidth  = 1;
constraints.fill       = GridBagConstraints.NONE;
constraints.weightx    = 0.0;
addFormComponent(gridbag, ageLabel, constraints);
constraints.gridwidth  = GridBagConstraints.REMAINDER;
constraints.weightx    = 1.0;
addFormComponent(gridbag, ageField, constraints);

// Create and add a world view label and a single checkbox
// for a true/false value.

makeWorldViewField();

constraints.gridwidth  = 1;
constraints.weightx    = 0.0;
addFormComponent(gridbag, worldViewLabel, constraints);
constraints.gridwidth  = GridBagConstraints.REMAINDER;
constraints.weightx    = 1.0;
addFormComponent(gridbag, worldViewField, constraints);

// Create and add a coffee consumption label and text field.

makeCoffeeField();

constraints.gridwidth  = 1;
constraints.weightx    = 0.0;
addFormComponent(gridbag, coffeeLabel, constraints);
constraints.gridwidth  = GridBagConstraints.REMAINDER;
```

```
    constraints.weightx    = 1.0;
    addFormComponent(gridbag, coffeeField, constraints);

    // Create and add a fashion sense label and a checkbox
    // group that has three mutually exclusive values.

    makeFashionField();

    constraints.gridwidth = GridBagConstraints.REMAINDER;
    constraints.weightx    = 0.0;
    constraints.weighty    = 0.0;
    addFormComponent(gridbag, fashionLabel, constraints);

    // The three checkboxes that represent fashion sense.

    addFormComponent(gridbag, low, constraints);
    addFormComponent(gridbag, medium, constraints);
    addFormComponent(gridbag, high, constraints);

    // The Occupation field is output only.

    makeOccupationField();

    constraints.gridwidth = 1;
    constraints.weightx    = 0.0;
    constraints.weighty    = 1.0;
    constraints.fill       = GridBagConstraints.NONE;
    addFormComponent(gridbag, occupationLabel, constraints);
    constraints.fill       = GridBagConstraints.HORIZONTAL;
    constraints.gridwidth = GridBagConstraints.REMAINDER;
    constraints.weightx    = 1.0;
    addFormComponent(gridbag, occupationField, constraints);

    // Display the initial Unknown occupation.

    recalculateOccupation();

    resize(400, 250);
}
```

The `paint()` method for this applet just calls the `paintComponents()` method, which is defined by the `Container` class. It causes all the components visible within the `Container` to be painted:

```
public void paint(Graphics g) {
  paintComponents(g);
}
```

```
// When any action occurs within the form we do the same thing:
// recalculate the person's occupation.

public boolean action(Event event, Object arg) {
  recalculateOccupation();
  return true;
}

// A helper function that associates constraints with a component
// and adds it to the form.

private void addFormComponent(GridBagLayout grid,
    Component comp, GridBagConstraints c) {
  grid.setConstraints(comp, c);
  add(comp);
}
```

The recalculateOccupation() method fetches the values of each component
and computes an occupation based on some truly inane heuristics:

```
private void recalculateOccupation() {

  // If we don't have a name yet we might incorrectly categorize
  // the CEO!

  if (nameField.getText() == "") {
     occupationField.setText("Unknown");
  }

  // Fetch other important values that we'll use in our
  // calculations.

  int      age;
  int      coffeeConsumption;
  boolean  binaryView = worldViewField.getState();

  // Try to fetch integer values for age and coffeeConsumption.
  // If the values in the fields can't be parsed as integers,
  // set the occupation to Unknown.

  try {
     age               = Integer.parseInt(ageField.getText());
     coffeeConsumption =
           Integer.parseInt(coffeeField.getText());
  } catch (Exception e) {
     occupationField.setText("Unknown");
     return;
  }
```

```
// Check for the CEO.

String name = nameField.getText();

if (name.endsWith("II")   ||
    name.endsWith("III")  ||
    name.endsWith("IV")) {

    if (age < 35 || coffeeConsumption < 4) {
        occupationField.setText("Junior Executive");
    } else {
        occupationField.setText("CEO");
    }

    return;
}
```

Fashion sense is a critical piece of information. The `getCurrent()` method of `CheckboxGroup` returns whichever `Checkbox` in the group is currently selected. Only one can be selected at a time as shown in Example 16-2:

Listing 16-2 `CheckboxGroup` **returns selected** `Checkbox`

```
Checkbox fashionValue = fashionGroup.getCurrent();

if (fashionValue == low || fashionValue == medium) {

    // There are two kinds of people in the world: those who
    // divide people into two kinds and those who don't.

    if (binaryView && coffeeConsumption >= 4) {
        occupationField.setText("Engineer");

    } else if ((age > 40 && binaryView) ||
               (age < 40 && coffeeConsumption >= 4)) {
        occupationField.setText("Engineering Manager");

    } else {
        occupationField.setText("Product Manager");
    }

} else {

    // High fashion sense. Not an engineer!

    if (binaryView || coffeeConsumption >= 4) {
        occupationField.setText("Vice President");
```

```java
    } else {
        occupationField.setText("Product Marketing");
    }
  }
}

// Helper functions to create form components.

private void makeNameField() {
  nameLabel = new Label("Name: ");
  nameField = new TextField(40);
}

private void makeAgeField() {
  ageLabel  = new Label("Age: ");
  ageField  = new TextField(3);
}

private void makeOccupationField() {
  occupationLabel = new Label("Occupation: ");
  occupationField = new TextField(40);
}

private void makeWorldViewField() {
  worldViewLabel  = new Label("Binary World View: ");
  worldViewField  = new Checkbox();
}

private void makeCoffeeField() {
  coffeeLabel  = new Label("Coffee consumption: ");
  coffeeField  = new TextField(3);
}

private void makeFashionField() {
  fashionLabel = new Label("Fashion sense: ");
  fashionGroup = new CheckboxGroup();
  low          = new Checkbox("Low   ", fashionGroup, false);
  medium       = new Checkbox("Medium", fashionGroup, true);
  high         = new Checkbox("High  ", fashionGroup, false);
}

// Text fields.

private TextField    nameField;
private TextField    ageField;
private TextField    coffeeField;
private TextField    occupationField;
```

```
// Labels.

private Label          nameLabel;
private Label          ageLabel;
private Label          coffeeLabel;
private Label          fashionLabel;
private Label          worldViewLabel;
private Label          occupationLabel;

// Checkboxes.

private Checkbox       worldViewField;
private Checkbox       low;
private Checkbox       medium;
private Checkbox       high;

// The fashion sense checkbox group.

private CheckboxGroup fashionGroup;
}
```

Output from the Occupational Oracle Applet

Figure 16-2 shows sample output from the `OccupationOracle` applet.

```
┌─────────────────────────────────────────────────────┐
│ ▽   Applet Viewer: OccupationOracle.class             │
├─────────────────────────────────────────────────────┤
│ Applet                                                │
├─────────────────────────────────────────────────────┤
│ Name:          │ Sam Son                            │ │
│                                                       │
│ Age:           │ 48 │                                 │
│                                                       │
│ Binary World View:   ■                                │
│                                                       │
│ Coffee consumption:  │ 8 │                            │
│                                                       │
│ Fashion sense:                                        │
│ ◇Low                                                  │
│ ◇Medium                                               │
│ ◆High                                                 │
│                                                       │
│ Occupation:    │ Vice President                     │ │
│ applet started                                        │
└─────────────────────────────────────────────────────┘
```

Figure 16-2 An Applet With Multiple Components
In this case, the Occupation Oracle predicts a 48 year old fellow who consumes 8 cups of coffee a day, has a binary view of the world, and a high sense of fashion is a Vice President.

Summary

Working with forms involves incorporating multiple components into an applet. The sample applet in this chapter shows use of radio buttons, text fields, and check boxes. This applet shows use of one of Java's default LayoutManagers—`GridBagLayout`. The applet uses `GridBagLayout` to arrange components vertically and horizontally in the display. In later applets, we'll show alternatives to using `GridBagLayout`.

CHAPTER 17

Animation in Applets

Incorporating Animation

One of the things that excites a lot of people about Java is the potential for lively pages on the world-wide web—not just pictures and sound, but movement as well. Java provides ample support for such animated applets. We'll focus our discussion of animation in applets on one of the most popular applets in use: the ticker-tape.

A Ticker-tape Applet

This `Ticker` applet will scroll a message across the screen like the news tickers in airports or at sports arenas. This is a configurable applet, so you can specify parameters in the HTML file to override the default values for the text, the font, and the foreground and background colors of the ticker-tape.

The key point of this applet is the use of *double buffering* to produce flicker-free animation. Double buffering refers to the technique of first drawing an image offscreen and then displaying it. In the example, the scrolling text is first written to an instance of `Image`, which is then displayed on the screen.

Other interesting characteristics of this applet to note are the use of the `Graphics.draw3DRect` call to draw an indented rectangle for a border and the use of the `java.util.StringTokenizer` class to divide a string at specified delimiters.

Following is the code for the `Ticker` class:

```java
import java.awt.*;
import java.util.StringTokenizer;
import java.applet.Applet;

// The Ticker class displays a ticker tape of text that scrolls
// across the screen in a loop. When the text scrolls completely
// off one end it reappears on the other end. The text, font,
// foreground and background can be set via parameters. The font is
// specified by fontname, fontsize, fontweight and fontslant. The
// colors may be entered by name or by rgb values. To avoid
// flickering, the text is first drawn into an offscreen image and
// the image is then displayed all at once.

public class Ticker extends Applet implements Runnable {

    // The init() method initializes the Ticker. It sets the text,
    // font, foreground and background. The background is defaulted
    // to pink, the foreground to black, and the font to Helvetica.

    public void init() {

    tape       = "Java by Example: The Java Book for Programmers";
    String param = getParameter("text");

    if (param != null) {
        tape   = param;
    }

    // Get the user's font parameters, with 12 point Helvetica
    // font as the default.

    textFont   = getFont("Helvetica", Font.PLAIN, 12);

    // We use the font height and font descent to draw the text
    // centered in the scrolling area. The width is used to
    // determine how far to scroll before starting over.

    FontMetrics metrics = getFontMetrics(textFont);

    textHeight = metrics.getHeight();
    textDescent= metrics.getDescent();
    textWidth  = metrics.stringWidth(tape);

        // Get the colors specified by the user with black as the
        // default foreground and pink as the default background.

        getColors(Color.black, Color.pink);
```

```
  // Initialize the size, number of scrolling steps and the
  // offscreen image used to draw the text.

  setupTape();
}

// The start() method create a new thread to scroll the text and
// starts it.

public void start() {
  scrollThread = new Thread(this);
  scrollThread.start();
}

// The stop() method stops the scrolling thread.

public void stop() {
  scrollThread.stop();
}

// The Ticker update() method just calls paint() since we are
// covering the background with our offscreen image.

public void update(Graphics g) {
  paint(g);
}
```

The paint() method first checks if the Ticker has grown wider or taller. If it has grown taller, it is resized back to the right height for the font. If it has grown wider, setupTape() will create a new and wider offscreen image and reset the number of steps required to scroll all the way across. After checking for the value of resize, the paint() method draws the string into the offscreen image at the current scroll position and then draws the image on the display:

```
public void paint(Graphics g) {

  // Adjust for resize if necessary.

  setupTape();

  // Draw the string into the offscreen image.

  Graphics offg = offscreenImage.getGraphics();

  offg.setColor(getBackground());
  offg.fillRect(0, 0, size().width - (RECTMARGIN * 2), textHeight);
  offg.setColor(getForeground());
  offg.setFont(textFont);
```

previousWidth is the width of the displayed area in pixels. The text starts at the right edge of the Ticker at a position previousWidth pixels from the left. Each time it is repainted, the text is drawn one pixel farther to the left:

```
offg.drawString(tape, previousWidth - tapeIndex,
    textHeight - textDescent);
```

totalTapeSteps is set to the width of the display area plus the width of the text. After scrolling the width of the display area, the text is at the left end of the display and it must scroll its own width to complete one traversal:

```
tapeIndex = (tapeIndex + 1) % totalTapeSteps;

// Draw a 3D rectangle just within the display area for a border.

g.draw3DRect(RECTMARGIN, RECTMARGIN,
  size().width - RECTMARGIN,
  size().height - RECTMARGIN,
  false);

// Draw the offscreen image within the rectangle.

g.drawImage(offscreenImage, RECTMARGIN + 1,
  RECTMARGIN + TEXTMARGIN + 1,
  this);
}

// The run() method just pauses briefly between repaints.

public void run() {
  while (true) {
    try {
      scrollThread.sleep(SCROLLPAUSE);

    }catch (InterruptedException e) {
    }
    repaint();
  }
}
```

The getColors() method retrieves color parameters from the user for foreground and background colors. If either is unspecified in the HTML file calling this applet, the arguments are used as defaults:

```
private void getColors(Color foreground, Color background) {

  // Get either a named foreground color or an rgb value.
```

```
String param = getParameter("foreground");

if (param != null) {
   setForeground(lookupColor(param, foreground));

} else {
   param = getParameter("foreground-rgb");

   if (param != null) {
      setForeground(lookupRGBColor(param, foreground));

   } else {

      // If no parameter, use the default.

      setForeground(foreground);
   }
}

// Get either a named background color or an rgb value.

param = getParameter("background");
if (param != null) {
   setBackground(lookupColor(param, background));

} else {
   param = getParameter("background-rgb");

   if (param != null) {
      setBackground(lookupRGBColor(param, background));

   } else {

      // If no parameter, use the default.

      setBackground(background);
   }
}
}
```

The `lookupColor()` method looks up a color by name. All the predefined colors in the `Color` class are available, except the shades of gray. The `colors` array holds { *"colorname"*, *color*} pairs. If the name argument does not match any color in the array, the `defaultColor` argument is used:

```java
private Color lookupColor(String name, Color defaultColor) {
   for (int i = 0; i < colors.length; i++) {
     if (name.equals(colors[i][0])) {
       return (Color)colors[i][1];
     }
   }

   return defaultColor;
}
```

The `lookupRGBColor()` method takes a string that is expected to have the form: *rval, gval, bval*, where *rval, gval* and *bval* are integers between 0 and 255. If the string matches this format, a color is returned with the specified RGB values; otherwise, `defaultColor` is returned. The Java `StringTokenizer` class is used to split the `description` argument into separate red, green, and blue values:

```java
private Color lookupRGBColor(String description, Color
   defaultColor) {
   try {

     // If any error occurs trying to parse the string, return
     // the default color. Possible errors are that there are
     // not enough tokens or that there are malformed integers.

     StringTokenizer tokens = new StringTokenizer(description,
         ",");

     int red     = Integer.parseInt(tokens.nextToken());
     int green   = Integer.parseInt(tokens.nextToken());
     int blue    = Integer.parseInt(tokens.nextToken());

     // Ignore any extra stuff

     return new Color(red, green, blue);

   } catch (Exception e) {
     return defaultColor;
   }
}
```

The `getFont()` method retrieves user-specified font parameters. Any parameter not set by the user is replaced by the corresponding default argument. The `style` argument subsumes the `fontweight` and `fontslant` parameters:

```
private Font getFont(String name, int style, int pointSize) {
  String param = getParameter("fontname");

  if (param != null) {
    name = param;
  }
```

Since the Java font model combines slant and weight into `style`, so we need to keep track of whether or not any `style` parameters have been specified. If `fontweight` has been specified, then we need to do a logical OR between `fontslant` and `fontweight`. Otherwise, `fontslant` should completely replace the default:

```
  boolean styleSpecified  = false;
  param                   = getParameter("fontweight");

  if (param != null) {
    styleSpecified = true;

    if (param.equals("bold") || param.equals("BOLD")) {
      style = Font.BOLD;

    } else {

      // Since the only two weights are bold and plain, set the
      // style to plain if it isn't bold.

      style = Font.PLAIN;
    }
  }
  param = getParameter("fontslant");

  if (param != null) {
    if (param.equals("italic") || param.equals("ITALIC")) {
      if (styleSpecified) {
        style |= Font.ITALIC;
      } else {
        style = Font.ITALIC;
      }

    } else if (!styleSpecified) {

      // Since the only two slants are italic and plain,
      // we'll set the style to plain if it isn't italic.
```

```
        style = Font.PLAIN;
    }
}

param = getParameter("fontsize");

if (param != null) {
  pointSize = Integer.parseInt(param);
}

return new Font(name, style, pointSize);
}
```

The setupTape() method adjusts the state of the Ticker after a resize. If the height has changed, it is reset to the appropriate height for the selected font. If the width has changed, the number of steps required for a complete scroll traversal is reset, and a new offscreen image is created to draw into:

```
private void setupTape() {
  Dimension dim = size();

  // resize() does nothing if the size hasn't changed.

  resize(dim.width, textHeight + (TEXTMARGIN * 2) + (RECTMARGIN *
    2));

  // If the width hasn't changed, we're done.

  if (dim.width == previousWidth) {
    return;
  }

  // Save the width to compare against next time.

  previousWidth  = dim.width;

  // Reset the tape to the beginning.

  tapeIndex  = 0;

  // The total steps required for a scroll traversal is the width
  // of the display area + the width of the text.

  totalTapeSteps = dim.width + textWidth;

  // If there is already an existing offscreen image, destroy it.

  if (offscreenImage != null) {
```

```
   offscreenImage.flush();
}

// Create a new image to fit the current display area.

offscreenImage = createImage(dim.width - (RECTMARGIN * 2),
  textHeight);
}

// Constants.

private static final int TEXTMARGIN   = 3;
private static final int RECTMARGIN   = 1;
private static final int SCROLLPAUSE  = 15;

// The offscreen image we write text into before displaying it.

private Image offscreenImage              = null;
// How wide the Ticker was the last time we drew it.

private int    previousWidth = -1;

private Thread scrollThread;     // Thread that scrolls text.
private String tape;             // Text being displayed.
private Font   textFont;         // The displayed font.
private int    tapeIndex;        // The current index into
                                 // the text.
private int    totalTapeSteps;   // The number of steps
                                 // required to traverse a
                                 // complete scroll.
private int    textWidth;        // The width of the text in
                                 // pixels.
private int    textHeight;       // The height of the text in
                                 // pixels.
private int    textDescent;      // How far the text goes below
                                 // the font's baseline in
                                 // pixels.

// Colors indexed by name.Used by lookupColor() to select a color
// value.
```

```
private Object[][] colors = {{ "white",    Color.white  },
                             { "WHITE",    Color.white  },
                             { "gray",     Color.gray   },
                             { "GRAY",     Color.gray   },
                             { "black",    Color.black  },
                             { "BLACK",    Color.black  },
                             { "red",      Color.red    },
                             { "RED",      Color.red    },
                             { "pink",     Color.pink   },
                             { "PINK",     Color.pink   },
                             { "orange",   Color.orange },
                             { "ORANGE",   Color.orange },
                             { "yellow",   Color.yellow },
                             { "YELLOW",   Color.yellow },
                             { "green",    Color.green  },
                             { "GREEN",    Color.green  },
                             { "magenta", Color.magenta },
                             { "MAGENTA", Color.magenta },
                             { "cyan",     Color.cyan   },
                             { "CYAN",     Color.cyan   },
                             { "blue",    Color.blue   },
                             { "BLUE",    Color.blue   } };
}
```

Output From the Ticker-tape Applet

Figure 17-1 shows output from the Ticker applet.

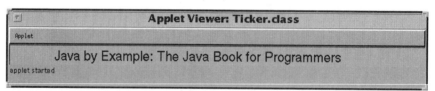

Figure 17-1 Ticker Applet Display

The Animator Class

The JDK 1.0.2 release includes a demo of an `Animator` class (look in the jdk/demo directory). This class provides direct support for animated display sequences. Using the `Animator` class is the simplest solution for tasks such as basic animated presentations. The `Animator` class can display a sequence of images with sounds stored in individual frames. Each frame can have its own position and duration of display.

The `Animator` class included with the JDK 1.0.2 release is optimized for smooth, flicker-free displays.

Summary

The ticker-tape applet is a common and useful one. The key point illustrated in this example is the use of double buffering to prevent the screen display from flickering. The ticker-tape applet also shows how to draw an indented rectangle for a border and the use of the `java.util.StringTokenizer` class to divide a string at specified delimiters.

CHAPTER 18

- Using a Custom Layout Manager

- Developing a Complex Applet

- Using synchronized in an Applet

Putting the Applet Pieces Together

Introduction

To complete discussion of applets, we'll describe a complex applet that will use techniques applied in previous examples. This applet will use interfaces, event handling, multiple threads of execution, and add some interesting new features.

This example will be the longest program we discuss and should help understand how to construct large Java applications or applets. The applet is a *cellular automaton construction kit*. That sounds like a mouthful, but don't be put off by the name. You may already be familiar with a particular cellular automaton—the computer game of Life. In the game of Life, the cells of a grid structure are filled, as if under their own power. In this chapter, we'll build an applet (the cellular automaton construction kit) that lets you define new automata and watch them evolve.

Constructing the Cellular Applet

This applet uses a two-dimensional grid of cells, a set of possible cell values, and a rule that tells how cell values change over time. The rule determines the next value contained in a cell. The next value is based on the cell's current value and the current values of the eight cells that surround it, as illustrated in Figure 18-1.

N	N	N
N	C	N
N	N	N

Figure 18-1 Cellular Applet Grid

In the grid, C is the current cell and N is a neighbor cell. The next value of a cell is based on the cell's current value and the current values of the eight cells that surround it.

The game of Life has two possible cell values—off and on—and a simple rule that says:

```
IF the current cell is off
  IF exactly 3 of the current cell's neighbors are on
    Turn the current cell on.
  ELSE
    Leave the current cell off.

ELSE (the current cell is on)
  IF 2 or 3 of the current cell's neighbors are on
    Leave the current cell on.
  ELSE
    Turn the current cell off.
```

By changing the rule and changing the set of values we can define different automata that have completely different—and sometimes surprising—behavior.

Applet Overview

The Cellular applet consists of four different parts:

- A user interaction piece that displays the automata and takes user input
- A layout manager that arranges the display canvas and controls for the applet
- An *arena* in which the evolution of the automata takes place
- A rule module that provides support for defining rules and sets of cell values

These parts correspond to the program structure, which we'll show later in the chapter in our discussion of applet class structure. Before doing that, let's look at how it works.

Operation of the Applet

The applet can run in two modes:

1. An interactive mode in which the user can select a set of rules and define the starting configuration of cells before launching the automaton.

2. A scripted mode in which the applet runs automatically according to a pre-defined set of rules and configurations.

When the applet is run in its interactive mode, four controls are provided to start and stop the evolution, clear the canvas, and switch to a different rule set, as illustrated in Figure 18-2.

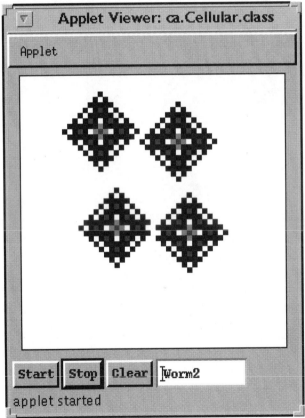

Figure 18-2 Cellular Applet in Interactive Mode
In interactive mode, the user can start, stop, or clear the board.
The user can also enter a new set of rules in the text field.

When the applet is running in scripted mode, it looks something like this:

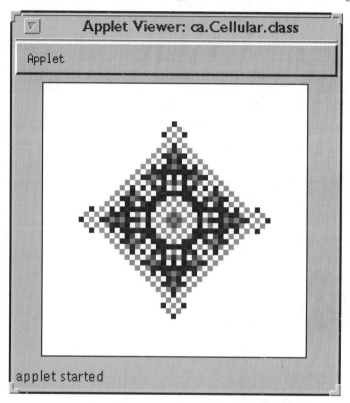

Figure 18-3 Cellular Applet in Scripted Mode
In scripted mode, the applet plays according to a predefined
script. There are no controls for user interaction.

A user can zoom in on the activity by making the applet bigger. This makes each individual cell larger, so it's easier to see the pattern of changing cells.

The Cellular applet also employs some special techniques and features worth noting before looking in detail at the code. These include use of the synchronized keyword, a custom layout manager, an easy-to-modify rule set, and the scripting capability we already alluded to. It is helpful to look at each of these to better understand how the entire applet works.

Use of synchronized in the Applet

The Cellular applet is the first example in which we've used the Java `synchronized` keyword. We use it to synchronize changes to the cells of an automaton. The user can change the values of cells by using the mouse, but the ongoing thread that handles the evolution of the automaton may be about to change that cell as well, or the cell might be about to repainted. So we use the `synchronized` keyword to avoid conflicts.

A Custom Layout Manager

This applet is unable to make use of any of the default layout managers discussed in *Layout Managers* on page 268. The problem is that, when resizing the applet canvas, the width and height must always be integral multiples of the number of cells on a side. Otherwise, there would be leftover bits of cells around the edges. The default layout managers don't provide any way to handle this particular resizing problem. As a result, we have written our own layout manager called `BoardLayout`.

The `BoardLayout` layout manager arranges a board and a set of controls, and it handles the resizing problem. It's called `BoardLayout` because it could easily be used to manage a board for a game like chess or checkers. This layout manager tries to make a square board as large as possible within the space provided by its parent and arranges the controls in the remaining space. If the controls won't fit when the board is reduced to its minimum size, they are not shown.

Defining Rules

The Cellular applet is designed to make it easy to define new rules. Each rule set is a class that must define three methods, as described in Table 18-1.

Table 18-1 Cellular Applet Rule Methods

Rule Methods	Description
`getColors()`	Returns an array of colors representing cell values.
`getInitialValue()`	Returns the index into the color array of the starting value for cells.
`apply()`	Returns the new value for a cell.

Several helper methods are provided to obtain the values of the current cell and its neighbors. Here is the rule set for the game of Life:

```
// All rule sets should be in the ca.rules package.

package ca.rules;

// All rule sets must extend the ca.Rules class. The process() method
// of the ca.Rules class initializes the set of neighbors and the
// value of the current cell before calling a rule set's apply()
// method. The ca.Rules class also provides support methods for
// selecting particular neighbors and determining how many
// neighboring cells have a particular value.

import ca.Rules;
import java.awt.Color;

public class Life extends Rules {
  public Life() {
    colors    = new Color[2];
    colors[0] = Color.white;
    colors[1] = Color.black;
  }

  // Return the set of colors this rule set wants to display for
  // its cell values.

  public Color[] getColors() {
    return colors;
  }

  // Cells should be initialized to the zero'th color in this rule
  // set's color array (i.e. white).

  public int getInitialValue() {
    return 0;
  }

  // The apply() method determines the new value for a cell given
  // its current value and the values of its neighbors.

  public int apply() {

    // The numCells() method returns the number of neighbors that
    // currently have the value passed as its argument. In this
    // case, it returns the number of cells that have the value "1"
    // (the cells which are on).
```

```
int num = numCells(1);

// The self() method returns the current value of the current
// cell.

if (self() == 0) {

    // If the current cell is off, there must be exactly three
    // neighbors that are on before it gets turned on.

    if (num == 3) {
        return 1;

    } else {
        return 0;
    }

} else {

    // If the current cell is on, there must be two or three
    // neighbors that are on or it gets turned off.

    if (num == 2 || num == 3) {
        return 1;

    } else {
        return 0;
    }
  }
 }
  private Color colors[];
}
```

In this rule set, note the use of the numCells() method to determine how many neighbors have a particular value. numLinear() and numDiag() methods are also provided. These methods determine how many cells have specified values in the *rook move* and *bishop move* directions on the board.

Different rule sets can be dynamically loaded into the applet by typing their names into the text field at the bottom of the applet (see Figure 18-2 on page 293).

Scripting the Applet

Automata are entertaining to watch. For those wishing to be mesmerized, it's possible to use HTML code to script the applet so that it executes a predefined set of rules and patterns. The two HTML parameters for the applet are script and numcells. The script parameter allows you to specify rules and configurations. The numcells parameter determines the *grain size* of the applet (that is, the number of cells across one side of the applet). The width of the applet divided by the number of cells specified determines the minimum size of a cell on the screen. The cells can be made larger by increasing the size of the applet, but they cannot be made smaller than their initial size. More cells allows for more generations and more of a birds-eye view of the automaton, but it also makes each generation take longer to calculate.

Example 18-1 shows a sample HTML script for the Cellular applet.

Example 18-1 Sample Cellular Script

```
<applet code="ca.Cellular.class" width=300 height=300>
<param  name="script"
value="Worm2:edge:25,25,1;Life:10:25,23,1:25,24,1:25,25,1:25,26,1
:25,27,1">
<param  name="numcells" value="51">
</applet>
```

For each entry in the script, you can define three parameters: the rule set to use, when to stop running the rule set, and the initial configuration of cells. Here's the syntax of a script entry:

<Rule set name> : *<bound behavior>* : *<initial configuration>*

So, in the following single script entry:

```
Worm2:edge:25,25,1;
```

the script says to start the applet with the `Worm2` rule and execute it until it reaches the edge or until its pattern stops changing. This entry also says to start the applet with a single cell set to color number 1 at location `25,25`.

The *<initial configuration>* parameter (and the colon preceding it) are optional. An *<initial configuration>* consists of triples separated by colons. Each triple is of the form: *x*, *y*, *color*.

After executing the first script entry, the applet then switches to the `Life` rule set, as specified in Example 18-1. The `Life` rule set initializes cells to color number 1 at 5 locations. The color and locations are specified in a series of triples separated by colons. The `Life` rule set runs for 10 generations or until its pattern stops changing. Then the applet repeats executing from the beginning.

The execution pattern display can terminate two ways:

- When the pattern reaches the edge of the canvas
- After a certain number of steps

Also, the pattern can run continuously, unless it stops changing. (The evolution of an automaton always stops if it does not change between two generations.)

Applet Class Structure

As previously mentioned, the Cellular applet has four functional parts: a user interaction part, a layout part, an arena part, and a rule part. Figure 18-4 on the next page shows the high-level organization of the classes that provide these four parts.

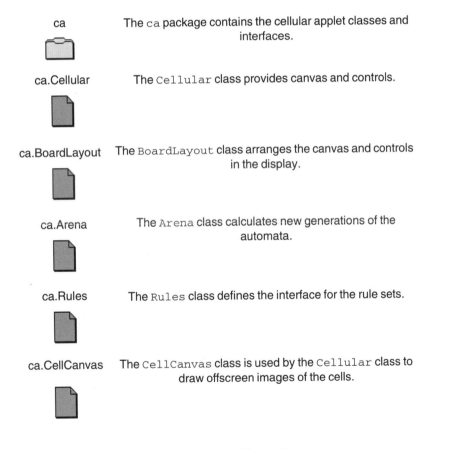

Figure 18-4 The Cellular Applet's Class Structure
All of these classes are in the ca package.

Table 18-2 describes these classes in more detail.

Table 18-2 Cellular Applet Class Summary

`Cellular` **Class**	
Package	`ca`

Imports	`java.applet.Applet`
	`java.awt.*`
	`java.util.*`

Interfaces	`Runnable`
Subclass of	`Applet`
Description	The `Cellular` class is the top-level class for the applet. It reads parameters and provides a canvas and controls for manipulating components of the applet.

`BoardLayout` **Class**	
Package	`ca`
Imports	`java.util.*` `java.awt.*`
Interfaces	`LayoutManager`
Subclass of	`Object`
Description	The `BoardLayout` class implements the `LayoutManager` interface. It arranges the display canvas and controls for the applet, reshaping them if necessary when the display is resized.

`Arena` **Class**	
Package	`ca`
Imports	None
Interfaces	None
Subclass of	`Object`
Description	The `Arena` class takes care of actually calculating new generations for the automata. It loops through the current array of cells, saves new values for each cell in a separate array, and then swaps the arrays.

Table 18-2 Cellular Applet Class Summary (Continued)

`Rules` **Class**	
Package	`ca`
Imports	`java.awt.Color`
Interfaces	None
Subclass of	`Object`
Description	The `Rules` class is an *Abstract* class that defines the interface for rule sets and provides support methods for defining rules. (For a review of abstract classes, see *Abstract Methods* on page 30.)

`CellCanvas` **Class**	
Package	`ca`
Imports	None
Interfaces	None
Subclass of	`Canvas`
Description	The `CellCanvas` is *not* `public` as it is only useful within the context of the `Cellular` class. `CellCanvas` does the actual display of automata. It calls the arena's `apply()` method repeatedly and redraws the cells that have changed. All drawing is done to an offscreen image, which is then displayed on the screen. When the display is resized, the offscreen image is recreated and the `cellSize` and `cellSide` are recomputed.

The Cellular Applet

We've gone into a fairly lengthy discussion of the Cellular applet—what's going on in it and how it works. Now let's take a look at the code.

The Cellular Class

The `Cellular` class provides the canvas for displaying and controls for manipulating cellular automata. It can be used in two modes:

- A running display mode that automatically steps through predefined patterns

- A manual mode with controls for starting, stopping, and clearing the display and changing the automaton rules and initial cell configuration

This applet uses the `BoardLayout` layout manager to place the canvas and controls. Following is the code for the `Cellular` class:

```
package ca;

import java.applet.Applet;
import java.awt.*;
import java.util.*;

// The Cellular applet provides a canvas and controls for
// manipulating and displaying cellular automata.

public class Cellular extends Applet implements Runnable {
```

The init() method retrieves parameter values from the user and creates the components of the applet. If the applet is running in automatic mode, no controls are added to the layout. The components of the applet are:

- A canvas for displaying automata
- A start button to initiate the evolution of an automaton
- A stop button to suspend the evolution
- A clear button that clears the display and suspends evolution
- A text field holding the name of the current rule set. This value can be changed to load a new rule set

```
    public void init() {

    // The initial size of the canvas defaults to the size of the
    // applet. It may change later to become an integral
    // multiple of the number of cells on a side.

    canvasWidth  = size().width;

    // Retrieve the number of cells on a side of the display. This
    // value combined with the canvasWidth is used to determine
    // the size of a single cell on the display in pixels.

    String param = getParameter("numcells");

    int numSideCells;

    if (param != null) {
       numSideCells = Integer.parseInt(param);

    } else {

    // If the number of cells is not specified, compute it
    // from the width of the canvas and the default cell size.
```

```
    numSideCells = canvasWidth / DEFAULT_CELL_SIZE;
  }

  cellSize = canvasWidth / numSideCells;

  if (cellSize == 0) {
    cellSize = 1;
  }

  // We recompute the canvasWidth so that it is an integral multiple
  // of the number of cells.

  canvasWidth= numSideCells * cellSize;
```

It is necessary to obtain the patterns defined by the user. If no pattern is defined, a default pattern is used. A pattern consists of:

- The name of a rule set
- The bounds of the pattern. This is either a number of steps to run, the string edge, indicating the pattern should stop upon reaching the edge of the canvas, or the string none, indicating the pattern should continue running until no more changes occur.
- An optional initial configuration of cells

The syntax of these patterns is described in Example 18-2.

Example 18-2   getPatterns( ) method

```
  Vector patterns= getPatterns();

  // If the first pattern has an initial configuration, start
  // automatically; otherwise, create the canvas and add a set
  // of controls so that the user can specify a configuration.

  Pattern firstPattern = (Pattern)patterns.firstElement();

  startAutomatically =
    (firstPattern.getConfiguration().size() > 0);

  // Set the font for the buttons and rule set name field.

  setFont(new Font("Courier", Font.BOLD, 12));
```

We create the layout manager for the applet. The BoardLayout will guarantee that the canvas is always resized to an integral multiple of the number of cells on a side.

```
  BoardLayout boardLayout = new BoardLayout();
  setLayout(boardLayout);

  // Create the canvas and add it to the applet.
```

```
cellCanvas  = new CellCanvas(canvasWidth, cellSize, cellThread,
        patterns);
add(cellCanvas);

// Add the canvas to the layout as the board.

boardLayout.addBoard("Canvas", cellCanvas, numSideCells,
        canvasWidth, BORDER_WIDTH);

if (!startAutomatically) {

  // If we're not running through predetermined patterns,
  // add a set of controls to the applet and layout.

  startButton     = new Button("Start");
  stopButton      = new Button("Stop");
  clearButton     = new Button("Clear");

  String ruleName = firstPattern.getRuleName();
  ruleField       = new RuleTextField(ruleName, RULENAME_SIZE,
                        cellCanvas);
  add(startButton);
  add(stopButton);
  add(clearButton);
  add(ruleField);

  boardLayout.addControl("start", startButton);
  boardLayout.addControl("stop", stopButton);
  boardLayout.addControl("clear", clearButton);
  boardLayout.addControl("rules", ruleField);
}

// Resize to the preferred size for the applet. This will be
// determined by the preferredLayoutSize() method of the
// layout manager.

resize(preferredSize());
}

// The start() method creates a thread for recalculating cell
// values.

public void start() {
  if (cellThread.isAlive()) {
    cellThread.resume();

  } else {
```

```java
    cellThread.setPriority(Thread.MIN_PRIORITY);
    cellThread.start();
  }
}

// The stop() method simply suspends the recalculation thread so
// that the applet won't consume resources while offscreen.

public void stop() {
  cellThread.suspend();
}

// The destroy method actually stops the recalculation thread
// since we won't be needing it anymore.

public void destroy() {
  cellThread.stop();
}

// The run() method checks if the applet is starting
// automatically and, if not, suspends the thread.

public void run() {
  if (!startAutomatically) {
    cellCanvas.suspend();
  }

  cellCanvas.execute();
}

// The update() method paints the border around the board then
// paints the board and controls using the paintComponents()
// method defined in awt.Container.

public void update(Graphics g) {
  paint(g);
  paintComponents(g);
}

// Paint the border around the board.

public void paint(Graphics g) {
  Rectangle r = cellCanvas.bounds();

  g.setColor(Color.black);
  g.draw3DRect(r.x - 1, r.y - 1,
    r.width + 1, r.width + 1, false);
}
```

```
// The action() method handles button presses for the start,
// stop, and clear buttons.

public boolean action(Event event, Object arg) {

  // Call the resume, suspend, and clear methods of the canvas
  // depending on which button was pressed.

  if (event.target instanceof Button) {
    if (event.target.equals(startButton)) {
      cellCanvas.resume();
    } else if (event.target.equals(stopButton)) {
      cellCanvas.suspend();
    } else {
      cellCanvas.clear();
    }

    return true;

  } else {
    return false;
  }
}
```

The getPatterns() method retrieves the script parameter from the user's
HTML code and builds a Vector of Pattern structures based on its value. If
there is no script specified in the HTML code, a default pattern is used:

```
private Vector getPatterns() {

  // Create a vector to hold the patterns read from the user. The
  // vector will be returned as the value of this method.

  Vector patterns = new Vector();
  String param    = getParameter("script");

  // If no script was specified, load rules for Life by default.

  if (param == null) {
    Pattern pat = new Pattern();
    pat.setRuleName("Life");
    pat.setRules(Rules.loadRules("Life"));
    patterns.addElement(pat);

  } else {

    // Use StringTokenizers to break up the pattern strings
    // from the script. Patterns are separated by semicolons.
```

```
StringTokenizer pats = new StringTokenizer(param, ";");

// For each pattern, break it up into name, boundary
// behavior and configuration.

while (pats.hasMoreTokens()) {

    // The parts of a pattern are separated by colons.

    StringTokenizer patValues =
        new StringTokenizer(pats.nextToken(), ":");

    try {

        // Get the name of the rule set and try to load it.
        // If the load fails, skip to the next pattern.

        String ruleName = patValues.nextToken();
        Rules patRules  = Rules.loadRules(ruleName);

        if (patRules == null) {
            continue;
        }

        // Create a new pattern.

        Pattern pat = new Pattern();

        // Set the rule name and rules for the new pattern.

        pat.setRuleName(ruleName);
        pat.setRules(patRules);
```

The setStop() method means the pattern should stop upon hitting the edge of the display. The setSteps() method sets the maximum number of generations to run before stopping:

```
        // Set up the boundary behavior for the pattern.

        String steps = patValues.nextToken();

        if (steps.equals("edge")) {
            pat.setStop(true);
        } else if (steps.equals("none")) {
            pat.setStop(false);
        } else {
            pat.setSteps(Integer.parseInt(steps));
        }
```

```
                // Collect all the cell values for the initial
                // configuration. The x position, y position,
                // and color index are separated by commas.

                while (patValues.hasMoreTokens()) {
                    StringTokenizer patCells =
                        new StringTokenizer(
                            patValues.nextToken(), ",");

                    int cellX =
                        Integer.parseInt(patCells.nextToken());
                    int cellY =
                        Integer.parseInt(patCells.nextToken());
                    int color =
                        Integer.parseInt(patCells.nextToken());

                    pat.addCellValue(
                        new CellValue(cellX, cellY, color));
                }

                // Add the new pattern to the set of patterns.

                patterns.addElement(pat);

            } catch (Exception e) {
                e.printStackTrace();
            }
        }

        // If all the patterns in the script failed to load, use
        // the default pattern.

        if (patterns.size() == 0) {
            Pattern pat = new Pattern();
            pat.setRuleName("Life");
            pat.setRules(Rules.loadRules("Life"));
            patterns.addElement(pat);
        }
    }
    return patterns;
}
// Constants.

private static final int DEFAULT_CELL_SIZE= 4;
private static final int BORDER_WIDTH    = 1;
private static final int RULENAME_SIZE   = 10;

// The thread used to recalculate cell values.
```

```java
    private Thread        cellThread   = new Thread(this);

// The canvas on which the automata are displayed.

    private CellCanvas     cellCanvas;

    // The start, stop, and clear controls.

    private Button          startButton;
    private Button          stopButton;
    private Button          clearButton;

    // The text field with which to enter a rule name.

    private RuleTextField ruleField;

    // The width of the cell canvas in pixels.

    private int            canvasWidth;

    // The width of a cell in pixels.

    private int            cellSize;

    // Whether or not to start running the display immediately.

    private boolean        startAutomatically;
}
```

The CellCanvas Class

The `CellCanvas` class does the actual display of automata. It calls the arena's `apply()` method repeatedly and redraws the cells that have changed. All drawing is done to an offscreen image, which is then displayed on the screen. When a resize occurs, the offscreen image is recreated and the `cellSize` and `cellSide` are recomputed:

```
class CellCanvas extends Canvas {

    // Create a new CellCanvas. The instance variables are
    // initialized and the current pattern is set to be the first
    // pattern in the pattern vector.

    CellCanvas(int width, int newCellSize, Thread thread, Vector
        patterns) {
```

`mySide` is compared to the current width at repaint time. If it is different, the offscreen image is rebuilt and dimensions are recomputed. Its value is set to –1 the first time to force a rebuild:

```
        mySide      = -1;
        cellSide    = width / newCellSize;
        cellSize    = newCellSize;
        cellThread  = thread;
        cellPatterns = patterns;

        Pattern firstPattern = (Pattern)patterns.firstElement();
        setPattern(firstPattern);
    }

    // The update() method for a CellCanvas just calls paint() since
    // there is no background showing.

    public void update(Graphics g) {
        paint(g);
    }

    // The paint() method first adjusts dimensions if the applet has
    // been resized. Then it draws changed cells into an offscreen
    // image and displays it.

    public void paint(Graphics g) {

        // If the current width of the canvas is different then the
        // remembered width, rebuild the offscreen image and recompute
        // the cellSize. Save the new width for next time.
```

```
if (size().width != mySide) {

    // Save the new width.

    mySide    = size().width;

    // recompute the cell size.

    cellSize = mySide / cellSide;

    // If there is an existing offscreen image, free its
    // resources.

    if (offscreen != null) {
        offscreen.flush();
    }

    // Create a new image with the current dimensions.

    offscreen = createImage(mySide, mySide);
}

// Use the graphics object for the offscreen image for drawing
// cells.

Graphics og = offscreen.getGraphics();

synchronized (arena) {
```

When the user clicks with the mouse on a cell in the display, `singleCell` is set so that only that cell is redrawn. The `mouseUp()` method sets `paintColor`, `cellX`, and `cellY`:

```
if (singleCell) {
    og.setColor(paintColor);
    og.fillRect(cellX, cellY, cellSize, cellSize);
    g.drawImage(offscreen, 0, 0, this);
    singleCell = false;

} else if (specific) {
```

After a generation is computed, we only draw the cells that have changed. The `changed` array includes flags indicating which cells have changed. If nothing changes for a generation, we move on to the next pattern if there is one or suspend the cell computation thread if there isn't:

```
boolean somethingChanged = false;
```

```java
for (int i = 0; i < cellSide; i++) {
    for (int j = 0; j < cellSide; j++) {

        // If cell(i,j) has changed, draw it.
        // Note the change if this is the first one.

        if (arena.getChanged(i, j)) {

            if (!somethingChanged) {
                somethingChanged = true;
            }

            // If the stopAtEdge flag is set and
            // we're at one of the edges, stop.

            if (stopAtEdge &&
                (i == 0 || j == 0   ||
                i == cellSide - 1 ||
                j == cellSide - 1)) {
                atEdge = true;
                return;
            }

            // Draw the changed cell.

            og.setColor(getColors()[arena.getCell(i, j)]);
            og.fillRect(i * cellSize, j * cellSize,
                cellSize, cellSize);
        }
    }
}

// Display the updated image on the screen.

g.drawImage(offscreen, 0, 0, this);
specific = false;

// Check for a change. If nothing changed, nothing ever
// will so stop the current pattern and go to the next
// one if there is one.

if (!somethingChanged) {
    if (cellPatterns.size() > 1) {
        noChange = true;
    } else {
        suspend();
    }
```

```
    } else {

        // Redraw all the cells. This is used after a resize
        // and at startup.

        for (int i = 0; i < cellSide; i++) {
            for (int j = 0; j < cellSide; j++) {
                og.setColor(getColors()[arena.getCell(i, j)]);
                og.fillRect(i * cellSize, j * cellSize,
                    cellSize, cellSize);
            }
        }

        g.drawImage(offscreen, 0, 0, this);
    }
  }
}
```

The mouseUp() method increments the color value in the cell pointed to by the mouse. If the color value exceeds the maximum, it wraps around to 0. This method is synchronized on the arena so that a new value added by the user won't be lost:

```
public boolean mouseUp(Event evt, int x, int y) {
  synchronized (arena) {

    // Find the current cell.

    int xoffset = x / cellSize;
    int yoffset = y / cellSize;

    // If we're outside the board, do nothing. This can occur
    // if someone presses the mouse within the canvas then
    // drags it out before releasing.

    if (xoffset < 0 || xoffset >= cellSide ||
        yoffset < 0 || yoffset >= cellSide) {
        return true;
    }

    // Get the current value out of the cell.

    int val = arena.getCell(xoffset, yoffset);

    val = (val + 1) % colors.length;

    // Write the updated value.
```

```
        arena.setCell(xoffset, yoffset, val);

        // Set the new parameters so that repaint can redraw the
        // right cell in the right color.

        paintColor    = getColors()[val];
        cellX         = xoffset * cellSize;
        cellY         = yoffset * cellSize;

        // Set singleCell to true so that repaint() will only
        // draw one cell.

        singleCell = true;

        repaint();
        return true;
    }
}


    // The resume() method resumes the calculation thread if it is
    // suspended.

    void resume() {
      if (threadSuspended) {
        threadSuspended = false;
        cellThread.resume();
      }
    }
```

The suspend() method just sets a flag so that when the execute() method has completed the calculation of the current generation it will suspend the calculation thread:

```
    void suspend() {
      if (!threadSuspended) {
        threadSuspended = true;
      }
    }
```

The clear() method first checks to see if the calculation thread is running. If it is, it just sets a flag telling execute() to clear the display and call suspend() so that calculation will stop after the display is cleared. If the calculation thread is not running, the arena is cleared and the applet is repainted.

```
    void clear() {
      synchronized(arena) {
        if (threadSuspended) {
           arena.clear();
           specific = false;
```

```
          repaint();
        } else {
          clearArena = true;
          suspend();
        }
      }
    }
```

The `setRules()` methods are used to change the current rule set. They change the rule set of the current arena (which also clears it). Like `clear()`, if the calculation thread is not running, the rule set change is done immediately; otherwise, a flag is set that `execute()` can act on. When `setRules()` is called from `nextPattern()`, it sets the `suspendFlag` to false since there won't be any pending calculation or repaint waiting:

```
void setRules(Rules newRules) {
  setRules(newRules, true);
}

void setRules(Rules newRules, boolean suspendFlag) {
  if (arena != null) {
    synchronized(arena) {
      if (!suspendFlag || threadSuspended) {
        arena.setRules(newRules);
        setColors(newRules.getColors());
        specific = false;
        repaint();

      } else {
        rules = newRules;
        suspend();
      }
    }

  } else {

    // If this is the first time, create a new arena.

    arena = new Arena(cellSide, cellSide, newRules);
    setColors(newRules.getColors());
    setBackground(getColors()[newRules.getInitialValue()]);
  }
}
```

The `execute()` method is the master method for the canvas. It recalculates new generations and performs various actions based on flags set by other methods. If the `clearArena` flag is set, the arena is cleared. If the rules variable is not `null`, the rule set is changed to its value. If `threadSuspended` is set, the calculation thread is suspended. Finally, if the number of steps for the current pattern has run out, the pattern reached the edge of the display with `stopAtEdge` set, or the pattern remained unchanged through a generation, `execute()` advances to the next pattern.

```java
void execute() {
  while (true) {

    // Clear the arena.

    if (clearArena) {
        arena.clear();
        clearArena = false;
        repaint();

    } else if (rules != null) {

        // Switch to a new rule set.

        arena.setRules(rules);
        setColors(rules.getColors());
        rules = null;
        repaint();
    }

    // If a method has requested that the thread be suspended,
    // suspend it.

    if (threadSuspended) {
        cellThread.suspend();
    }

    // Check if it's time to end the current pattern. If so,
    // reset the flags and step count.

    if (steps++ == maxSteps || atEdge || noChange) {
        steps = 0;
        atEdge = false;
        noChange = false;
        nextPattern();
        repaint();
    }

    // Calculate the next generation.

    synchronized(arena) {
        arena.apply();
    }
```

```
    // Paint the cells that have changed.

    specific = true;
    repaint();

    // Be a good citizen and sleep briefly.

    try {
        cellThread.sleep(SLEEP_TIME);
    } catch (InterruptedException e) {
    }
  }
}

// The nextPattern() method advances the current pattern to the
// next pattern in the set. If it reaches the end, it goes
// back to the first pattern.

private void nextPattern() {
  pattern = (pattern + 1) % cellPatterns.size();

  Pattern current = (Pattern)cellPatterns.elementAt(pattern);
  setPattern(current);
}

// setPattern() sets the boundary flags, the rule set and the
// initial cell configuration based on a new pattern.

private void setPattern(Pattern current) {

  // We stop at the edge of the display if there are multiple
  // patterns or the single pattern says to.

  stopAtEdge = cellPatterns.size() > 1 || current.stop();
  maxSteps   = current.steps();

  setRules(current.getRules(), false);
  setInitialConfiguration(current.getConfiguration());
  }
```

The `setInitialConfiguration()` method sets an initial set of cells in the arena to prespecified values. This is used for the applet's automatic display mode:

```
private void setInitialConfiguration(Vector cells) {
  Enumeration e = cells.elements();

  while (e.hasMoreElements()) {
    CellValue c = (CellValue)e.nextElement();
```

```
      arena.setCell(c.x, c.y, c.color);
  }
}

// Return the array of colors obtained from the current rule set.

private Color[] getColors() {
  return colors;
}

// Set the current array of colors.

private void setColors(Color colorArray[]) {
  colors = colorArray;
}

// The amount of time to sleep between calculations.

private static final int SLEEP_TIME = 10;

// The offscreen image where cells are drawn.

private Image    offscreen    = null;

// The thread used to recalculate cell values.

private Thread cellThread;

// The rule set that will become current at the next time
// through execute().

private Rules    rules      = null;

// The array of colors obtained from the current rule set.

private Color    colors[];

// Flags passed to repaint().

private boolean singleCell  = false;
private boolean specific    = false;

// The color and location of a particular cell to repaint().

private Color    paintColor;
private int      cellX;
private int      cellY;
```

```
// The number of cells on a side of the canvas.

private int     cellSide;

// The width of a single cell in pixels.

private int     cellSize;

// The width of the canvas in pixels.

private int     mySide;

// The number of generations that have been computed for the
// current pattern.

private int     steps    = 0;

// The maximum number of generations before stopping the current
// pattern. It's initialized to -1 by default so that steps will
// likely never reach it.

private int     maxSteps    = -1;

// The current index into the vector of patterns.

private int     pattern    = 0;

// Flags passed to execute.

private boolean threadSuspended= false;
private boolean clearArena     = false;
private boolean stopAtEdge     = false;
private boolean atEdge         = false;
private boolean noChange       = false;

// The current set of patterns.

private Vector  cellPatterns;

// The arena which calculates cell values.

private Arena   arena    = null;
}
```

The RuleTextField Class

The `RuleTextField` class holds the name of the current rule set for the `Cellular` applet. It overrides `keyDown` to load a new rule set when a newline or carriage return is pressed. If no rule set can be found with the new name, the field reverts to its previous value:

```
class RuleTextField extends TextField {

  // Create a new RuleTextField. The canvas it's associated with is
  // saved so that its setRules() method can be called.

  RuleTextField(String text, int size, CellCanvas canvas) {
    super(text, size);
    previousText = text;
    myCanvas     = canvas;
  }

  // Check the key that was just pressed. If it was a newline or a
  // carriage return, try to load the rule class named in the
  // text field. If the load fails, restore the previous rule class
  // name.

  public boolean keyDown(Event evt, int key) {
    if (key == '\n' || key == '\r') {
      Rules rules = Rules.loadRules(getText());

      if (rules != null) {
        myCanvas.setRules(rules);
        previousText = getText();

      } else {
        setText(previousText);
      }

      return true;
    }

    return false;
  }

  // The rule name from the last successful load.

  private String    previousText;

  // The canvas whose rules we set.

  private CellCanvas myCanvas;
```

```
}
```

The CellValue Class

The CellValue class encapsulates x and y positions and a color index for a cell so that they may be manipulated as a unit:

```
class CellValue {

   // Create a new CellValue.

   CellValue(int cellX, int cellY, int cellColor) {
      x     = cellX;
      y     = cellY;
      color = cellColor;
   }

   int x;
   int y;
   int color;
}
```

The Pattern Class

The `Pattern` class holds a rule set, a rule name, boundary behavior information, and a set of `CellValue` objects representing an initial automaton configuration:

```
class Pattern {
  // Set and get the rule set.

  void setRules(Rules newRules) {
    rules = newRules;
  }

  Rules getRules() {
    return rules;
  }

  // Set and get the rule name.

  void setRuleName(String name) {
    ruleName = name;
  }

  String getRuleName() {
    return ruleName;
  }

  // Add another cell value to the initial configuration.

  void addCellValue(CellValue cval) {
    cellValues.addElement(cval);
  }

  // Get the initial configuration.

  Vector getConfiguration() {
    return cellValues;
  }

  // Set and get the flag indicating whether or not to stop at the
  // edge of the canvas.

  void setStop(boolean flag) {
    stopFlag = flag;
  }

  boolean stop() {
    return stopFlag;
  }
```

```
// Set and get the maximum number of generations for the pattern.

void setSteps(int steps) {
  numSteps = steps;
}

int steps() {
  return numSteps;
}

Rules    rules;
String   ruleName;
Vector   cellValues    = new Vector();
boolean  stopFlag      = false;
int      numSteps      = -1;
}
```

The BoardLayout Class

The applet has sizing requirements that are not adequately handled by Java's default layout managers, so we create a custom layout manager for the Cellular applet. The `BoardLayout` class implements the `LayoutManager` interface. It arranges the display canvas and controls for the applet, reshaping them if necessary when the display is resized.

The layout is divided into two areas: the board and the controls. The board is guaranteed to be sized into a square whose side is an integral multiple of the side of a single square on the board. A border can be specified for the board that will be taken into account when it is laid out. The user controls flow into the space below the board. If the controls cannot be made to fit in the space below the board, they are not displayed. If the board cannot fit even when shrunk to its minimum size, it will be clipped at the right and bottom:

```
package ca;

import java.util.*;
import java.awt.*;

// The BoardLayout class provides layout support for grids of cells
// as might be used in a board game.

public class BoardLayout implements LayoutManager {
```

The two `addBoard()` methods add the board component to the layout. The long form `addBoard(String, Component, int, int, int)` allows the three board parameters to be set at the same time:

```
public void addBoard(String name, Component newBoard, int
        numCellsOnSide, int boardSide, int borderWidth) {
  board = newBoard;
  setCellParameters(numCellsOnSide, boardSide, borderWidth);
}

public void addBoard(String name, Component newBoard) {
  board = newBoard;
}
```

The `setCellParameters()` method sets the three defining values for a board:

- The number of cells on a side

- The minimum allowed length of a side in pixels

- The width of the border around the board

```
public void setCellParameters(int numCellsOnSide, int
        minBoardSide, int borderWidth) {
  cells   = numCellsOnSide;
  minSide = minBoardSide;
  border  = borderWidth;
}
```

The `addControl()` method is a more descriptive name for the generic `addLayoutComponent()` that all `LayoutManager` objects must implement. It adds a control to the layout (usually a button, text item, and so on):

```
public void addControl(String name, Component comp) {
  addLayoutComponent(name, comp);
}

// addLayoutComponent() just adds a component to the Vector of
// controls.

public void addLayoutComponent(String name, Component comp) {
  controls.addElement(comp);
}

// removeLayoutComponent() will remove a control from the
// Vector of controls and hide it.

public void removeLayoutComponent(Component comp) {
  controls.removeElement(comp);
  comp.hide();
}
```

The `layoutContainer()` method formats the board and controls. It is called automatically when an applet is resized. The approach for this layout is to make the board as large as possible while leaving room for the controls. If the controls will not fit, either horizontally or vertically, they are not displayed. The vertical space taken up by the controls depends on the width of the applet. As many controls as possible are placed in each control row:

```
public void layoutContainer(Container parent) {

    // The area available for board and controls is the size of the
    // parent minus the parent's insets and the border width
    // specified in the layout parameters. Insets are padding
    // around the edges of some Containers.

    Insets insets   =   parent.insets();

    // The width available for the board is the parent's width
    // minus the left and right insets and a border on two sides of
    // the board.

    int    innerWidth  = parent.size().width -
        (insets.left + insets.right + border * 2);

    // The height available for the board and controls is the
    // parent's height minus the top and bottom insets and a
    // border on two sides of the board.

    int    innerHeight = parent.size().height -
        (insets.top + insets.bottom + border * 2);

    // The maximum height available for controls is the
    // innerHeight minus the minimum height of the board.

    int    maxControlHeight= innerHeight - minSide;

    // The maximum width available for controls is the maximum
    // board width plus the borders since the controls are not
    // constrained by the borders around the board.

    int    maxControlWidth = innerWidth + (border * 2);

    // Fetch the width, height, rowHeights, and rowLengths for
    // the controls given the maximum width.

    ControlParameters cParams =
        controlParameters(maxControlWidth);
```

```
    // If the controls will not fit, remove them and just show the
    // board.

    if (cParams.width  > maxControlWidth ||
        cParams.height > maxControlHeight) {
        layoutBoardOnly(insets, innerWidth, innerHeight);
        return;
    }
```

Now we determine how big the board will be. We know the board at its minimum size will fit vertically from our previous calculations for controls. If the minimum board width is greater than the available width, draw the board at its minimum size and let it be clipped at the right:

```
    int side;

    if (innerWidth < minSide) {

        // If the available space is smaller than the minimum board
        // size, use the minimum board size (the board will be
        // clipped).

        side = minSide;

    } else {

        // If there is room for the board horizontally, round the
        // smaller of the width and height dimensions down to
        // a multiple of the number of cells.

        side = Math.min(innerWidth, (innerHeight -
            cParams.height)) / cells * cells;
    }

    // Reshape the board. If the board is too wide for its area,
    // position it at 0 and let it be clipped; otherwise, center
    // it in the available space.

    board.reshape(
        Math.max(innerWidth  - side, 0) / 2 + insets.left + border,
        (innerHeight - cParams.height - side) / 2 + insets.top +
            border, side, side);

    // Make the board visible.

    board.show();

    // Place the controls. The ControlParameters object cParams
```

```
// contains all the information necessary: the lengths of the
// rows and their heights, and the total height of the
// controls.

Enumeration e    = controls.elements();
int    cols      = 0;
int    row       = 0;

// Horizontally, the controls start at the very left of the
// area inside the container's padding.

int    xoffset = insets.left;

// Vertically, the controls start just below the board and its
// border. i.e. after the top inset, the top border, the
// board, and the bottom border.

int    yoffset = (innerHeight - cParams.height) + insets.top +
    (border * 2);
```

Here, we step through the controls and place them. The row lengths from the
`ControlParameters` are used to determine when to move to the next row. The
row heights from the `ControlParameters` are used to determine how tall to
make each control. The minimum width is used for each control:

```
while (e.hasMoreElements()) {
    Component c   = (Component)e.nextElement();
    Dimension d   = c.minimumSize();

    // The height of the current row.

    int    rHeight =
        ((Integer)cParams.heights.elementAt(row)).intValue();

    // The length of the current row.

    int    rLength =
        ((Integer)cParams.lengths.elementAt(row)).intValue();

    // Reshape the current component. Place it at the current
    // x and y offsets and make it minimum width and the height
    // of the current row.

    c.reshape(xoffset, yoffset, d.width, rHeight);

    // Make the component visible.

    c.show();
```

```
    // Advance to the next column. If we're at the end of the
    // current row, reset the column to 0 and the x offset to
    // the left inset then add the height of the current row
    // to the y offset.

    if (++cols >= rLength) {
        cols = 0;
        xoffset = insets.left;
        yoffset+= rHeight;
        row++;

    } else {

        // If we haven't reached the end of the row, just add
        // the width of the current component to the x offset.

        xoffset += c.size().width;
    }
  }
}
```

The `preferredLayoutSize()` method is used by the enclosing `Container` objects to determine how much space to allocate to a `Component`. For the board layout, we'll treat `preferred` and `minimum` the same because there isn't any well-defined preferred size for a board:

```
public Dimension preferredLayoutSize(Container parent) {
  return minimumLayoutSize(parent);
}
```

The `minimumLayoutSize()` method returns the smallest area the layout can occupy without violating its structure in some way. For the board layout, this is an area that is as wide as the greater of the board's minimum width and the maximum width of any control, and as tall as the minimum board height plus the controls. It's possible that a smaller area could be generated by making the layout wider rather than taller, but we're not pursuing that approach. The minimum width will always be as small as possible:

```
public Dimension minimumLayoutSize(Container parent) {

    // Find the widest control. We can't make the board layout
    // any narrower than that.

    int        minControlWidth = maxWidthOfControls();

    Inset      insets     = parent.insets();
    Dimension d           = new Dimension();
```

```
// Set the minimum width to the greater of the minimum size
// of the board and the width of the widest control.

int innerWidth = Math.max(minSide, minControlWidth);

// The actual minimum size of the layout has to take into
// account the insets and the borders of the board.

d.width  = insets.left + innerWidth + insets.right + border *
    2;

// The minimum height of the layout is the top and bottom
// insets plus the minimum height of the board plus the
// borders plus the calculated height of the controls given
// the width.

d.height = insets.top + minSide +
    controlParameters(innerWidth).height + insets.bottom +
        border * 2;

return d;
}
```

The `layoutBoardOnly()` method displays the board when there is no room for the controls. It makes the controls invisible and devotes all the available space to the board:

```
private void layoutBoardOnly(Insets insets, int innerWidth,
    int innerHeight) {

// Set the size of the board to the maximum that will fit or
// to the boards minimum size if it won't fit.

int side = Math.max(Math.min(innerWidth, innerHeight),
    minSide) / cells * cells;

// Reshape the board. If the board is too large for the
// available space, clip it on the right and bottom.

board.reshape(
    Math.max(innerWidth  - side, 0) / 2 + insets.left + border,
    Math.max(innerHeight - side, 0) / 2 + insets.top + border,
    side, side);

// Make the board visible.

board.show();
```

326 *Java by Example*

```
  // Make the components invisible.

  Enumeration e = controls.elements();

  while (e.hasMoreElements()) {
    Component c  =  (Component)e.nextElement();

    c.hide();
  }
}


// The maxWidthOfControls() method simply steps through the set
// of controls and returns the minimum width of the widest
// control.

private int maxWidthOfControls() {
  Enumeration e  = controls.elements();
  int          max = 0;

  while (e.hasMoreElements()) {
    Component c = (Component)e.nextElement();
    max           = Math.max(max, c.minimumSize().width);
  }

  return max;
}
```

The controlParameters() method determines the width, height, row lengths
and row heights for a set of controls. It adds controls to a row until the maximum
width is reached, then it adds another row. The row height for a row is set to the
maximum height of any element in the row.

```
private ControlParameters controlParameters(int maxWidth) {
  int rowWidth    = 0;  // The width of the current row.
  int totalHeight = 0;  // The total height of all controls.
  int rowHeight   = 0;  // The height of the current row.
  int totalWidth  = 0;  // The total width of all controls.
  int numColumns  = 0;  // The number of columns in a row.

  // We keep track of the heights and lengths of each row.

  Vector rowHeights = new Vector();
  Vector rowLengths = new Vector();

  Enumeration e = controls.elements();

  while (e.hasMoreElements()) {
    Component c  = (Component)e.nextElement();
```

```
      Dimension d   = c.minimumSize();
      rowWidth      += d.width;
```

For each component, if its width does not overflow the maximum width for a row, increment the number of columns for the row and adjust the row height to the height of the new component if it is taller than any of the previous components in the row:

```
      if (rowWidth <= maxWidth) {
         numColumns++;
         rowHeight = Math.max(rowHeight, d.height);

      } else {

         // If the current component makes the row too wide,
         // end the row. Add the current height and number
         // of columns for the row to the vectors of row
         // parameters, adjust the maximum width of controls
         // if necessary, and reset the row width, row height,
         // and number of columns to start a new row.

         rowHeights.addElement(new Integer(rowHeight));
         rowLengths.addElement(new Integer(numColumns));

         totalWidth    = Math.max(totalWidth, rowWidth -
                           d.width);
         totalHeight  += rowHeight;
         rowWidth      = d.width;
         rowHeight     = d.height;
         numColumns    = 1;
      }
   }

   // End the final row.

   rowHeights.addElement(new Integer(rowHeight));
   rowLengths.addElement(new Integer(numColumns));

   totalWidth   = Math.max(totalWidth, rowWidth);
   totalHeight += rowHeight;

   // Return an instance of ControlParameters that contains all
   // the information about the controls.

   return new ControlParameters(totalWidth, totalHeight,
            rowHeights, rowLengths);
}
```

These are the instance variables used by the layout. The layout keeps track of the board, the set of controls, the number of cells on one side of the board, the minimum length of a side of the board, and the width of the border around the board:

```
    private Component board;
    private Vector    controls = new Vector();
    private int       cells;
    private int       minSide;
    private int       border;
}
```

The `ControlParameters` class is a helper class that wraps up several values associated with the layout of a set of controls so that they can be returned from a function as a single value. This is similar to the use of `Dimension`, `Point`, `Rectangle`, and so on, in the awt package:

```
class ControlParameters {

  // Create a new instance of ControlParameters.
  ControlParameters(int cWidth, int rHeight, Vector rowHeights,
      Vector rowLengths) {
    width    = cWidth;
    height   = rHeight;
    heights  = rowHeights;
    lengths  = rowLengths;
  }

  // The parameters of interest.

  int    width;
  int    height;
  Vector heights;
  Vector lengths;
}
```

The Arena Class

The `Arena` class takes care of actually calculating new generations for the automata. It loops through the current array of cells, saves new values for each cell in a separate array, and then swaps the arrays. Two copies of the cell array are maintained so that the current state of each cell may be used in computing the next states of its neighbors:

```
package ca;

// The Arena class creates an array of cells and applies a set of
// rules to each cell.
```

```java
public class Arena {

    // Create a new Arena with dimensions x and y and a new rule set.
    // Each cell is initialized with the result of the rule set's
    // getInitialValue() method.

    public Arena(int x, int y, Rules newRules) {
        cellWidth   = x;
        cellHeight  = y;

        // The cells array holds the current cell values.

        cells     = new int[x][y];

        // the newCells array is where newly computed values
        // are placed.

        newCells = new int[x][y];

        // The changed array keeps track of which cells have changed
        // and will need to be redrawn.

        changed   = new boolean[x][y];

        setRules(newRules);
    }

    // The setRules() method associates a new set of rules with the
    // arena and calls the clear() method to initialize the cells to
    // the rule set's initial value.

    public void setRules(Rules newRules) {
        rules      = newRules;
        clear();
    }

    // The clear() method steps through each cell and initializes its
    // value to the initial value for the current rule set.

    public void clear() {
        int initialValue = getInitialValue();

        for (int i = 0; i < cellWidth; i++) {
            for (int j = 0; j < cellHeight; j++) {
                cells[i][j] = initialValue;
            }
        }
    }
```

```java
// Return the initial value obtained from the arena's current
// rule set.

public int getInitialValue() {
  return rules.getInitialValue();
}


// Return the value of a cell.

public int getCell(int x, int y) {
  return cells[x][y];
}


// Set the value of a cell.

public void setCell(int x, int y, int val) {
  cells[x][y] = val;
}


// Return the changed flag associated with a particular cell.
// The entry in the changed array for a cell is set to true if
// the value calculated for it during an apply is different from
// its current value.

public boolean getChanged(int x, int y) {
  return changed[x][y];
}
```

The `apply()` method steps through the cells and calls the current rule set's process method on each cell. The result is placed in the `newCells` array. If the result is different than the current value of the cell, an entry is made for the cell in the changed array. After all the cells have been processed, the roles of the `cells` and `newCells` arrays are reversed so that the `newCells` array becomes the `cells` array for the next `apply()`:

```java
public void apply() {
  for (int i = 0; i < cellWidth; i++) {
    for (int j = 0; j < cellHeight; j++) {

      int result       = rules.process(cells, i, j);
      newCells[i][j]    = result;
      changed[i][j]     = (cells[i][j] != result);
    }
  }

  // Reverse the roles of the cells and newCells arrays.
  swap();
}
```

```
// The swap() method exchanges the cells and newCells arrays.
private void swap() {
  int[][] tempcells  = cells;
  cells            = newCells;
  newCells         = tempcells;
}

private int       cellWidth;      // Width of the cells array.
private int       cellHeight;     // Height of the cells array.
private int[][]   cells;          // The array of current cell
                                  // values.
private int[][]   newCells;       // The array of new cell
                                  // values.
private boolean[][]changed;       // Flags to indicate which
                                  // cells have changed.
private Rules     rules;          // The current rule set.
}
```

The Rules Class

The `Rules` class is an abstract class that defines the interface for rule sets and provides support methods for defining rules. (For a review of abstract classes, see *Abstract Methods* on page 30.) Several helper methods are defined in the `Rules` class that make it easier to write rules. An `apply()` method can use the methods in formulating rules. All the helper methods are declared `protected` since they only make sense when called by the `apply()` method of a subclass:

```
package ca;

import java.awt.Color;

// The Rules class supports the definition of different rule sets for
// a cellular automaton. Each new rule set extends the Rules class
// and defines three methods:
//
// getColors()        -- Return an array containing the colors used
//                       by a rule set.
//
// getInitialValue()-- Return the index of the initial color
//                       value for the cells.
//
// apply()            -- Return a new color index for a cell based
//                       on the values of its neighbors. This is
//                       called for each cell in the grid.

public abstract class Rules {
```

```
// The three methods that all subclasses of Rules must define.

public abstract Color[] getColors();
public abstract int     getInitialValue();
public abstract int     apply();
```

The `loadRules()` method looks up the name of a subclass of `Rules` in the `ca.rules` package and returns an instance of the class if it's found; otherwise it returns `null`:

```
public static Rules loadRules(String name) {
  try {
    Class ruleClass = Class.forName("ca.rules." + name);
    return (Rules)ruleClass.newInstance();

  } catch (Exception e) {
    return null;
  }
}
```

The `process()` method is called by an instance of `Arena` for each cell. It initializes the set of neighbors for the cell, and then it calls the `apply()` method. `cellVal` will wrap around to the other side of the board if it is called at an edge:

```
public int process(int [][] cells, int i, int j) {
  neighbors[0] = cellVal(cells, i - 1, j - 1);
  neighbors[1] = cellVal(cells, i, j - 1);
  neighbors[2] = cellVal(cells, i + 1, j - 1);
  neighbors[3] = cellVal(cells, i - 1, j);
  neighbors[4] = cellVal(cells, i + 1, j);
  neighbors[5] = cellVal(cells, i - 1, j + 1);
  neighbors[6] = cellVal(cells, i, j + 1);
  neighbors[7] = cellVal(cells, i + 1, j + 1);
  selfValue    = cellVal(cells, i, j);

  return apply();
}

// Helper functions that return the values of particular
// neighboring cells.

// Upper left.

protected int ul() {
  return neighbors[0];
}

// Upper center.
```

```
protected int uc() {
  return neighbors[1];
}

// Upper right.

protected int ur() {
  return neighbors[2];
}

// Left.

protected int l() {
  return neighbors[3];
}

// Right.

protected int r() {
  return neighbors[4];
}

// Lower left.

protected int ll() {
  return neighbors[5];
}

// Lower center.

protected int lc() {
  return neighbors[6];
}

// Lower right.

protected int lr() {
  return neighbors[7];
}

// The current cell.

protected int self() {
return selfValue;
}
```

The `getNeighbors()` method returns the entire array of neighbor values in case a rule set wants to perform some operation that iterates over the set of neighbors:

```java
protected int[] getNeighbors() {
  return neighbors;
}

// The anyCell() method returns true if any of the neighbors have
// the value val.

protected boolean anyCell(int val) {
  for (int i = 0; i < numNeighbors; i++) {
    if (neighbors[i] == val) {
        return true;
    }
  }
  return false;
}

// The numCells() method returns the number of neighbors that
// have the value val.

protected int numCells(int val) {
  int result = 0;

  for (int i = 0; i < numNeighbors; i++) {
    if (neighbors[i] == val) {
        result++;
    }
  }

  return result;
}

// The numLinear() method returns the number of rook move
// neighbors that have the value val.

protected int numLinear(int val) {
  int result = 0;

  if (uc() == val) {
    result++;
  }

  if (l() == val) {
    result++;
  }
```

```
   if (r() == val) {
      result++;
   }

   if (lc() == val) {
      result++;
   }

   return result;
}


// The numDiag() method returns the number of bishop move
// neighbors that have the value val.

protected int numDiag(int val) {
   int result = 0;

   if (ul() == val) {
      result++;
   }

   if (ur() == val) {
      result++;
   }

   if (ll() == val) {
      result++;
   }

   if (lr() == val) {
      result++;
   }

   return result;
}
```

The `cellVal()` method encapsulates the behavior of the automaton at the edge of the board. Negative x and y positions and position values that are too large wrap around to the opposite side of the board:

```
private int cellVal(int[][] cells, int x, int y) {

   if (x < 0) {
      x = cells.length + x;
   } else if (x >= cells.length) {
      x = x - cells.length;
   }
```

```
   if (y < 0) {
      y = cells[0].length + y;
   } else if (y >= cells[0].length) {
      y = y - cells[0].length;
   }

  return cells[x][y];
}


// The number of neighbors for a cell. This can be used in
// apply methods that iterate through the set of neighbors.

protected static final int numNeighbors = 8;

// The array of neighbors. This array is filled by the process
// method before an apply method is called.

private int[] neighbors = new int[numNeighbors];

// The value of the current cell. It is set by the process method
// before an apply method is called.

private int   selfValue;
}
```

Summary

This chapter and final example applet bring together many features of the Java language discussed throughout this book—arrays, interfaces, event handling, type comparisons, threaded execution, and so on. The Cellular applet emphasizes use of packages to organize Java programs into functional groups. Also, since the Cellular applet places demands on sizing that the default Java layout managers can't support, we develop a custom BoardLayout class. Not only does this class support the Cellular applet, but it could also be used for other board-oriented games such as chess or checkers.

This completes our discussion and examples of Java applets. In *Part 3— Appendixes*, we provide a high-level introduction to object-oriented programming and a quick reference to the Java language.

Appendixes

PART THREE

APPENDIX A

- Classes

- Instances

- Inheritance

- Encapsulation

- Overloading

- Polymorphism

Object-Oriented Programming

Overview

Although Java's syntax will be familiar to C programmers, its object-oriented features may not. In this appendix, we'll cover some basic characteristics of object-oriented (OO) programming as it pertains to Java. For C++ programmers and others already familiar with OO programming, you may want to skip this appendix. It is just a summary of Java's basic OO language features, and they are quite similar to those in C++. For C programmers who are new to object-oriented programming, successfully working with Java means you'll have to grasp a few OO concepts:

- **Classes** — The fundamental structure in Java. Classes are similar to structured types in C.

- **Instances** — Similar to a value of a structured type

- **Inheritance** — Language construct that allows for classes to be related to one another so that a subclass can *inherit* features of its superclass

- **Encapsulation** — Language construct that enables programmers to limit access to parts of a program

- **Overloading** — The ability to use the same name for multiple methods (Java methods are similar to C functions)

- **Polymorphism** – Ability to deal with multiple types based on a common feature

We'll talk briefly about each of these in this appendix.

Note that we only intend to provide a simple introduction to object-oriented programming.

Classes

The fundamental structure in Java is a *class*, and a Java program consists of a set of class definitions. A class is a data structure, similar to a `record` in Pascal or a `struct` in C, with some extra features. A Java program is a set of class definitions, with at least one of those class definitions containing a function (called a *method*) named `main`.

In traditional programming languages, functions and statements are the primary elements. Data structures serve a secondary purpose. FORTRAN and the original version of Basic are extreme examples of this, providing only simple arrays as data structures. This primary emphasis on functions and secondary emphasis on data structures is reversed in an object-oriented language like Java. In Java, the class is primary.

Unlike C and other traditional programming languages, Java does not support free-standing functions. All functions in Java are associated with classes. Instead of building a program around a set of interrelated functions, you build a Java program out of a set of data structures and their affiliated operations.

Let's look at an example. Suppose we want to write a word processing program. Using a traditional approach, we would probably begin by thinking about the operations the program needs to perform. Our list of operations might look something like this:

- Read files
- Write files
- Accept user input
- Support cursor movement
- Insert and delete text
- Format paragraphs

We would then write a program with functions to carry out these operations.

Object-oriented programming languages such as Java encourage a different approach. Instead of thinking about the operations the word processor needs to perform, we would start by determining the sorts of objects the word processor needs to manipulate. If we were working with an object-oriented language, our list would look something like this:

- Files

- Characters

- Lines of text

- Paragraphs

The advantage of the object-oriented approach is that the code we write will tend to be more generic and reusable than code written in the traditional way. Instead of writing code that is narrowly focussed on completing the current task, we'll develop a set of general-purpose operations that make sense for an object such as a file or a line of text.

Instances

Classes in Java correspond to structured types in a language such as C or Pascal. A member of a class, like a member of a structured type, is called an *instance* of the class. (Note that the use of the term member here should not be confused with the use of member in C++, which refers to the attributes of an object.) Creating an instance is referred to as *instantiating* the class. At the time a class is instantiated, memory is allocated for the new instance and that memory is initialized with appropriate values.

Inheritance

Classes can be related to one another. One class may be a *subclass* of another class. For example, say we had a class describing wagons, and we called it the Wagon class. Then, if we want a class describing red wagons—the RedWagon class—we could make it a subclass of Wagon. (Wagon—or any parent class—is referred to as a *superclass*.) This means that all the attributes and operations defined for the Wagon class would also be applicable to the RedWagon class. (This is generally referred to as *single inheritance*.)

Using inheritance can eliminate a lot of code redundancy since many operations need only be defined once and can be used for free within subclasses. Membership in a subclass implies membership in the superclass. That is, a RedWagon is a Wagon. Some object-oriented languages allow a class to be a direct subclass of more than one other class. (This is generally referred to as *multiple inheritance*.) This is *not* allowed in Java. However, Java does provide a facility that approximates the behavior of multiple inheritance. We discuss this facility in detail in *Interfaces as Types* on page 69.

Encapsulation

Java provides the ability to limit access to parts of a program. A programmer can provide an abstraction such as a stack or a tree without letting the user of the abstraction see inside it. Not only does this prevent the user from accidentally breaking a program by changing its internal state in an incorrect way, but it also prevents them from writing code that depends on the implementation details of such an abstraction. This makes code much easier to maintain and modify since a programmer knows exactly which code will be affected if the implementation of an abstraction is changed.

As a result of encapsulation, the code you write tends to be modular. As a general rule, programs should be organized into discrete groups so that information is shared on a need-to-know basis. That way, when a feature changes, you only need to update the parts of the program that really depend on that feature. An object-oriented approach makes this kind of programming straightforward by grouping all the operations that need to know about the internals of a data structure within that data structure. For example, with our word processing example in mind, only the operations defined for a line of text are given access to the internals of that structure. Example A-1 shows how such a structure might look in Java.

Example A-1 Encapsulation in a Class

```java
public class LineOfText {
  // Return the length of the line.
  public int getLength() {
    return length;
  }

  // Return the current index.
  public int getCurrentIndex() {
    return index;
  }.

  // Advance the current index by one if it's not already
  // at the end.
  public void forwardCharacter() {
    if (index < length - 1) {
      index++;
    }
  }

  private int length;
  private int index;
  private String buffer;
```

The important point to make about this example is that the LineOfText object has length, index, and buffer fields that are *not* exposed to any piece of code outside of this particular class. These fields are private, and are specified so by use of the private keyword. Only the getLength(), getCurrentIndex(), and forwardCharacter() methods in the LineOfText class are visible to other parts of the program that use this class.

Overloading

Overloading refers to using the same name for multiple methods (Java methods are similar to C functions) within a class. In Java, we can do this. The only stipulation is that the argument list and return type for each method must be unique. The selection of the correct method to call is based on the types of the arguments in a call expression. For example, in Example A-2, the class Example has two methods called doubleIt.

Example A-2 Method Overloading

```
  class Example {
❶     public static int doubleIt(int x) {
          return x * 2;
      }

❷     public static String doubleIt(String x) {
          return x + x;
      }
  }
```

In Example A-2, lines ❶ and ❷ both define methods named doubleIt. However, as long as the argument lists in each have different types, each method is distinct, and there is no confusion. A program can call both methods without a problem, as illustrated in Example A-3.

Example A-3 Calling an Overloaded Method

```
❶ int intResult    = Example.doubleIt(3);
❷ String stringResult= Example.doubleIt("wow");
```

In this example, the method doubleIt is *overloaded*. Specifically:

❶ Is a call to the doubleIt() method (in the Example class) that returns an integer. intResult would hold the integer 6.

❷ Is a call to the `doubleIt()` method (in the `Example` class) that returns a string. `stringResult` would hold the string wowwow.

Polymorphism

In C, functions can only operate on a specific set of argument types. This is inconvenient and can lead to code redundancy. For example, the following code shows a C function that checks to see if its argument's color is blue:

```c
/* take an automobile and return true if it's blue */

int
is_blue(struct car *c)
{
    return c->color == BLUE;
}
```

Unfortunately, this function only works for cars. It would be nice if we could have a generic test for the quality of "blueness," but C has no way of expressing this. In Java, we could write a method like this one:

```java
class Example {
  static boolean isBlue(ColoredObject o) {
    return o.getColor() == Colors.blue;
  }
}
```

This is polymorphism at work. Any class could declare itself to be a `ColoredObject` and its instances could then be passed to the `isBlue()` method. A method that can operate on arguments of multiple types is referred to as polymorphic. This ability to deal with multiple types based on a common feature is very powerful, as illustrated in the chapter on *Interfaces as Types* on page 69.

APPENDIX
B

- Java for C Programmers

- Java for C++ Programmers

- Data Types

- Operators

- Control Flow and Iteration

- Comments

- Keywords

- Java Classes and Interfaces

- HTML applet and param Tags

Quick Reference

Java for C Programmers

Table B-1 compares some typical C syntax and the Java equivalents.

Table B-1 Java Syntax Equivalents for C Programmers

C Syntax	Java Equivalent
`char *foo;`	`String foo;`
`char **foo;`	`String[] foo;`
`int *foo = (int *) malloc(` `    5 * sizeof(int));`	`int[] foo = new int[5];`
`int foo[3][4];`	`int[][] foo = new int[3][4];`
`#define foo 5`	`static final int foo = 5;`
`printf(` `    " Value equals: %d\n",val);`	`System.out.println(` `    " Value equals: " + val);`
`char c = getc(stdin);`	`char c = (char)System.in.read();`
`free(ptr);`	`N/A`
`int x = foo.bar;` `int x = foo->bar;`	`int x = foo.bar;` `int x = foo.bar;`
`int main (int argc, char **argv);`	`public static void main (String[] args);`

Java by Example

Java for C++ Programmers

Table B-2 compares some typical C++ syntax and the Java equivalents.

Table B-2 Java Syntax Equivalents for C++ Programmers

C++ Syntax	Java Equivalent
`char* foo;`	`String foo;`
`char** foo;`	`String[] foo;`
`int* foo = new int[5];`	`int[] foo = new int[5];`
`int** foo = new int[3][4];`	`int[][] foo = new int[3][4];`
`const int foo = 5`	`static final int foo = 5;`
`cout    << "The answer is: "` `        << answer;`	`System.out.println(` `    "The answer is: " + answer);`
`char c; cin >> c;`	`char c = (char)System.in.read();`
`delete ptr;`	`N/A`
`int x = foo.bar;` `int x = foo->bar;`	`int x = foo.bar;` `int x = foo.bar;`
`int main (int argc, char **argv);`	`public static void main (String[] args);`

Data Types

Table B-3 describes the Java data types and their default values.

Table B-3 Simple Data Types

Data Type	Sizes	Description	Default Value
byte	1 byte	Machine independent and signed integers	0
short	2 bytes	Signed, twos complement	0
int	4 bytes	Signed, twos complement	0
long	8 bytes	Signed, twos complement	`0L`
float	4 bytes	Single precision float	`0.0f`
double	8 bytes	Double precision float	`0.0d`
char	2 bytes	Unsigned integer that uses the Unicode character set	`'\u0000'`
boolean	1 bit	Contains a `true` or `false` value; not a number	`false`

Operators

Table B-4 describes the Java operators.

Table B-4 Java Operators

Type	Operator	Data Type	Description
Additive Operators	x + y	x,y: Arithmetic types	Sum of x and y.
	x - y	x,y: Arithmetic types	Difference of x and y.
Multiplicative Operators	x * y	x,y: Arithmetic types	Product of x and y.
	x / y	x,y: Arithmetic types y != 0	Quotient of x and y.
	x % y	x,y: Arithmetic types y != 0	Remainder of x and y.
Equality Operators	==	x,y: Arithmetic types	x equals y.
		x,y: Boolean	x and y both true or false.
		x,y: Object	x and y refer to the *same* object.
Increment/ Decrement Operators	x++	x: Arithmetic types	Add one to x, returning the previous value.
	++x	x: Arithmetic types	Add one to x, returning the new value.
	x--	x: Arithmetic types	Subtract one from x, returning the previous value.
	--x	x: Arithmetic types	Subtract one from x, returning the new value.
Other Unary Operators	~x	x: Integral	Bitwise complement of x.
	!x	x: Boolean	Logical complement of x.
	+x	x: Arithmetic types	Unary plus.
	-x	x: Arithmetic types	0 - x.

Java by Example

Table B-4 Java Operators (Continued)

Type	Operator	Data Type	Description
String Concatenation Operator	x + y	x or y: `String`	If either x or y is a `String`, the other is converted to a `String` and then they are concatenated. `null` converts to "null". `booleans` convert to "true" and "false". An object reference is converted using its `toString()` method.
Bitwise & Logical Operators	x & y	x: Integral or boolean.	x AND y.
	x ^ y	x: Integral or boolean.	x XOR y.
	x | y	x: Integral or boolean.	x OR y.
Relational Operators	x < y	x,y: Arithmetic	x less than y.
	x > y	x,y: Arithmetic	x greater than y.
	x <= y	x,y: Arithmetic	x less than or equal to y.
	x >= y	x,y: Arithmetic	x greater than or equal to y.

Table B-4 Java Operators (Continued)

Type	Operator	Data Type	Description
Shift Operators	x << y	x,y: Integral	x * (2 ** y).
	x >> y	x,y: Integral	x / (2 ** y).
	x >>> y	x,y: Integral	The bits of x are shifted right y places with zero extension.
Assignment Operators	x = y	x,y: Arithmetic	The value of y is placed in x.
	x += y	x,y: Arithmetic	x = x + y.
	x -= y	x,y: Arithmetic	x = x - y.
	x *= y	x,y: Arithmetic	x = x * y.
	x /= y	x,y: Arithmetic	x = x / y.
	x %= y	x,y: Arithmetic	x = x % y.
	x <<= y	x,y: Integral	x = x << y.
	x >>= y	x,y: Integral	x = x >> y.
	x >>>= y	x,y: Integral	x = x >>> y.
	x &= y	x,y: Integral or boolean	x = x & y.
	x ^= y	x,y: Integral or boolean	x = x ^ y.
	x |= y	x,y: Integral or boolean	x = x | y.
Conditional Operators	x && y	x,y: Boolean	True if x and y both true.
	x || y	x,y: Boolean	True if x or y true.
	x ? y : z	x: Boolean	If x is true, then y, otherwise, z.
		y,z: Arithmetic, boolean, or object references.	

Control Flow and Iteration

The control structures in Java are largely the same as C or C++ with a few exceptions. For one, there is no goto statement. Another difference is that break and continue can take a single argument, indicating which of a set of nested loops they refer to. The loop must have a label which is used as the argument. For example, consider the following program:

```java
import java.io.*;

public class LoopTest {
    public static void main(String[] args) {

    outer:
    for (int i = 0; i < 3; i++) {
        for (int j = 0; j < 3; j++) {
            if (i + j == 3) {
                continue outer;
            }

            System.out.println("i = " + i + "; j = " + j);
        }
    }
    }
}
```

This program would print the following:

```
i = 0; j = 0
i = 0; j = 1
i = 0; j = 2
i = 1; j = 0
i = 1; j = 1
i = 2; j = 0
```

Comments

Table B-5 shows the comment forms you can use in Java code.

Table B-5 Java Comments

Comment Form	Notes
`/* A comment */`	C-style comment. All text between /* and */ is ignored.
`// A comment`	C++ style comment. All text from // to the end of the line is ignored.
`/** A comment */`	Comment used before a declaration. Running the `javadoc` program on the file will automatically generate HTML documentation for any comment in this form.

Keywords

Table B-6 shows Java keywords and summarizes their use.

Table B-6 Java Keywords

Keyword	Description
`abstract`	A class or method modifier. An `abstract` class is used for classes that include `abstract` methods. An `abstract` method is used for methods that are generic and that will have their operations fully defined in subclasses of the class. An interface is implicitly abstract, since the methods in it have their operations defined in the classes that implement the interface.
`boolean`	One of Java's primitive types. By default, initialized to `false`.
`break`	Standard control transfer statement. Passes control to the end of an enclosing iteration.
`byte`	One of Java's primitive types. By default, initialized to 0.
`case`	Standard control flow in a `switch` statement.
`cast`	Not used in Java 1.0.
`catch`	Keyword used in exception handling. (See *try and catch* on page 103.)
`char`	One of Java's primitive types. By default, initialized to `'\u0000'`.
`class`	Keyword used to introduce a new type. (See *Classes and Methods* on page 21.)
`const`	Not used in Java 1.0.
`continue`	Standard control transfer statement. Passes control to the loop-continuation point of an iteration statement.
`default`	Standard default action of a `switch/case` block.

Table B-6 Java Keywords (Continued)

Keyword	Description
`do`	Standard loop. Executes until value of its expression is `boolean` false.
`double`	One of Java's primitive types. By default, initialized to `0.0`.
`else`	Standard conditional control flow.
`extends`	Keyword that specifies the superclass or superclasses of the class or interface being declared.
`final`	A class, method, or variable modifier. A `final` class cannot be subclassed. A `final` method cannot be overridden. A `final` variable cannot have its initialized value changed.
`finally`	Keyword used in exception handling. (See *The finally Statement* on page 104.)
`float`	One of Java's primitive types. By default, initialized to `0.0f`.
`for`	Standard loop. Executes until value of its test expression is false. You can omit the test expression, in which case the implied test expression is `true`.
`future`	Not used in Java 1.0.
`generic`	Not used in Java 1.0.
`goto`	Not used in Java 1.0.
`if`	Standard conditional control flow.
`implements`	Keyword that specifies the interface(s) that will be provided by the class being declared.
`import`	Keyword that specifies packages or classes that can be used within a program.
`inner`	Not used in Java 1.0.
`instanceof`	A type comparison operator.
`int`	One of Java's primitive types. By default, initialized to `0`.
`interface`	Keyword used to introduce a new interface. (See *Interfaces as Types* on page 69.)
`long`	One of Java's primitive types. By default, initialized to `0L`.
`native`	A method modifier. A native method indicates the method body will be written in C and linked into the interpreter.
`new`	Keyword used to create an instance of a class.
`null`	Keyword indicating the absence of a reference.
`operator`	Not used in Java 1.0.
`outer`	Not used in Java 1.0.

Table B-6 Java Keywords (Continued)

Keyword	Description
package	Keyword used to name a group of related classes.
private	A constructor, method, or variable modifier. A private constructor, method, or variable can be accessed only within the same class.
protected	A constructor, method, or variable modifier. A protected constructor, method, or variable can be accessed by other methods in the class, methods in subclasses of the class, or methods in classes in the same package as the class.
public	A class, constructor, method, or variable modifier. A public class, constructor, method, or variable can be directly accessed or imported from other packages.
rest	Not used in Java 1.0.
return	Standard control transfer statement. Passes control to the caller of the current method.
short	One of Java's primitive types. By default, initialized to 0.
static	A method or variable modifier. A static method is used to declare a class method. (See *Class Methods* on page 26.) A static variable is used to declare a class variable, which will be shared among all instances of a class.
super	Keyword used to reference a class's immediate superclass or a constructor defined in the superclass.
switch	Standard conditional control flow.
synchronized	A method or block modifier. A synchronized method or block acquires a lock on a resource, executes the specified code, and releases the lock. Used for multithreading.
this	Keyword used to reference the current class or a constructor defined in the current class.
throw	Standard control transfer statement. Indicates a runtime exception. By convention, the argument to throw is a subclass of the Exception class.
throws	A method keyword that lists all the exceptions the method can throw.
transient	A variable modifier indicating the variable is not part of the persistent state of an object.
try	Keyword used in exception handling. (See *try and catch* on page 103.)
var	Not used in Java 1.0.

Table B-6 Java Keywords (Continued)

Keyword	Description
void	Standard null return type.
volatile	A variable modifier indicating the variable may be asynchronously modified.
while	Standard loop. Executes until value of its test expression is boolean false.

The Java Classes and Interfaces

In the following section, we've extracted key information about the Java classes and interfaces. There is a section for each of the major Java packages:

- java.applet — Provides support for Java programs that will execute within a web browser.

- java.awt — Provides support for graphics in Java programs.

- java.io — Provides support for input/output in Java programs.

- java.lang — Provides the base classes of the Java language. This package is always available without being imported.

- java.net — Provides support for network applications.

- java.util — Provides useful classes such as hashtables, stacks, and so on.

The java.applet Package

Table B-7 shows the classes and interfaces that comprise the java.applet class library.

Table B-7 java.applet Classes and Interfaces

Class Name	Description
Applet	The base applet class.
AppletContext	Interface that corresponds to an applet's environment. It can be used by an applet to obtain information from the applet's environment—usually the browser or the applet viewer.
AppletStub	Interface used to implement an applet viewer. (Not normally used by applet programmers.)
AudioClip	Interface used to implement audio applets.

The java.awt Package

Table B-8 shows the classes and interfaces that comprise the java.awt class library.

Table B-8 java.awt **Classes and Interfaces**

Class Name	Description
AWTError	Class that represents an error occurring within the awt. AWTError extends the Error class.
AWTException	Class that signals an Abstract Window Toolkit exception has occurred.
BorderLayout	Class that lays out a container, using components labeled North, South, East, West, and Center.
Button	A labeled button component.
Canvas	A generic component. Primarily available to be subclassed.
CardLayout	Class that serves as a layout manager for a container. The container contains several cards, with only one card visible at a time.
Checkbox	A GUI element with a boolean state.
CheckboxGroup	Class used to create a set of Checkbox buttons with the same CheckboxGroup object. This means that only one of those Checkbox buttons will be active at a time.
CheckboxMenuItem	A Checkbox object that represents a choice in a menu.
Choice	A pop-up menu of choices. The current choice is displayed as the title of the menu.
Color	Class that encapsulates RGB colors.
Component	A generic Abstract Window Toolkit (awt) component.
Container	A generic Abstract Window Toolkit (awt) container object which is a component that can contain other awt components.
Dialog	A window that takes input from the user. The default layout for a dialog object is BorderLayout
Dimension	Class that encapsulates a width and a height.
Event	Class that encapsulates platform-independent events from the local GUI.

Table B-8 `java.awt` **Classes and Interfaces (Continued)**

Class Name	Description
FileDialog	Class that displays a file selection dialog. It is a modal dialog. It blocks the calling thread when the `show()` method is called to display it. It releases the resource when the user has chosen a file.
FlowLayout	Class used to layout buttons in a panel. It arranges buttons left to right until no more buttons fit on the same line.
Font	Class representing fonts.
FontMetrics	Class that holds information about the dimensions of a font.
Frame	Class representing a window with a title. The default layout for a `Frame` is `BorderLayout`.
Graphics	Abstract class for graphics contexts.
GridBagConstraints	Class used to specify constraints for components laid out using the `GridBagLayout` class.
GridBagLayout	Complex layout manager that supports relative positioning and assigning weights to individual components.
GridLayout	A layout manager for a container that lays out grids.
Image	Abstract class for obtaining platform-specific images.
Insets	The insets of a container. Used to lay out containers.
Label	A component that displays a single line of read-only text.
LayoutManager	Interface implemented by classes that lay out containers.
List	A scrolling list of text items.
MediaTracker	Class used to track the status of a number of media objects, including images and audio clips. Create an instance and then call `addImage()` for each image to be tracked.
Menu	A component of a menu bar.

Table B-8 `java.awt` **Classes and Interfaces** (Continued)

Class Name	Description
MenuBar	Class that encapsulates the platform's concept of a menu bar bound to a `Frame`. To associate the `MenuBar` with an actual `Frame`, call the `Frame.setMenuBar()` method.
MenuComponent	Superclass of all menu-related components.
MenuContainer	Superclass of all menu-related containers.
MenuItem	A `String` item that represents a choice in a menu.
Panel	A generic container.
Point	An x,y coordinate.
Polygon	A list of x, y coordinates.
Rectangle	A rectangle that is defined by x, y, width, and height.
Scrollbar	A scrollbar component.
TextArea	A multiline area that displays text. The area can be set to allow editing or be set to be read-only.
TextComponent	A component that allows the editing of text.
TextField	A component that allows the editing of a single line of text.
Toolkit	Class used to bind the abstract awt classes to a particular native toolkit implementation.
Window	Class that implements a top-level window with no borders and no menu bar. It could be used to implement a pop-up menu. The default layout for a window is `BorderLayout`.
image/ColorModel	Abstract class that encapsulates the methods for translating from pixel values to alpha, red, green, and blue color components for an image.
image/CropImageFilter	Class that extends the basic `ImageFilter` class. `CropImageFilter` extracts a given rectangular region of an existing image and provides a source for a new image containing just the extracted region. Meant to be used in conjunction with a `FilteredImageSource` object to produce cropped versions of existing images.

Table B-8 `java.awt` **Classes and Interfaces (Continued)**

Class Name	Description
`image/DirectColorModel`	Class that specifies a translation from pixel values to alpha, red, green, and blue color components for pixels that have the color components embedded directly in the bits of the pixel itself. This color model is similar to an X11 TrueColor visual.
`image/FilteredImageSource`	Class that implements the `ImageProducer` interface. This takes an existing image and a filter object and uses them to produce image data for a new filtered version of the original image.
`image/ImageConsumer`	Interface for objects expressing interest in image data through the `ImageProducer` interfaces. When a consumer is added to an image producer, the producer delivers all the data about the image using the method calls defined in this interface.
`image/ImageFilter`	Class that implements a filter for the set of interface methods that are used to deliver data from an `ImageProducer` to an `ImageConsumer`. Meant to be used in conjunction with a `FilteredImageSource` object to produce filtered versions of existing images.
`image/ImageObserver`	Interface for receiving asynchronous notifications about image information as the `Image` is constructed.
`image/ImageProducer`	Interface for objects that can produce the image data for `Image` objects. Each image contains an `ImageProducer` that is used to reconstruct the image whenever it is needed.
`image/IndexColorModel`	Class that specifies a translation from pixel values to alpha, red, green, and blue color components for pixels that represent indices into a fixed colormap. An optional transparent pixel value can be supplied that indicates a completely transparent pixel, regardless of any alpha value recorded for that pixel value. This color model is similar to an X11 PseudoColor visual.

Table B-8 `java.awt` **Classes and Interfaces (Continued)**

Class Name	Description
`image/MemoryImageSource`	Class that implements the `ImageProducer` interface, which uses an array to produce pixel values for an `Image`.
`image/PixelGrabber`	Class that implements an `ImageConsumer`, which can be attached to an `Image` or `ImageProducer` object to retrieve a subset of the pixels in that image.
`image/RGBImageFilter`	Abstract class that provides an easy way to create a `ImageFilter` that modifies the pixels of an image in the default RGB ColorModel. Meant to be used in conjunction with a `FilteredImageSource` object to produce filtered versions of existing images.

The java.io Package

Table B-9 shows the classes and interfaces that comprise the `java.io` class library.

Table B-9 `java.io` **Classes and Interfaces**

Class Name	Description
`BufferedInputStream`	A stream from which you can read in characters. The data is read into a buffer, and subsequent reads benefit from fast buffer access.
`BufferedOutputStream`	A stream to which you can write characters. The data is stored in a buffer. The data is written to the actual stream only when the buffer is full or when the stream is flushed.
`ByteArrayInputStream`	A buffer that can be used as an `InputStream`.
`ByteArrayOutputStream`	A buffer that can be used as an `OutputStream`. The buffer grows when data is written to the stream. The data can be retrieved using `toByteArray()` and `toString()`.
`DataInput`	Interface that describes streams that can read input in a machine-independent format.
`DataOutput`	Interface that describes streams that can write output in a machine-independent format.

Table B-9 `java.io` **Classes and Interfaces (Continued)**

Class Name	Description
`DataInputStream`	Class for reading primitive Java data types from a stream in a portable way.
`DataOutputStream`	Class for writing primitive Java data types to a stream in a portable way.
`EOFException`	Class that signals an EOF has been reached unexpectedly during input.
`File`	Class that represents a file name of the host file system. File names can be relative or absolute. They must use the file name conventions of the host platform.
`FileDescriptor`	A file handle to an open file or an open socket.
`FileInputStream`	Class that can be used to construct an input stream from a file descriptor or a file name.
`FileNotFoundException`	Class that signals that a file was not found.
`FileOutputStream`	Class that can be used to construct an output stream from a file descriptor or a file name.
`FilenameFilter`	Interface for filtering file names.
`FilterInputStream`	Abstract class that represents a filtered input stream of bytes. This class allows multiple input stream filters to be chained together, each providing additional functionality.
`FilterOutputStream`	Abstract class that represents a filtered output stream of bytes. This class allows multiple output stream filters to be chained together, each providing additional functionality.
`IOException`	Class that signals that an I/O exception has occurred.
`InputStream`	Abstract class that represents an input stream of bytes. All `InputStream` objects are based on this class.
`InterruptedIOException`	Class that signals that an I/O operation has been interrupted.
`LineNumberInputStream`	Class that keeps track of line numbers.
`OutputStream`	Abstract class that represents an output stream of bytes. All `OutputStream` objects are based on this class.

Table B-9 `java.io` **Classes and Interfaces (Continued)**

Class Name	Description
`PipedInputStream`	Class that enables a thread reading from a `PipedInputStream` to receive data from a thread writing to the `PipedOutputStream`.
`PipedOutputStream`	Class that enables a thread writing to a `PipedOutputStream` to send data to a thread reading from a `PipedInputStream`.
`PrintStream`	Class that implements an output stream that has additional methods for printing. You can specify that the stream be flushed every time a newline character is written.
`PushbackInputStream`	Class that produces an input stream that has a 1-byte push-back buffer.
`RandomAccessFile`	Class that constructs a random access file from a file descriptor, file name, or file object. You would use this class to append data to an existing file.
`SequenceInputStream`	Class that converts a sequence of input streams into an `InputStream`.
`StreamTokenizer`	Class that converts an input stream into a stream of tokens.
`StringBufferInputStream`	A `String` buffer that can be used as an `InputStream`.
`UTFDataFormatException`	Class that signals that a malformed UTF-8 string has been read in a `DataInputStream`.

The java.lang Package

Table B-10 shows the classes and interfaces that comprise the `java.lang` class library.

Table B-10 `java.lang` **Classes and Interfaces**

Class Name	Description
`AbstractMethodError`	Class that signals an attempt to call an abstract method.
`ArithmeticException`	Class that signals an arithmetic error has occurred.
`ArrayIndexOutOfBoundsException`	Class that signals an invalid array index has been used.
`ArrayStoreException`	Class that signals an attempt has been made to store the wrong type of object to an array.
`Boolean`	Class that provides an object wrapper for `boolean` data values and serves as a place for boolean-oriented operations. A wrapper is useful because most of Java's utility classes require the use of objects. Since booleans are not objects in Java, they need to be *wrapped* in a `Boolean` instance.
`Character`	Class that provides an object wrapper for `Character` data values and serves as a place for character-oriented operations. A wrapper is useful because most of Java's utility classes require the use of objects. Since characters are not objects in Java, they need to be *wrapped* in a `Character` instance.
`Class`	Class that represents runtime classes. Every object in the system is an instance of some `Class`, and for each `Class` there is one of these descriptor objects. A `Class` descriptor is not modifiable at runtime.
`ClassCastException`	Class that signals that an invalid cast has occurred.
`ClassCircularityError`	Class that signals that a circularity has been detected when initializing a class.

Table B-10 `java.lang` **Classes and Interfaces (Continued)**

Class Name	Description
ClassFormatError	Class that signals an invalid file format has occurred.
ClassLoader	Abstract class that can be used to define a policy for loading Java classes into the runtime environment. By default, the runtime system loads classes that originate as files by reading them from the directory defined by the CLASSPATH environment variable. (This is platform dependent.) The default mechanism does not involve a class loader.
ClassNotFoundException	Class that signals that a class could not be found.
CloneNotSupportedException	Class that signals that an attempt has been made to clone an object that cannot be cloned.
Cloneable	Interface indicating that this object may be copied or cloned.
Compiler	Class that allows programs to call the Java compiler directly.
Double	Class that provides an object wrapper for Double data values and serves as a place for double-oriented operations. A wrapper is useful because most of Java's utility classes require the use of objects. Since doubles are not objects in Java, they need to be *wrapped* in a Double instance.
Error	Class that is a subtype of Throwable for abnormal events that should not occur.
Exception	Class that is a form of Throwable that normal programs may wish to catch.
Float	Class that provides an object wrapper for Float data values, and serves as a place for float-oriented operations. A wrapper is useful because most of Java's utility classes require the use of objects. Since floats are not objects in Java, they need to be *wrapped* in a Float instance.

Table B-10 `java.lang` **Classes and Interfaces (Continued)**

Class Name	Description
`IllegalAccessError`	Class that signals that an illegal access exception has occurred.
`IllegalAccessException`	Class that signals that a particular method could not be found.
`IllegalArgumentException`	Class that signals that an illegal argument exception has occurred.
`IllegalMonitorStateException`	Class that signals that a monitor operation has been attempted when the monitor is in an invalid state. For example, trying to notify a monitor that you do not own would invoke this class.
`IllegalThreadStateException`	Class that signals that a thread is not in the proper state for the requested operation.
`IncompatibleClassChangeError`	Class that signals that an incompatible class change has occurred.
`IndexOutOfBoundsException`	Class that signals that an index of some sort is out of bounds.
`InstantiationError`	Class that signals that the interpreter has tried to instantiate an abstract class or an interface.
`InstantiationException`	Class that signals that an attempt has been made to instantiate an abstract class or an interface.
`Integer`	Class that produces a wrapper for integer values. In Java, integers are not objects and most of the Java utility classes require the use of objects. A wrapper is useful because most of Java's utility classes require the use of objects. Since integers are not objects in Java, they need to be *wrapped* in an `Integer` instance.
`InternalError`	Class that signals that an internal error has occurred.
`InterruptedException`	Class that signals that some thread has interrupted this thread.

Table B-10 `java.lang` **Classes and Interfaces (Continued)**

Class Name	Description
`LinkageError`	Class that indicates that a class has some dependency on another class; however the latter class is incompatible and has changed after the compilation of the former class.
`Long`	Class that provides an object wrapper for long data values, and serves as a place for long-oriented operations. A wrapper is useful because most of Java's utility classes require the use of objects. Since longs are not objects in Java, they need to be *wrapped* in a `Long` instance.
`Math`	Class that represents the standard `Math` library. For the methods in this class, error handling for out-of-range or immeasurable results is platform dependent. This class cannot be subclassed or instantiated because all methods and variables are `static`.
`NoClassDefFoundError`	Class that signals that a class could not be found.
`NoSuchFieldError`	Class that signals a particular field could not be found.
`NoSuchMethodError`	Class that signals that a particular method could not be found and there's no way to recover.
`NoSuchMethodException`	Class that signals that a particular method could not be found.
`NullPointerException`	Class that signals the illegal use of a null pointer.
`Number`	Abstract class for numeric scalar types. `Integer`, `Long`, `Float` and `Double` are subclasses of `Number` that bind to a particular numeric representation.
`NumberFormatException`	Class that signals that an invalid number format was detected when trying to parse a number.

Table B-10 `java.lang` **Classes and Interfaces (Continued)**

Class Name	Description
`Object`	Class that represents the root of the class hierarchy. Every class in the system has `Object` as its ultimate parent. Every variable and method defined here is available in every `Object`.
`OutOfMemoryError`	Class that signals you are out of memory.
`Process`	Class that is returned by variants of the `exec()` method in class `System`. From the `Process` instance, it is possible to: get the standard in and/or standard out of the subprocess, kill the subprocess, wait for it to terminate, and retrieve the final exit value of the process.
`Runnable`	Interface that provides a common protocol for objects that will execute code while they are active. For example, `Runnable` is implemented by class `Thread`. You can `implement Runnable` in a class to start threaded execution.
`Runtime`	Class with a single instance that provides system operations such as `exec` and `exit`.
`RuntimeException`	Class that signals an exception that can reasonably occur during the execution of a Java program by the Java virtual machine. A method need not declare any `RuntimeException` errors in the list of exceptions it might throw.
`SecurityException`	Class that signals that a security exception has occurred.
`SecurityManager`	Abstract class that can be subclassed to implement a security policy. It allows the inspection of the class loaders on the execution stack.
`StackOverflowError`	Class that signals that a stack overflow has occurred.
`String`	Class that represents character `String` objects. `String` objects are constant, and their values cannot be changed after creation. `String` objects are immutable, so they can be shared.

Table B-10 `java.lang` **Classes and Interfaces (Continued)**

Class Name	Description
StringBuffer	Class that produces a buffer for characters. It is mainly used to create String objects. The compiler uses it to implement the "+" operator.
StringIndexOutOfBoundsException	Class that signals that a String index is out of range.
System	Class that provides a system-independent interface to system functionality. One of the more useful things provided by this class is the standard input and output streams. The standard input stream is used for reading character data. The standard output streams are used for printing.
Thread	Class that represents a thread, which is a single sequential flow of control within a process. This means that while executing within a program, each thread has a beginning, a sequence, a point of execution occurring at any time during runtime of the thread, and an ending. Thread objects are the basis for multithreaded programming.
ThreadDeath	Class that is thrown when thread.stop() is called. This is not a subclass of Exception, but rather a subclass of Error because too many people already catch Exception. Instances of this class should be caught explicitly only if you are interested in cleaning up when being asynchronously terminated. If ThreadDeath is caught, it is important to rethrow the object so that the Thread will actually die. The top-level error handler will not print out a message if ThreadDeath falls through.

Table B-10 `java.lang` **Classes and Interfaces (Continued)**

Class Name	Description
ThreadGroup	Class that produces a group of Thread objects. A Thread group can contain a set of Thread objects as well as a set of other Thread groups. A Thread can access its Thread group, but it can't access the parent of its Thread group. This makes it possible to encapsulate a Thread in a Thread group and stop it from manipulating Thread objects in the parent group.
Throwable	Class that signals that an exceptional condition has occurred. All exceptions and errors are subclasses of Throwable. A Throwable contains a snapshot of the execution stack; this snapshot is used to print a stack backtrace. A Throwable also contains a message string.
UnknownError	Class that signals that an unknown but serious exception has occurred.
UnsatisfiedLinkError	Class that signals a failure when attempting to link in a native method.
VerifyError	Class that signals that an error occurred during bytecode verification.
VirtualMachineError	Class that indicates the Java virtual machine is broken or has run out of resources.

The java.net Package

Table B-11 shows the classes and interfaces that comprise the `java.net` class library.

Table B-11 `java.net` Classes and Interfaces

Class Name	Description
ContentHandler	Class to read data from a `URLConnection` and construct an object. Specific subclasses of `ContentHandler` handle specific mime types. It is the responsibility of a `ContentHandlerFactory` to select an appropriate `ContentHandler` for the mime-type of the `URLConnection`. Applications should never call `ContentHandlers` directly; rather they should use `URL.getContent()` or `URLConnection.getContent()`
ContentHandlerFactory	Interface that defines a factory for `ContentHandler` instances. It is used by the `URLStreamHandler` class to create `ContentHandlers` for various streams.
DatagramPacket	Class that represents a datagram packet containing packet data.
DatagramSocket	Class that implements unreliable datagrams.
InetAddress	Class that represents Internet addresses.
MalformedURLException	Class that signals that a malformed URL has occurred.
PlainSocketImpl	Class that provides a default socket implementation. This does not implement any security checks, and neither does it support any firewalls. Note this class should not be `public`.
ProtocolException	Class that signals when connect gets an EPROTO. This exception is specifically caught in class `Socket`.
ServerSocket	Class that uses a `SocketImpl` to implement the actual socket operations. This enables you to change socket implementations depending on the kind of firewall that is used. You can change socket implementations by setting the `SocketImplFactory`.
Socket	Class that produces a client `Socket`. It uses a `SocketImpl` to implement the actual socket operations. This enables you to change socket implementations depending on the kind of firewall that is used. You can change socket implementations by setting the `SocketImplFactory`.

Table B-11 `java.net` **Classes and Interfaces (Continued)**

Class Name	Description
`SocketException`	Class that signals that an error occurred while attempting to use a socket.
`SocketImpl`	Abstract class that implements sockets. This class must be subclassed to provide an actual implementation.
`SocketImplFactory`	Interface that defines a factory for `SocketImpl` instances. It is used by the socket class to create socket implementations that implement various policies.
`SocketInputStream`	Class that produces a stream that extends `FileInputStream` to implement a `SocketInputStream`. Note that this class should not be `public`.
`SocketOutputStream`	Class that produces a stream that extends `FileOutputStream` to implement a `SocketOutputStream`. Note that this class should not be `public`.
`URL`	Class that represents a Uniform Reference Locator, which is a reference to an object on the world-wide web. This is a `constant` object; once it is created its fields cannot be changed.
`URLConnection`	Abstract class that represents an active connection to an object represented by a URL.
`URLEncoder`	Class that turns `String` objects of text into *x-www-form* URL encoded format.
`URLStreamHandler`	Abstract class for URL stream openers. Subclasses of this class know how to create streams for particular protocol types.
`URLStreamHandlerFactory`	Interface that defines a factory for instances of `URLStreamHandler`. It is used by the URL class to create `URLStreamHandlers` for various streams.
`UnknownHostException`	Class that signals that the address of the server specified by a network client could not be resolved.
`UnknownServiceException`	Class that signals that an unknown service exception has occurred.

The java.util Package

Table B-12 shows the classes and interfaces that comprise the `java.util` class library.

Table B-12 `java.util` **Classes and Interfaces**

Class Name	Description
BitSet	A set of bits that automatically grows as more bits are needed.
Date	A wrapper for a date. Allows you to manipulate dates in a system-independent way. The date can be set and examined according to the local time zone.
Dictionary	Abstract class that is the parent of Hashtable, which maps keys to values. Any object can be used as a key and/or value.
EmptyStackException	Class that signals that an operation has been attempted on an empty stack.
Enumeration	Interface that specifies a set of methods that may be used to step through a set of values. For example, you might use it to print all the elements of a vector.
Hashtable	Class that maps keys to value. Any object can be used as a key or value.
NoSuchElementException	Class that signals that an enumeration is empty.
Observable	Class whose instances can be *observed* by other objects. The other objects are notified of changes to Observable objects.
Observer	Interface that allows instances of a class to be notified of changes to Observable objects.
Properties	Class that produces a hashtable that can be saved and/or loaded from a stream.
Random	Class that generates a stream of pseudo-random numbers.
Stack	Class that produces a Last-In-First-Out (LIFO) stack of objects.
StringTokenizer	Class that controls simple linear tokenization of a String. The set of delimiters, which defaults to common whitespace characters, may be specified at creation time or on a per-token basis.

Table B-12 `java.util` **Classes and Interfaces (Continued)**

Class Name	Description
Vector	Class that tries to optimize storage management by maintaining a capacity and a `capacityIncrement`. The capacity is always at least as large as the vector size; it is usually larger because as elements are added to the vector, the vector's storage increases in chunks the size of `capacityIncrement`. Setting the capacity to what you want before inserting a large number of objects will reduce the amount of incremental reallocation. You can safely ignore the capacity and the vector will still work correctly.

The HTML applet and param Tags

To call an applet from within a web page, you use the HTML `applet` tag. Minimally, you can use a single-line call, as in Example B-1. (Assume that we're calling the `StaticLabel` applet on page 237.)

Example B-1 The Basic HTML `applet` Tag

```
<applet code="StaticLabel.class" width=200 height=80> </applet>
```

You can also include a set of parameters to specify exactly how you want the applet displayed, as in Example B-2. Applet parameters are specified using the `param` tag. The syntax for the `param` tag is:

```
<param name="name" value="value">
```

All parameters are passed to an applet as strings.

If specified within the web page, these HTML parameters override the default parameters specified in an applet. For instance, the `StaticLabel` applet described on page 237 has default parameters for `label`, `fontname`, `fontslant`, `fontweight`, and `fontsize`. However, the param tags in Example B-2 would override those default values.

Example B-2 The HTML `param` Tag

```
<applet code="StaticLabel.class" width=200 height=80> <param
name=label value="I'm a static label.">
<param name=fontname value="Courier">
<param name=fontslant value="italic">
<param name=fontweight value="bold">
<param name=fontsize value="24">
</applet>
```

Index

...ALSO AVAILABLE FROM SUNSOFT PRESS

SUNSOFT PRESS

Prentice Hall PTR is pleased to publish SunSoft Press books. This year's SunSoft catalog has unprecedented breadth and depth, covering not only the inner workings of Sun operating systems, but also guides to multiprocessing, internationalization of software, networking, and other topics important to anyone working with these technologies.

These and other Prentice Hall PTR books are available at your local Magnet Store. To locate the store nearest you fax (201) 236-7123 or visit our web site at:

http://www.prenhall.com

ALL ABOUT ADMINISTERING NIS+, Second Edition
Rick Ramsey

Updated and revised for Solaris™ 2.3, this book is ideal for network administrators who want to know more about NIS+: its capabilities, requirements, how it works, and how to get the most out of it. Includes planning guidelines for both new installations and for transitions from NIS; detailed descriptions of the structure of NIS+ objects and security; and setup instructions for both standard NIS+ comands and NIS+ shell scripts. Presents modular, fully-tested, step-by-step instructions and many illustrations, examples, and tips.

1995, 480 pp., Paper, 0-13-309576-2 (30957-5)

AUTOMATING SOLARIS INSTALLATIONS
Paul Anthony Kasper and Alan L. McClellan

If you want to minimize the time you spend installing the Solaris environment on SPARC™ or x86 systems, this book is for you! It describes how to set up "hands-off" Solaris installations for hundreds of SPARC or x86 systems. It explains in detail how to configure your site so that when you install Solaris, you simply boot a system and walk away—the software installs automatically! Topics covered include setting up network booting, enabling automatic system configuration, setting up custom JumpStart files, booting and installing, debugging and trouble-shooting. A diskette containing working shell scripts that automate pre- and post-installation tasks is provided.

1995, 320 pp., Paper, 0-13-312505-X (31250-4) Book/Disk

CONFIGURATION AND CAPACITY PLANNING FOR SOLARIS SERVERS
Brian L. Wong

Written for MIS staff, this book provides information on planning and configuring Solaris servers for use in NFS™, DBMS, and timesharing environments. The material concentrates on applied computer architecture, case studies and experimentally-based, real-world results rather than on queueing models.

1996, 300 pp., Paper. 0-13-349952-9 (34995-1)

THE UNIX BOOK OF GAMES
Janice Winsor

A collection of classic games with complete rules and illustrated tips and hints. Includes commentary by the programmers who created each game. Includes complete source code and binaries for SCO and Linux.

1997, 256 pp., Paper, 0-13-490079-0 (49007-8) Book/CD-ROM

MANAGING THE NEW ENTERPRISE:
The Proof, Not The Hype

Harris Kern, Randy Johnson, Andrew Law, and Michael Hawkins with William Kennedy

In this follow-up to the best selling *Rightsizing the New Enterprise*, the authors discuss how to build and manage a heterogeneous client/ server environment. *Managing the New Enterprise* describes in detail the key technology support infrastructures, including networking, data centers, and system administration, as well as how Information Technology must change in order to manage the New Enterprise. This is an indispensable reference for anyone within Information Technology who is facing the challenges of building and managing client/server computing.

1996, 240 pp., Cloth, 0-13-231184-4 (23118-3)

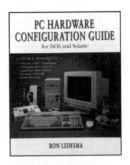

PC HARDWARE CONFIGURATION GUIDE:
For DOS and Solaris

Ron Ledesma

This book eliminates trial-and-error methodology by presenting a simple, structured approach to PC hardware configuration. The author's time-tested approach is to configure your system in stages, verify and test at each stage, and troubleshoot and fix problems before going on to the next stage. Covers both standalone and networked machines. Discusses how to determine x86 hardware configuration requirements, how to configure hardware components (MCA, ISA, and EISA), partitioning hard disks for DOS and UNIX, and installing DOS and/or UNIX (Solaris x86). Includes configuration instructions, checklists, worksheets, diagrams of popular SCSI host bus, network, and video adapters, and basic installation troubleshooting.

1995, 352 pp., Paper, 0-13-124678-X (12467-7)

NEW!

NETWORKING THE NEW ENTERPRISE:
The Proof, Not The Hype

Harris Kern and Randy Johnson

The final volume in the New Enterprise Trilogy, this book focuses on planning network projects, developing architectures, and implementations of expanding distributed computing and client server technologies. A must for any business in today's growing marketplace.

Networking the New Enterprise includes in-depth ideas for developing network architectures; including, key methods, and strategies for network management, security and design; details on implementing Network Management Systems; Methods for enhancing, securing and optimizing Networks.

1997, 350 pages, paper, 0-13-263427-9 (26342-6)

INTERACTIVE UNIX OPERATING SYSTEM:
A Guide for System Administrators

Marty C. Stewart

Written for first-time system administrators and end users, this practical guide describes the common system administration menus and commands of the INTERACTIVE UNIX System V/386 Release 3.2, Version 4.0 and SVR 3.2 UNIX in general. Loaded with step-by-step instructions and examples, it discusses how to install and configure the INTERACTIVE UNIX system, including the hardware requirements. It describes the unique CUI menu interface, basic OS commands, administration of new user accounts, configuration of customized kernels, and working with the INTERACTIVE UNIX system as an end user.

1996, 320 pp., Paper, 0-13-161613-7 (16161-2)

MULTIPROCESSOR SYSTEM ARCHITECTURES:
A Technical Survey of Multiprocessor / Multithreaded Systems Using SPARC, Multi-level Bus Architectures and Solaris (SunOS)
Ben Catanzaro

Written for engineers seeking to understand the problems and solutions of multi-processor system design, this hands-on guide is the first comprehensive description of the elements involved in the design and development of Sun's multiprocessor systems. Topics covered include SPARC processor design and its implementations, an introduction to multilevel bus architectures including MBus and XBus/XDBus, an overview of the Solaris/SunOS™ multithreaded architecture and programming, and an MBus Interface Specification and Design Guide. This book can serve as a reference text for design engineers as well as a hands-on design guide to MP systems for hardware/software engineers.

1994, 528 pp., Paper, 0-13-089137-1 (08913-6)

PANIC! UNIX System Crash Dump Analysis
Chris Drake and Kimberley Brown

PANIC! is the first book to discuss in detail UNIX system panics, crashes and hangs, their causes, what to do when they occur, how to collect information about them, how to analyze that information, and how to get the problem resolved. *PANIC!* presents this highly technical and intricate subject in a friendly, easy style which even the novice UNIX system administrator will find readable, educational and enjoyable. It is written for systems and network administrators and technical support engineers who are responsible for maintaining and supporting UNIX computer systems and networks. Includes a CD-ROM containing several useful analysis tools, such as adb macros and C tags output from the source trees of two different UNIX systems.

1995, 496 pp., Paper, 0-13-149386-8 (14938-5) Book/CD-ROM

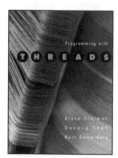

PROGRAMMING WITH THREADS
Steve Kleiman, Devang Shah, and Bart Smaalders

Written by senior threads engineers at Sun Microsystems, Inc., this book is the definitive guide to programming with threads. It is intended for both novice and more sophisticated threads programmers, and for developers multithreading existing programs as well as for those writing new multithreaded programs. The book provides structured techniques for mastering the complexity of threads programming with an emphasis on performance issues. Included are detailed examples using the new POSIX threads (Pthreads) standard interfaces. The book also covers the other UNIX threads interface defined by UNIX International.

1996, 250 pp., Paper, 0-13-172389-8 (17238-9)

RIGHTSIZING THE NEW ENTERPRISE:
The Proof, Not The Hype
Harris Kern and Randy Johnson

A detailed account of how Sun Micro-systems implemented its rightsizing strategy going from a mainframe data center to a heterogeneous client/server distributed environment. This book covers the key infrastructures of an IT organization (the network, data center, and system administration), the rightsizing/management tools, and the training/resource issues involved in transitioning from mainframe to UNIX support. The facts contained in this book provide you with the PROOF that 'rightsizing' can be done.and has been done.

1995, 352 pp., Cloth, 0-13-490384-6 (49038-3)

RIGHTSIZING FOR CORPORATE SURVIVAL:
An IS Manager's Guide
Robert Massoudi, Astrid Julienne, Bob Millradt, and Reed Hornberger

This book provides IS managers with "hands-on" guidance for developing a rightsizing strategy and plan. Based upon research conducted through customer visits with multinational corporations, it details the experiences and insights gained by IS professionals that have implemented systems in distributed, client-server environments. Topics covered include:

- Why rightsize?
- What business results can rightsizing produce?
- Key technologies critical to rightsizing
- Good starting points for rightsizing
- What is the process to rightsize an information system?
- Cost considerations and return on investment (ROI) analysis

• How to manage the transition

Throughout the book, case studies and "lessons learned" reinforce the discussion and document best practices associated with rightsizing.

1995, 272 pp., Paper,
0-13-123126-X (12312-5)

READ ME FIRST!
A Style Guide for the
Computer Industry
Sun Technical Publications

A comprehensive look at documenting computer products, from style pointers to legal guidelines, from working with an editor to building a publications department—in both hard copy and electronic copy with an on line viewer, FrameMaker templates for instant page design, and a detailed guide to establishing a documentation department and its processes. Based on an internationally award-winning Sun Microsystems style guide (Award of Excellence in the STC International Technical Publications Competition, 1994)

1996, 300 pp., Paper,
0-13-455347-0 (45534-6)
Book/CD-ROM

SOLARIS IMPLEMENTATION:
A Guide for System Administrators
George Becker, Mary E. S. Morris and Kathy Slattery

Written by three expert Sun system administrators, this book discusses real world, day-to-day Solaris 2 system administration for both new installations and for those migrating an installed Solaris 1 base. It presents tested procedures to help system administrators to improve and customize their networks by eliminating trial-and-error methodologies. Also includes advice for managing heterogeneous Solaris environments and provides autoinstall sample scripts and disk partitioning schemes (with recommended sizes) used at Sun.

1995, 368 pp., Paper,
0-13-353350-6 (35335-9)

CREATING WORLD WIDE WEB SOFTWARE:
SOLARIS, Second Edtion
Bill Tuthill and David Smallberg

Written for software developers and business managers interested in creating global applications for the Solaris environment (SPARC and x86), this second edition expands on the first edition and has updated information on international markets, standards organizations, and writing international documents. New topics in the second edition include CDE/Motif, NEO (formerly project DOE)/ OpenStep, Universal codesets, global internet applications, code examples, and success stories.

1996, 250 pp., Paper,
0-13-494493-3 (49449-2)

SOLARIS PORTING GUIDE,
Second Edition
SunSoft Developer Engineering

Ideal for application programmers and software developers, the *Solaris Porting Guide, Second Edition*, provides a comprehensive technical overview of the Solaris 2.x operating environment and its related migration strategy. The second edition is current through Solaris 2.4 (both the SPARC and x86 platforms) and provides all the information necessary to migrate from Solaris 1 (SunOS 4.x) to Solaris 2 (SunOS 5.x). Other additions include a discussion of emerging technologies such as the Common Desktop Environment (CDE), hints for application performance tuning, and extensive pointers to further information, including Internet sources.

1995, 752 pp., Paper,
0-13-443672-5 (44367-1)

SUN PERFORMANCE AND TUNING:
SPARC and Solaris
Adrian Cockcroft

An indispensable reference for anyone working with Sun workstations running the Solaris environment, this book provides detailed performance and configuration information on all SPARC machines and peripherals, as well as on all operating system releases from SunOS 4.1 through Solaris 2.4. It includes hard-to-find tuning information and offers insights that cannot be found elsewhere. This book is written for developers who want to design for performance and for system administrators who have a system running applications on which they want to improve performance.

1995, 288 pp., Paper,
0-13-149642-5 (14964-1)

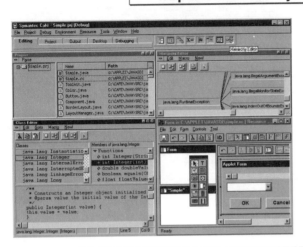

State Sales/Use Tax

In the following states, add sales/use tax: CO-3%; GA, LA, NY-4%; VA-4.5%; KS-4.9%; AZ, IA, IN, MA, MD, OH, SC, WI-5%; CT, FL, ME, MI, NC, NJ, PA, TN-6%; CA, IL, TX-6.25%; MN, WA-6.5%;DC-5.75%.

Please add local tax for AZ, CA, FL, GA, MO, NY, OH, SC, TN, TX, WA, WI.

Order Information:

- Please allow 2-4 weeks for processing your order.
- Please attach the order form with your payment.
- No P.O. boxes and no C.O.D.s accepted.
- Order form good in the U.S. only.
- If you are tax exempt, please include exemption certificate or letter with tax-exempt number.
- Resellers not eligible.
- Offer not valid with any other promotion.
- One copy per product, per order.

THE ARCHIVE UTILITY FOR WINDOWS

Windows 95
FEATURES INCLUDE
long filename support and the ability to zip and unzip files without leaving the Explorer

WINZIP ®►►►

Nico Mak Computing, Inc.

Have you ever used the Internet, a BBS, or CompuServe? If so, you've probably encountered .ZIP, .TAR, .GZ, and .Z files. Are you a Windows user? If so, WinZip is the way to handle these archived files.

WinZip brings the convenience of Windows to the use of ZIP files without requiring PKZIP and PKUNZIP. It features an intuitive point-and-click drag-and-drop interface for viewing, running, extracting, adding, deleting, and testing files in ZIP, LZH, ARJ, and ARC files. Optional virus scanning support is included. Windows and Windows 95 versions are included in the same package.

Shareware evaluation versions of WinZip are available on better bulletin boards and online services everywhere. Be sure to get version 6.0 or later.

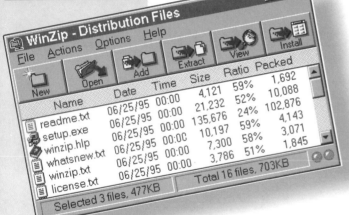

"These days everyone needs a good unzipping utility. This is the best."
PC Computing, 12/95

"Recommended download"
Windows Magazine, 9/95

"Cadillac of unzippers"
PC Magazine, 3/95

Voted "Best Utility"
1994 Annual Shareware Industry Awards

SPECIAL OFFER!

IMPORTANT—READ CAREFULLY BEFORE OPENING SEALED CD-ROM

This CD-ROM contains the Java Development Kit and sample code from Java By Example, as well as other copyrighted software.

SUN MICROSYSTEMS LICENSE AGREEMENT

This is a legal agreement between the purchaser of this book/CD-ROM package ("You") and Sun Microsystems, Inc. By opening the sealed CD-ROM you are agreeing to be bound by the terms of this agreement. If you do not agree to the terms of this agreement, promptly return the unopened book/CD-ROM package to the place you obtained it for a full refund.

SOFTWARE LICENSE FOR SAMPLE CODE

1. Grant of License. Sun Microsystems grants to you ("Licensee") a non-exclusive, non-transferable license to use the software programs (sample code) included on the CD-ROM without fee. The software is in "use" on a computer when it is loaded into the temporary memory (i.e. RAM) or installed into the permanent memory (e.g. hard disk, CD-ROM, or other storage device). You may network the software or otherwise use it on more than one computer or computer terminal at the same time.

2. Copyright. The CD-ROM is copyrighted by Sun Microsystems, Inc. and is protected by United States copyright laws and international treaty provisions. Therefore, you must treat the CD-ROM like any other copyrighted material. Individual software programs on the CD-ROM are copyrighted by their respective owners and may require separate licensing. The Java Development Kit is copyrighted by Sun Microsystems, Inc. and is covered by a separate license agreement provided on the CD-ROM and reprinted below.

3. Java By Example Sample Code. Sun Microsystems, Inc. grants you a royalty-free right to reproduce and distribute the sample code or applets provided that you: (a) distribute the sample code or applets only in conjunction with and as a part of your software application; (b) do not use Sun Microsystems, Inc. or its authors' names, logos, or trademarks to market your software product; and (c) agree to indemnify, hold harmless and defend Sun Microsystems, Inc. and its authors and suppliers from and against any claims or lawsuits, including attorneys fees, that arise or result from the use or distribution of your software product.

DISCLAIMER OF WARRANTY

The SOFTWARE (including instructions for its use) is provided "AS IS" WITHOUT WARRANTY OF ANY KIND. SUN MICROSYSTEMS and any distributor of the SOFTWARE FURTHER DISCLAIM ALL IMPLIED WARRANTIES INCLUDING WITHOUT LIMITATION ANY IMPLIED WARRANTIES OF MERCHANTABILITY OR OF FITNESS FOR A PARTICULAR PURPOSE. THE ENTIRE RISK ARISING OUT OF THE USE OR PERFORMANCE OF THE SOFTWARE OR DOCUMENTATION REMAINS WITH YOU.

IN NO EVENT SHALL SUN MICROSYSTEMS, ITS AUTHORS, OR ANY ONE ELSE INVOLVED IN THE CREATION, PRODUCTION, OR DELIVERY OF THE SOFTWARE BE LIABLE FOR ANY DAMAGES WHATSOEVER (INCLUDING, WITHOUT LIMITATION, DAMAGES FOR LOSS OF BUSINESS PROFITS, BUSINESS INTERRUPTION, LOSS OF BUSINESS INFORMATION, OR OTHER PECUNIARY LOSS) ARISING OUT OF THE USE OF OR INABILITY TO USE THE SOFTWARE OR DOCUMENTATION, EVEN IF SUN MICROSYSTEMS HAS BEEN ADVISED OF THE POSSIBILITY OF SUCH DAMAGES, BECAUSE SOME STATES/COUNTRIES DO NOT ALLOW THE EXCLUSION OF LIMITATION OF LIABILITY FOR CONSEQUENTIAL OR INCIDENTAL DAMAGES, THE ABOVE LIMITATION MAY NOT APPLY TO YOU.

U.S. GOVERNMENT RESTRICTED RIGHTS

The SOFTWARE and documentation are provided with RESTRICTED RIGHTS. Use, duplication, or disclosure is subject to restrictions as set forth in subparagraph (c)(1)(ii) of The Rights in Technical Data and Computer Software clause at DFARS 252.227-7013 or subparagraphs (c)(1) and (2) of the Commercial Computer Software—Restricted Rights 48 CFR 52.227-19.

Java Development Kit, Version 1.0.2, Binary Code License

This binary code license ("License") contains rights and restrictions associated with use of the accompanying software and documentation ("Software"). Read the License carefully before installing Software. By installing Software, you agree to the terms and conditions of this License.

1. Limited License Grant. Sun grants to you ("Licensee") a non-exclusive, non-transferable limited license to use Software without fee. Licensee may re-distribute complete and unmodified Software to third parties provided that this License conspicuously appear with all copies of the Software and that Licensee does not charge a fee for such re-distribution of Software.

2. Java Platform Interface. In the event that Licensee creates any Java-related API and distributes such API to others for applet or application development. Licensee must promptly publish an accurate specification for such API for free use by all developers of Java-based software. Licensee may not modify the Java Platform Interface ("JPI," identified as classes contained within the "java" package or any subpackages of the "java" package), by creating additional classes within the JPI or otherwise causing the addition to or modification of the classes in the JPI.

3. Restrictions. Software is confidential copyrighted information of Sun and title to all copies is retained by Sun and/or its licensors. Licensee shall not modify, decompile, disassemble, decrypt, extract, or otherwise reverse engineer Software. Software may not be leased, assigned, or sublicensed, in whole or in part. Software is not designed or intended for use in on-line control of aircraft, air traffic, aircraft navigation or aircraft communications; or in the design, construction, operation or maintenance of any nuclear facility. Licensee warrants that it will not use or redistribute the Software for such purposes.

4. Trademarks and Logos. Licensee acknowledges that Sun owns the Java trademark and all Java-related trademarks, logos, and icons including the Coffee Cup and Duke ("Java Marks") and agrees to: (i) comply with the Java Trademark Guidelines at http://java.com/trademarks.html; (ii) not do anything harmful to or inconsistent with Sun's rights in the Java Marks; and (iii) assist Sun in protecting those rights, including assigning to Sun any rights acquired by Licensee in any Java Mark.

5. Disclaimer of Warranty. Software is provided "AS IS," without a warranty of any kind. ALL EXPRESS OR IMPLIED REPRESENTATIONS AND WARRANTIES, INCLUDING ANY IMPLIED WARRANTY OF MERCHANT-ABILITY, FITNESS FOR A PARTICULAR PURPOSE OR NON-INFRINGEMENT, ARE HEREBY EXCLUDED.

6. Limitation of Liability. SUN AND ITS LICENSORS SHALL NOT BE LIABLE FOR ANY DAMAGES SUF-FERED BY LICENSEE OR ANY THIRD PARTY AS A RESULT OF USING OR DISTRIBUTING SOFTWARE. IN NO EVENT WILL SUN OR ITS LICENSORS BE LIABLE FOR ANY LOST REVENUE, PROFIT OR DATA, OR FOR DIRECT, INDIRECT, SPECIAL, CONSEQUENTIAL, INCIDENTAL OR PUNITIVE DAMAGES, HOWEVER CAUSED AND REGARDLESS OF THE THEORY OF LIABILITY, ARISING OUT OF THE USE OF OR INABILITY TO USE SOFTWARE, EVEN IF SUN HAS BEEN ADVISED OF THE POSSIBILITY OF SUCH DAMAGES.

7. Termination. Licensee may terminate this License at any time by destroying all copies of Software. This License will terminate immediately without notice from Sun if Licensee fails to comply with any provisions of this License. Upon such termination, Licensee must destroy all copies of Software.

8. Export Regulations. Software, including technical data, is subject to U.S. export control laws, including the U.S. Export Administration Act and its associated regulations, and may be subject to export or import regulations in other countries. Licensee agrees to comply strictly with all such regulations and acknowledges that it has the responsibility to obtain licenses to export, re-export, or import Software. Software may not be downloaded, or otherwise exported or re-exported (i) into, or to a national or resident of, Cuba, Iraq, Iran, North Korea, Libya, Sudan, Syria or any country to which the U.S. has embargoed goods; or (ii) to anyone on the U.S. Treasury Department's list of Specially Designated Nations or the U.S. Commerce Department's Table of Denial Orders.

9. Restricted Rights. Use, duplication or disclosure by the United States government is subject to the restrictions as set forth in the Rights in Technical Data and Computer Software Clauses in DFARS 252.227-7013(c) (1) (ii) and FAR 52.227-19(c) (2) as applicable.

10. Governing Law. Any action related to this License will be governed by California law and controlling U.S. federal law. No choice of law rules of any jurisdiction will apply.

11. Severability. If any of the above provisions are held to be in violation of applicable law, void, or unenforceable in any jurisdiction, then such provisions are herewith waived to the extent necessary for the License to be otherwise enforceable in such jurisdiction. However, if in Sun's opinion deletion of any provisions of the License by operation of this paragraph unreasonably compromises the rights or increase the liabilities of Sun or its licensors, Sun reserves the right to terminate the License and refund the fee paid by License, if any, as Licensee's sole and exclusive remedy.

Read before opening CD package!

LICENSE AGREEMENT
AND LIMITED WARRANTY

This CD-ROM is a standard ISO-9660 disc. Software on this CD-ROM requires Windows 95, Windows NT, Solaris 2.x or Macintosh (System 7.5).

Windows 3.1 IS NOT SUPPORTED